Generous Enemies

EARLY AMERICAN STUDIES

Daniel K. Richter and Kathleen M. Brown, Series Editors

Exploring neglected aspects of our colonial, revolutionary, and early national history and culture, Early American Studies reinterprets familiar themes and events in fresh ways. Interdisciplinary in character, and with a special emphasis on the period from about 1600 to 1850, the series is published in partnership with the McNeil Center for Early American Studies.

A complete list of books in the series is available from the publisher.

Generous Enemies

Patriots and Loyalists in Revolutionary New York

Judith L. Van Buskirk

PENN

UNIVERSITY OF PENNSYLVANIA PRESS

Philadelphia

Copyright © 2002 University of Pennsylvania Press
All rights reserved
Printed in the United States of America on acid-free paper

10 9 8 7 6 5 4 3 2 1

First paperback edition 2004

Published by
University of Pennsylvania Press
Philadelphia, Pennsylvania 19104-4011

Library of Congress Cataloging-in-Publication Data
Van Buskirk, Judith L.
  Generous enemies : patriots and loyalists in Revolutionary New York /
Judith L. Van Buskirk.
    p. cm. — (Early American studies)
  Includes bibliographical references and index.
  ISBN 0-8122-3675-0 (acid-free paper).—ISBN 0-8122-1822-1 (pbk. : alk. paper)
    1. New York (N.Y.)—History—Revolution, 1775–1783. 2. New York
(N.Y.)—History—Revolution, 1775–1783—Social aspects. 3. Revolutionaries—
New York (State)—New York—History—18th century. 4. American loyalists—
New York (State)—New York—History. 5. United States—History—Revolution,
1775–1783—Social aspects. I. Title. II. Series.

E263.N6 V36   2002
973.3′4471—dc21

2002024391

For my mother, Regina Van Buskirk

Contents

No. 1	South Ward
No. 2	West Do.
No. 3	North Do.
No. 4	Dock Do.
No. 5	East Do.
No. 6	Mon'gomery Do.
No. 7	Out Do.

City of New York, 1776

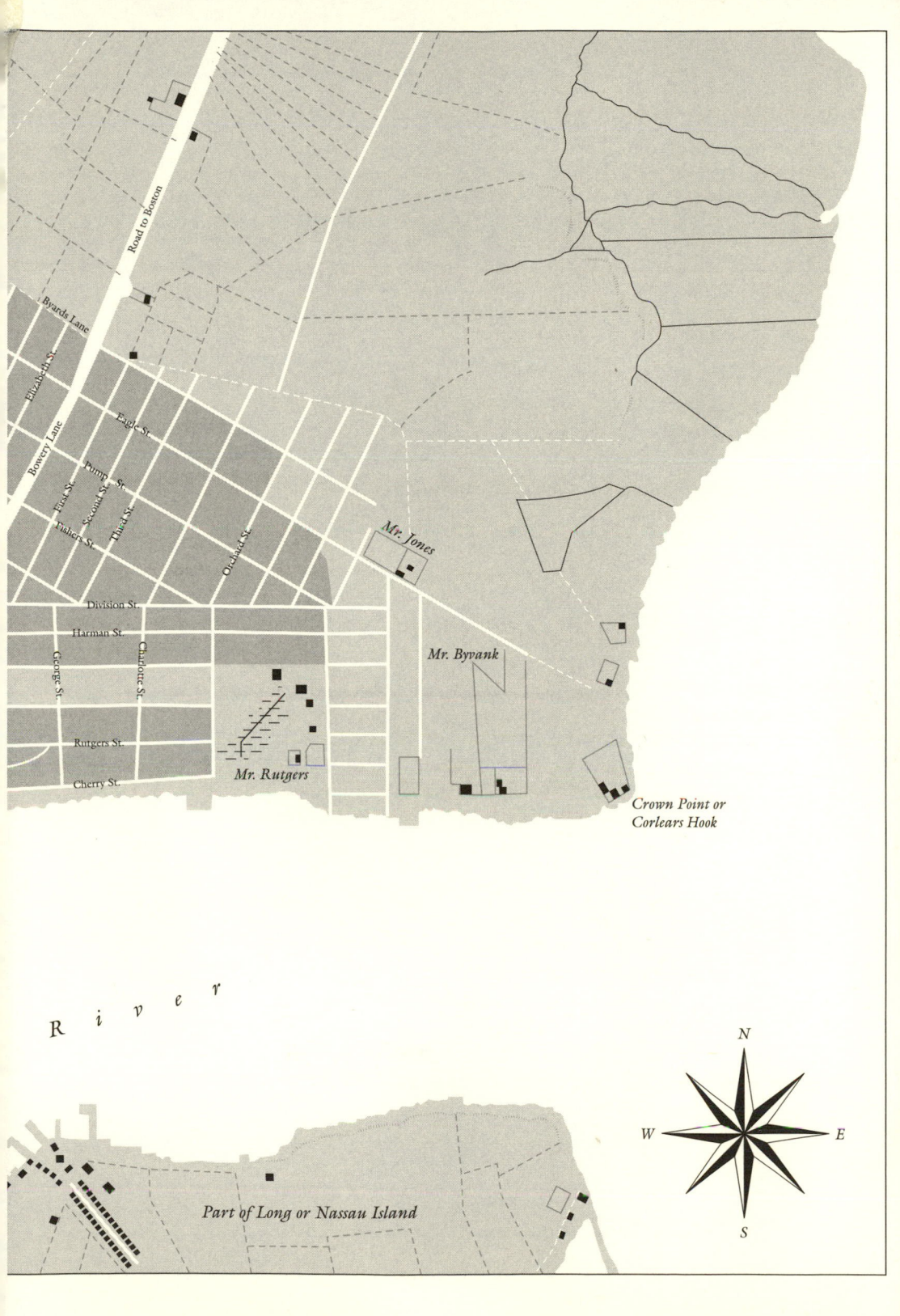

Road to Boston

Byards Lane

Elizabeth St.

Bowery Lane

Eagle St.

Pump St.

First St.

Second St.

Third St.

Fisher's St.

Orchard St.

Division St.

Harman St.

George St.

Charlotte St.

Rutgers St.

Cherry St.

Mr. Jones

Mr. Byvank

Mr. Rutgers

Crown Point or Corlears Hook

R i v e r

Part of Long or Nassau Island

N

W   E

S

City of New York and its environs

Introduction

ONE DECEMBER NIGHT in 1778, a group of Patriot men piled into whale-boats along the Connecticut shore with the express intention of raiding a Long Island town under British control.* The destination of the whaleboat contingent on this particular night was a village on Cow Bay in Queens County, Long Island. The raiders knew this hamlet very well, as they had lived there before the war. They were familiar with every cove; they knew the location of their former neighbors' farms; they were acquainted with the most prominent Tories in town. In the wee hours of the morning, the Patriot raiders pulled their boats up on the beach of Benjamin Sands's home and then fanned out to conduct their operation. They confiscated anything of value, from guns and grain to tools and boats. On this particular foray they also plucked a conspicuous Loyalist out of his home for transport back to Connecticut. Perhaps most remarkable, while spreading mayhem in this tiny village, the raiders dropped in to see parents, siblings, and cousins. In the midst of their military operation, they caught up on family news and perhaps shared a meal.

Such encounters were dangerous business for all concerned. Corresponding with the enemy was bad enough but welcoming him into one's home was a much more serious infraction. The warmth of that welcome varied from household to household. One care-worn father claimed later that he chided his son never to return again under such circumstances. However upsetting the various encounters were to these families of split loyalties, the relatives of the raiders did not report the visits to British authorities. Nonetheless, a neighbor, whose brother had been kidnapped during the raid, ran to the redcoats and identified certain of his neighbors for receiving the rebels. Five men, all reportedly members of the Queens

---

*This study will employ the terms "Patriot" and "Whig" to characterize those who supported the Continental Congress and American independence. The terms "Loyalist" and "Tory" will be used to identify those who supported the British during the war. It is important to remember, however, that Tories were as American as the Whigs and thought of themselves as patriots in that they loved their country as much as any supporter of American independence.

County [Loyalist] Militia, were subsequently accused of treasonable practices and keeping correspondence with the enemy.

At their trial, the accused defended their loyalty, pleading that they had no choice but to receive the rebels because they were family members. Benjamin Sands, Sr., testified that one of the intruders was "his nephew and three his cousins." Sam Cornell's brother and three of his cousins were raiders that night. Another of the accused recognized his brother, one cousin, and three neighbors' children in the rebel party. Hewlett Cornell summed up the defendants' dilemma when he related that he had been brought up in the same house with some of the raiders and that he "underwent a very severe tryal between Friendship and Duty," acknowledging himself blamable for not reporting their "coming over." The court remained unmoved, banishing four of the five men out of the British lines.[1]

The dilemma of the Sands and Cornell families that December night was shared by many families living in and around occupied New York City during the American Revolution. Public duty called them to one course of action; private attachment often pulled them the other way. The "tryal between Friendship and Duty" often resulted in family connection taking precedence over political conformity. In the act of waging war, staunch Whigs stopped by their friends' and relatives' homes for a chat and a meal, before (or perhaps after!) wrenching their hapless Tory neighbor out of his home for transport back to the Patriot lines.

In many respects, the American Revolution in the New York City region is Cow Bay writ large. Loyalists and rebels, typically depicted as hostile opponents, were, in fact, in constant contact throughout the war, crossing military lines to socialize, lend a helping hand to relatives and friends, or conduct a little business. Occupied New York was never Fortress Britannia, a bastion of solid opposition to the American rebels. Rather, it was the most volatile of places, whose fluid boundaries permitted a parade of Whigs, Loyalists, slaves, Hessians, and those of murky allegiance to interact throughout the war.[2]

This permeability of wartime boundaries and loyalties is a story largely untold in historical writings about the American Revolution. Indeed, to look at the situation around New York City, one would not expect such generous behavior between the two sides. The British occupied the islands of New York Bay—Manhattan, Staten, and western Long Island, where the Royal Navy could protect His Majesty's soldiers. Washington's Continentals and the state militias controlled the mainland around the British-occupied zone. The leaders of both armies secured their areas of operation by determining and reinforcing the allegiance of civilians living under their wing. They pointed their fingers across the Hudson and labeled those on the other side as enemies, pure and simple. In addition to trenches and fortifications, they erected a framework of laws that forbade communication with the enemy. It made sense to keep one's distance from adversaries bent on destroying one's cause. To read the public statements of the leaders of the war is to see two distinct and antagonistic groups who fought for their respective movements. The lines between them are clear.

But away from the legislatures and army headquarters, at the level of everyday experience, the lines begin to blur, the issues to soften. On the street, there was much confusion and fear and many uprooted people. Homes on both sides of the lines were filled to bursting with refugees; their hosts, of course, experienced the strain of this population shift and also the tension of living in close proximity to large numbers of soldiers. When looking for relief, they found little support from their government and army. These institutions simply demanded more sacrifice. And so this population in crisis tempered war's hardships by resorting to connections that had worked in the past. Some of those connections included people in enemy-occupied territory who might not share one's political beliefs. Through seven years of military occupation from 1776 to 1783, many individuals exercised liberality and a certain openhandedness to those on the other side with whom they could identify—whether that person was a relative, business associate, or a person of similar educational background or class. Even major Revolutionary figures in New York State had beloved connections on the other side. John Jay, a delegate to the Continental Congresses, had a brother whose political loyalties were indeterminate at best. The mother of Gouverneur Morris, a co-author of New York's first state constitution, chose to live behind enemy lines; his brother was a general in the British army. One of the daughters of Continental Army general William Alexander (Lord Stirling) lived in occupied New York with her prominent Loyalist husband. General Horatio Gates's brother-in-law was an officer in His Majesty's army. Such conflicts could be found up and down the social scale. Moreover, ties of family and friendship often proved more important to Americans caught in the coils of revolution than did military or political differences.

The episode at Cow Bay also highlights the murky political allegiance of the community in and about the occupied areas of New York City. While the raiders were active participants in the Patriot cause, the sentiments of their hosts on Long Island are less clear. Were they some shade of Loyalist? Or were they neutral, staying behind to protect their farms? Or were they sympathetic to the American cause? Clear-cut political allegiances of the civilian community in the New York City region are often difficult to establish with any confidence.

The drama of this story is further heightened by the fact that these complex characters were not content to stay home. They crossed the Sound from Connecticut; they made regular "jaunts" from New Jersey; they filed up the old coach road from Philadelphia; they crossed the rivers and bays into New Jersey. This book will follow the drama's characters wherever they go. And surprisingly, they often went where they were not supposed to—across to enemy-controlled territory. This movement was not an easy task, as two major armies were dug in on either side of the Hudson, giving support to their partisans. Occupying armies forced people to think about boundaries. Where was the line between collaboration and accommodation? To what extent could political and military authorities dictate one's actions in the personal sphere or the public one?

In order to understand the dilemmas faced by the people in this turbulent setting, it is important to imagine the place—New York and its environs during the Revolution—and to understand the experiences of Revolutionary-era Americans on the ground. From the nineteen-year-old poetess who posted her anti-British poems around Manhattan but later married a redcoat, to the enterprising trader who tried to persuade authorities that carrying a trunk to the enemy side filled with raccoon skins, needles, chintzes, and tea was not illegal trade, to the black man who witnessed the birth of his child thanks to his proximity to British-occupied New York—these resourceful people in a theater of war had to make difficult decisions about a number of critical issues. Most often, average people chose family, profit, or the best offer of freedom, reconciling those choices if possible with political ideology and civic virtue.

The existence of permeable boundaries in the New York theater of war was not unique in the American Revolution, but neither was it present everywhere. The situation in eastern seaboard cities contrasted sharply with locations along the frontier. Warfare to the west of the densely populated seacoast featured violent raids on both sides. Here, the American Indian nations joined the British and Americans as powerful players. As allies of the British for the most part, they incurred "murderous hatred" on the part of pro-Whig whites who killed neutral native leaders and summarily executed captured warriors. Along with frontier areas, the southern theater of war witnessed fewer examples of porous boundaries with respect to the enemy. The war between neighbors in the Carolinas featured few instances of old-fashioned chivalry, although determining allegiance was always a difficult task.[3]

The networks operating around New York City between 1775 and 1783 owe their strength to three important factors: the American Revolution around New York City was not a "total war"; the civilians in and around the city had to endure the presence of two major armies, each with fairly stable areas of operation, for seven years; the enemy looked like them, had a common background, and spoke the same language. With this combination of circumstances, New Yorkers lived with ambiguity as they struggled to prevail over their enemies. Using family letters, diaries, memoirs, soldier pensions, Loyalist claims, committee records, laws, newspapers, and church and meeting records, this book will allow its subjects to speak and, in doing so, will explain how a community sustained itself and attempted to shape and survive the American Revolution.

From the beginning of the war, political and military leaders tried to identify and separate the Whigs and the Tories. American authorities in New York City and its environs were the first to attempt such a threshing operation, but the chaos of a city on the brink of a major battle competed for their attention. I will adopt the perspective of the individual in the street to chart the confusion that reigned in the city from the news of Lexington and Concord in April 1775 to the eve of the battle of New York in August 1776. Most New Yorkers were too busy trying to read the signs of the time to bother about rooting out those who did not toe the Continental Congress's line. In a city known for its factious politics, the Committee of Safety worked furiously before the battle to identify internal enemies, for a noticeable number of these objectionable characters remained in the area ready to aid the British when they landed. The American authorities in control of New York before the battle had succeeded in displacing most of the civilian population but not in isolating and neutralizing those who rejected the notion of independence.

The outbreak of war drew clearer lines with respect to people's identities. Two armies now ranged the greater New York City area—the English and Hessians on the islands of the Bay and Washington's Continentals on the mainland around the city. Thousands of Loyalist refugees streamed into the British sector, while other thousands of displaced New Yorkers looked for shelter in areas outside the city. The lines between the two armies and the refugee communities were further etched geographically by water that surrounded the British strongholds. Despite these formidable obstacles, the soldiers and civilians of this drama managed to bridge the gap with lively networks of sociability, civility, and aid during the war. The war so taxed civilians that they began to look for succor from friends and acquaintances on the other side of the lines. The most intrusive presence in civilians' lives was not the enemy but their own occupying armies, who made enormous demands on them. Civilians in the New York City region had to weather the experience of sharing their lives with 50,000 young men of both sides who did not have much to do. The pent-up energy of such a conglomeration of armed youth resulted in many humiliating encounters and personal attacks for the neighborhood. Under such unrelenting pressure, the people living with the two armies looked for relief where they could find it.

And they found this relief in the networks that had worked so well for them before the war. Family connections across military lines meant needed medicine or extra grain. With the two major armies at a stand-off for the duration of the war, the people of New York City experienced greater long-term strain than did the citizens of Boston or Philadelphia, where military occupation was of much shorter duration. In this highly stressful situation, family ties often overcame the restrictions and demands of congresses and committees. Authorities on both sides—while according greater mobility to women as nurture providers and caregivers of their families—eventually realized that women were capable of carrying potentially damaging information across military lines. This concern was grafted onto laws that specifically mentioned women's movement.

While families carried on with old friends and relatives, the warriors of the conflict formed new networks as British and American soldiers peaceably crossed into each other's territory throughout the war. The movement of paroled officers sprang from an ancient European code that gave nothing to the rank and file. Americans both adopted and adapted this European way of war that created so much movement among the officers and made two distinct levels of experience in the Revolution: that of officers and that of the common soldier. These two experiences of the Revolution met in the high drama of the Arnold-André spy controversy, an event that further illuminates the codes of war and their consequences.

The Revolution provided profitable opportunities for commercial men and women bold enough to assume war's risks and able to develop a solid network of the right connections. Many enterprising individuals conducted trade between the hinterland and occupied New York with a relish unmitigated by laws prohibiting such activity with the enemy. These agile operators ranged from small-time actors who found the holes and bribed the right people to major characters profiting from patriotic piracy or privateering. In each case, the people making money from such questionable activities managed to concoct rationalizations for their doings.

The fact of war, and not the Declaration of Independence, provided new opportunities for the African American community. For the first time in American history, a powerful institution, the British army, supported the liberation of slaves. Many African Americans availed themselves of this opportunity by crossing the military lines to seek freedom. Though former slaves continued to experience a harsh existence behind British lines, they raised their voices and exercised control over their destinies in ways they had never done under the Americans.

Slaves

By the fifth year of occupation, these networks of self-interested individuals formed a steady fixture in the scene around New York City. The British defeat at Yorktown in late 1781 provided an added sense of urgency to these movements as it dawned on many that the Americans would eventually reclaim the city. Yorktown provided a two-year period in which Tory and Whig communities could take tentative steps to patch up their quarrels. In the last two years of occupation, Loyalist Americans developed a number of strategies to salvage what they could from a fast-deteriorating situation, including an effort to align themselves with conservative Whigs. The Loyalist presence in the new American city of 1784 was a divisive issue, yet an issue swiftly resolved in the early postwar years. The Revolutionaries would live and let live in part because they had participated in networks that tempered war's hardships and reminded them of the humanity of those on the other side.

life for loyalists post war

The seven-year stand-off around New York City saw two communities operate in close, sustained proximity, each testing the limits of political and military authority. The permeable boundaries between them, the need to make decisions in life-and-death situations, the privation and daily stress blurred their relationships with each other and their commitment to a cause. The war of the Revolution was won in the context of ordinary people's day-to-day lives. In light of the crushing demands made by both sides in this military theater, it is no wonder that people often chose a course outside the strictures of army or legislature. They learned to survive on their own terms and in so doing became generous enemies.

I

The Seat of War

As the first European explorers approached what became New York City in the sixteenth century, they smelled the sweetness of the land before setting eyes on their new home as the fragrance of wildflowers and fruit trees on the New York islands wafted miles out at sea. A century and a half later, the promise brought by ocean breezes was still realized by the land itself. It was "a most delightful part of the world," opined a newcomer in 1776.

Long Island's isolated hamlets lay in a sea of meadows, orchards, and fruit trees of all descriptions. On Staten Island, a tangle of wild grapes and cherries, chestnuts, laurel, olives, and various kinds of nuts mingled with wild roses and blackberry bushes. Wild peaches were so prolific that farmers dumped them into swine troughs. Cedars and sassafras trees the size of oaks graced the landscape. The island's numerous hills offered many a breathtaking view. One newcomer in 1776 visited regularly a particular perch from which he could see inbound ships from Europe slowly appear over the horizon. "The wide open ocean lay in front of us . . . the lovely fields of Long Island lay shimmering across from us [and] on the other side, were South Amboy and the lovely Pharos Tower."[1]

As those ships passed the narrows between Long and Staten Islands and into Upper New York Bay, passengers caught their first glimpse of Manhattan Island, on the tip of which stood the city of New York. The first noticeable feature of the city was its colors. The four, five, or six story brick-and-tile houses were crowned with cedar shingles, varnished and painted in a wide spectrum of hues.[2]

The buildings of New York's old city on the island's southern tip were of Dutch construction with distinctive steep-gabled facades, holdovers from the New Amsterdam days of the seventeenth century. The red brick edifices were sometimes painted white, as were many other buildings.

A View of New York in 1775, engraved by Sidney L. Smith, ca. 1906, after an aquatint in *The Atlantic Neptune*, 1781. Featuring New York's hills, trees, and church spires, this engraving also shows the logistical source of British strength—the city's harbor, which accommodated the great ocean-going vessels of His Majesty's navy. Eno Collection, Miriam and Ira D. Wallach Division of Art, Prints and Photographs, The New York Public Library, Astor, Lenox and Tilden Foundations.

On a sunny day, the vibrantly colored city must have gleamed between blue water and sky. Soldiers pouring into town in 1776 pronounced it splendid, extremely delightful, most beautiful, and magnificent. The streets were narrow, paved, and tree-lined, providing "shelter from the amazing heats in summer." The urban center extended just beyond the site of the World Trade Center, beyond which were farms, meadows, ponds, and country estates with terraced gardens flanked by orange, lime, pomegranate, and citron trees.[3]

Whether one sat in a terraced garden in the city's outskirts or on a roof in the center of town, the views were breathtaking. Homes often had "balconies on the roof, where company would sit in the summer evenings to enjoy the prospect of the opposite shores and harbour."[4] Here was visible the impressive expanse of New York's harbor, which welcomed the largest ships in the world and ushered them to the city's docks. From their rooftop balconies, New Yorkers also saw beyond the forests of masts at the town piers to the islands in the enormous bay beyond. An incoming West Indies schooner or a Hudson river sloop regularly pierced the horizon.

Balth. Frederic Leizelt, *La Nouvelle York*, ca. 1775. Although Leizelt was never in occupied New York, his series of contemporary images captures the energy of a bustling eighteenth-century port city. Eno Collection, Miriam and Ira D. Wallach Division of Art, Prints and Photographs, The New York Public Library, Astor, Lenox and Tilden Foundations.

Small oyster boats maneuvered among the grand full-rigged, three-masted ships bound for Europe. Greeted with such idyllic scenes, spectators were rarely disappointed.

The tranquility of the landscape belied the agitation of its inhabitants. Indeed, New York's ethnically and racially diverse population had been plunged into controversy and high emotions since the imposition of the first tax acts by the British in 1763. The thrust and parry of New Yorkers' relationship with the mother country had gradually crept into every corner of their lives and by 1775 anxiety and paranoia reigned in town. The April 24 edition of the *New York Mercury* informed city dwellers of the first major clash between British soldiers and American farmers at Lexington and Concord. On the heels of this news, a second Continental Congress convened in Philadelphia, organizing an army and advising local governments to suppress Crown authority.

At the local level, New Yorkers responded to the tax crises by forming committees that would coordinate the community's response to the mother country's latest moves. No ideologically seamless group sprang up to compose the revolutionary committees. Instead, the city's leadership featured radicals and conservatives who repeatedly reconfigured the revolutionary city committees, vying with one another to shape the debate and control the ever-careening course of events. By the time of Lexington and Concord, the radicals had managed to wrest control of the city committees from more conservative elements.[5]

The revolutionary movement in New York comprised a wide spectrum of political characters, from rioting sailors to scions of the city's wealthiest families. The latter often eyed the former with a flicker of fear. Conservative Whigs at first outnumbered their radical brethren and strove to find a compromise that would avoid armed conflict and a total cessation of trade with England. Future Continental Congress member, Gouverneur Morris, a young attorney at the time, was not even sure which was the greater of two evils, the mother country or the muscle-flexing lower sort who plucked outspoken opponents out of their houses in order to intimidate them.[6]

In addition to those loyal to King and Parliament, and Whigs of various persuasions, there was an even greater number of New Yorkers who refused to side with any particular faction, focusing instead on their daily activities. But as tensions intensified in 1775, politics increasingly impinged on the mundane so that even those who were neutral had to make plans for a possible sea-change in their lives. If musket balls could fly in Massachusetts, these people reasoned, they could fly in New York. In the whirlwind of changing conditions, even self-assured businessmen were confounded. Christopher Smith, a prominent merchant, was overwhelmed in his attempt to read the times and act accordingly. "The Dread I am now under for fear of our City being destroyed," he wrote to his friend in the Continental Congress, was such that he plaintively wondered, "how to act [I] do not know." Another bewildered man of affairs, Peter Keteltas, wrote of the confusion in town as early as May 1775. "I am so much out of humour with the times," he complained, "that I don't care to touch on them—the Congress has alarmed us more than anything by ordering us to prepare a place of safety for our Women and Children. I see no danger except we bring it on ourselves," he continued, "for I can't find that there are any troops destined for this place. We have been so alarmed from day to day with different stories about troops coming."[7]

In such a state of affairs, decisions had to be made about moving family members, furniture, and business inventories out of the city. Should ships be loaded immediately to avoid delay or possible confiscation in the event that armies and navies descended on the city? Could merchants sell tea that was ordered well before Congress banned its consumption? Should inventories be spirited away to neighboring colonies? In May 1775, Robert Ray, a member of the Committee of 100, contemplated sending his wife and sister to the country. Stealing a moment at midnight to write to a friend in upstate New York, he explained that he was "almost too confused to write" but expected that "all our ports will be shut up by the Continental Congress; all the vessels in our harbor are hurrying all they can to get away by that time."[8]

By the end of 1775, the rush of events kept average New Yorkers poised at a high pitch of nervousness with little time to digest each development before the next crisis swept into their lives. On May 26, the sixty-four-gun warship *Asia* sailed into the harbor and anchored opposite the Battery. Its provocative presence seemed a fulfillment of the rumors that the next battle would indeed be in New York. Despite assurances that the warship meant no aggression, its looming bulk increased anxiety and provided more grist for the radical Whigs' propaganda machine.

Three months later, the *Asia* shelled the city when Patriots removed British cannon off the Battery. While it was unclear who fired first, the exchange marked the first time that British guns had been used on New Yorkers. The effect was electric. Fifty years later, New York City veterans still recalled the event as one that sparked their commitment to the American cause. But while many a young man's blood boiled in defiance, other New Yorkers saw this event as proof that they should vacate the city. By October 1775, Christopher Smith of Long Island looked in vain for advice and assistance from his friends because so many had already moved out of New York. Those few who remained seemed as puzzled as Smith. "Within this few days past," he wrote, "many of the principal people are gitting their most valuable Furniture and Effects out of New York City. And I am told that yesterday, it look'd much the same as it did the day after the *Asia* fired on the town." Smith crossed the East River to see for himself that prominent men like Peter Keteltas, Jacobus Van Zandt, Leonard Lispenard, Francis Lewis, and Mayor Mathews were planning to vacate immediately. But what alarmed him most was "that the Governor does not seem satisfied to remain amongst us."[9] William Tryon, the Royal Governor, had indeed given up trying to control the events in town and felt so threatened that he fled to a British warship in the harbor on October 19.

By the end of 1775, there was no reason to hope for a peaceful resolution to the conflict.

That so many leaders left the city was not surprising. It was hard to gauge accurately the situation in New York between the time of Lexington and the Declaration of Independence. While New Yorkers read the Congressional declamations of loyalty to George III, they also perused weekly newspaper reports on the latest developments in the American invasion of Canada.[10] Confusion was exacerbated when Congress forbade any future trading with British fishing settlements in Canada, while the local Whig authorities permitted the victualling of British warships in New York harbor. For a merchant whose business was adversely affected by the Canadian restrictions, this turn of events was hard to figure.[11] Perhaps the most dramatic example of such confusion was the public demonstrations of June 1775, when New Yorkers greeted Royal Governor Tryon and the Continental army Commander-in-Chief, George Washington, with equal enthusiasm. Some witnesses said that many of the same people attended both demonstrations.[12]

The newly emergent political powers were also struggling to make sense of the accelerating chaos. A bewildering array of fledgling committees and congresses proclaimed their legitimacy and issued directives, but they were bodies with no history, no mandate, and no record of support from the community. In their daily lives, citizens now had to contend with this new galaxy of organizations including the Continental Congress in Philadelphia, the Convention in New York State, and local committees, some of which enforced the boycott and corresponded with other colonies, while others worked to uncover conspiracies and unmask internal enemies. In addition to legally constituted organizations, one could only ignore at one's peril the periodic appearance of groups of citizens who took matters into their own hands. In the early going, these various wings of the Revolutionary movement had not figured out who they were, what they were supposed to do, or where their responsibility ended and the next group's began. They were in the process of defining themselves in the midst of a full-fledged crisis that did not make for clear-cut distinctions or easily anticipated behavior.

On December 22, 1775, Great Britain stoked the Revolutionary flames and added to the chaotic situation in the colonies with passage of the Prohibitory Act. Heretofore, Mother England had protected her fledgling colonies, but when its recalcitrant children shouted in defiance of the tax

*British
tax
acts*

acts, she was impelled to administer harsh discipline. The act prohibited trade and commerce with the rebellious colonies, in effect declaring them outlaws and banishing them from the British family of nations. Indeed, their ships and goods were to be treated in the same way as any open enemy of Great Britain. The act was a godsend to the radical Whig leaders who proclaimed it a declaration of independence by act of Parliament. In their eyes, England made the break and declared American independence before the Americans did.[13]

In early 1776, as tensions increased, New Yorkers learned that the British had abandoned Boston, and that their town was the next likely point of confrontation. In the face of conflict, positions hardened among Whigs and Tories alike. As conciliatory rhetoric waned, New Yorkers continued to abandon the city. When General Charles Lee arrived in town with the first New England troops, even more decided it was time to leave. One city resident who had moved his family to Long Island claimed that "most of the Inhabitants left the city for Fear of another cannonading." The day after Lee's arrival, more British ships sailed into the harbor, including a 24-gun vessel carrying the British General, Henry Clinton. "The arrival of these vessels alarmed the Inhabitants of this City very sensibly," proclaimed a city newspaper. In response, more troops from New Jersey and Connecticut poured into town. "We are in daily expectation of having our city knocked down and burned by the Men of Warr," wrote a resident in February 1776. "Most all the effects are moved out of town; and at least

*people running from
the city in
droves*

half the families are gone and others agoing so that we are a compleat garrison town." Another New Yorker wrote of the "terror and confusion" in the city. "One-half of its inhabitants have withdrawn with their effects; hundreds without the means to support their families." William Smith noted the panic that reigned as hundreds of people fled with their belongings on a raw February day. As Smith looked over to the Jersey shore, he saw household goods everywhere, "there being not a sufficient number of carriages to take them away." Yet another resident noted that each event, whether it be Lee's arrival or the British ships' appearance, touched off another round of flight. "It is impossible to describe the consternation . . . pepol [are] moving as if it was the last day," Garish Harsin reported, "we are now a city of war."[14]

As the native civilian population of New York moved out, an increasing number of American military personnel from New England and New Jersey moved in, occupying the deserted homes of those who fled. "Oh, the houses in New York, if you could but see the insides of them!" lamented a New Yorker writing to London. "Occupied by the dirtiest people on the continent . . . If the owners ever get possession again, I am sure they must be years in cleaning them." [15] For the new residents, this trip was the first excursion outside their immediate region. With the assurance that they gathered at New York to serve their country, these foreigners to the Hudson region, released from the well-known routines of their homes, took in the new, the novel, and even the exotic features of the great city.

Isaac Bangs, a twenty-four-year-old lieutenant from Massachusetts, arrived in April to discover a city "which I found vastly surpassing my expectations." From the Battery at Manhattan's tip, Bangs beheld "a most beautiful prospect." There he looked north up the Broad Way and saw elegant buildings and several churches gracing both sides of the island's most spacious street. He was very impressed by George III's lead-and-gold-leaf equestrian statue that presided over "one-quarter of an acre of beautifull green." Its style reminded him of Roman emperors on horseback.

Lieutenant Bangs's life in New York was one endless round of entertainments. Frolics, elegant dinners, bowls tournaments, wine, grog and egg-pop gatherings filled his days, while curiosity took him to worlds both sacred and profane. He sampled the city's many churches, pronouncing the too-worldly Anglicans "Pedantick," the Dutch "devout," and the German Lutheran minister "A Poor Orator" (despite his inability to understand a word of the service). At a Quaker meeting, he grew weary of the two hours of silence and immediately thereafter refreshed himself with "a Bowl or two of Grog" before returning to camp. Bangs was utterly fascinated with the Jewish service at the city's small square synagogue, providing minute details about the layout of the building and the particulars of the service. To a Yankee from Congregational New England, the variety of religious establishments in New York provided many touristic venues to fill up more than a month of Sundays. [16]

Another source of fascination to Bangs was the red light district of New York, which he visited several times in one week. How could any man "so divest himself of Manhood as to desire an intimate Connexion with these worse than brutal creatures," mused this proper New England Christian. Bangs noted that "at first," he went "out of Curiousity," but neglected to articulate the reasons for his subsequent visits. [17]

Among the engagements of soldiers like Bangs were those connected with the principal reason for their presence in New York—to transform the city into a fortress. The men built breastworks across every street that led down to the water, erected imposing batteries along the Hudson and

North rivers, and fortified the already existing military complex at the tip of Manhattan. They tore up street paving to build walls, installed fireships, and sunk hulks in the rivers to frustrate the British navy.

The Provincial Congress had issued a directive that ordered "all male inhabitants . . . as well as all the Negro men in the city and county of New York" to work on the fortification sites. Corps commanders were to assemble one-third of the males in their respective districts each day with the proviso that servants and slaves could be substituted if it was not their day to serve.[18] It is easy to imagine that the better sort did not likely dig and build the battlements that protected their property from British guns.

The gaiety with which the young Americans encountered New York City in the face of an impending attack is understandable in light of their seemingly impregnable position behind these massive earthworks, barricades, and chevaux de frise. Yet their brimming self-assurance was shattered in July 1776 when two British warships and three smaller craft glided serenely up the Hudson river with nary a cannonball nick in their burnished oaken sides. Lieutenant Bangs explained, "The cannon from the City did very little execution, as not more than half the number of men belonging to them were present. The others were at their cups and at their usual place of abode"—the red light district. The nights of hilarity and frolics were about to end.[19]

As the Continental troops turned the New York islands into fortresses, the civilian wing of the revolutionary movement clicked into high gear, ferreting out and exposing adherents to the King's cause. A sizeable portion of the city's residents were Loyalists, and an even greater number had no great stake in the Whig cause at all. In July 1776, a correspondent wrote to John Adams from New York City, lamenting that "hundreds in this Colony are active against Us and such is the Weakness of the Government, (if it can deserve the Name) that the Tories openly profess their Sentiments in Favour of the Enemy, and live unpunished." Yet the confusing array of Patriot authorities made no harmony in their treatment of the Loyalists. While the Committee of Safety might appear downright obliging to suspicious persons, the army might summarily order high-profile Loyalists to be incarcerated out of town, and the mob might terrorize those of particularly obnoxious bent. Each organization had its own style of refashioning the community, whether by persuasion, intimidation, or brute force.[20]

The New York Committee on Intestine Enemies, for instance, composed of moderate Whigs like John Jay, Gouverneur Morris, and Philip Livingston, tolerated highly elusive answers from its suspects. William

Axtell, an officeholder under the colonial government, had his day before the committee on June 24, 1776. When asked if he was a Whig, Axtell replied that he was never unfriendly to his country. When asked if he approved of the actions of the Continental Congress, he let down his guard a bit and responded that he did not approve of all American opposition to Britain, particularly the Canadian campaign. When asked if he thought America had the right to defend its liberties by force of arms, Axtell claimed that he could not answer the question because he had the bulk of his fortune in Britain and the West Indies. Such slippery responses did not prevent the Committee from granting Axtell a parole requiring him never to oppose the measures of the Continental or Provincial Congresses. Axtell balked at the Committee's decision by claiming that the terms of the parole were too "broad." The unflappable Committee of Safety took no offense at Axtell's objections, giving him a copy of the parole to peruse at his leisure with the request that he return in three days with a definitive reply. When Axtell next appeared before the committee, he refused to sign the parole, as it "might be construed on the other side of the water [as] an overt act and made use of to forfeit his estates there." The substantial men of the Committee understood Axtell's "particular situation," but they did not have the authority to grant exceptions. They promised Axtell that they would take the matter up with the Congress of the colony.[21]

This accommodating behavior among gentlemen did not carry over into the streets, as mob violence intensified in the summer of 1776. Indeed, in the same month that the Committee on Intestine Enemies played cat and mouse with the likes of Axtell, the "people out of doors" plucked the more obnoxious Tories out of their homes to ride them on rails through the streets. One witness called these events "grand Toory rides" after which he gloated that "hardly a toory face to be seen this morning." During the same summer, an American soldier rounded a corner to see "a large mob" stripping its victims as it subjected the Tories to the rails. "Many officers endeavored to suppress them," noted Lieutenant Bangs, "but were unable [sic] only to disperse them for a little time." At nightfall, another mob deposited two Tories at an army post for safekeeping. The soldiers, finding no crime against their charges, released them. But the terrified men insisted on staying in their "safe haven" with the soldiers.[22]

In the midst of building a solid community behind an impregnable stronghold, New Yorkers awoke on the morning of June 29 to find that the British fleet had finally arrived in New York Bay. More than one hundred ships anchored off Sandy Hook on that June day to be followed by hundreds more. One Yankee soldier from New England sufficiently swallowed his fear to admire the "great display . . . of the vessels of all sizes." He was particularly taken with the picture presented by the fleet when it spread its sails to dry after a rainy day. "They [the sails] covered a large extent of the water," exclaimed the American soldier.[23] Even seasoned veterans of the British navy rhapsodized over the breathtaking assemblage of ships. According to Vice Admiral Sir George Collier, the masts of the British vessels appeared "as thick as trees in a forest." In July 1776, the Vice Admiral reported that at New York, "everything breathes the appearance of war. The number of transports are incredible. I believe there are more than 500 of different kinds besides the King's ships—a Force so formidable would make the first power in Europe tremble."[24] The effect of such a force, so beautiful and so deadly, was not lost on the Americans, who could not help taking in the fleet's splendor and disastrous potential.

With the enemy at hand, more Patriot soldiers streamed into the city and out to Long Island. "Throngs of men beyond reckoning are collecting," wrote an army chaplain to his wife in July. Whole streets in town were choked with men who set up camp, virtually stopping all wheeled and pedestrian traffic. City thoroughfares were "amazingly dirty," reported one newspaper, "it cannot be otherwise while a numerous army are in and about the city." A member of the Continental army described New York City in early August as "this shocking place." Garbage and urine could not drain into the Hudson fast enough to alleviate the oppressive odor permeating everything. "The air of the whole city seems infected," observed the soldier. "In almost every street there is a horrid smell." Appeals went out to those citizens remaining in town to pitch in and tidy up. Soldiers were ordered to bathe.[25]

The city authorities ruled over a logistical nightmare in placing and provisioning new regiments, and in regulating any maverick behavior on the part of soldiers and civilians. After listening to the first public reading of the Declaration of Independence, a party of zealous but raucous Patriots pulled down and mutilated the gilded statue of King George on the Broad Way. A general in the army applauded the idea but condemned the "appearance of riot." Businessmen, in the mad rush to settle accounts in a city emptying of its people and wealth, printed tickets to be used as a medium of money exchange, having no faith in the new congressional paper money. Here again, city authorities had to discourage such practice as tending to depreciate Continental currency. Some merchants refused to accept any newfangled money like the notes issued in Philadelphia, and so

Pulling Down the Statue of George III, by the "Sons of Freedom," at the Bowling Green City of New York July 1776. Painting by Johannes A. Oertal; engraved by John C. McRae, 1853. When news of the Declaration of Independence reached New York City, a crowd pulled down the statue of King George III on Bowling Green. Most of the mounted king was melted down for musket balls, but some of the statue survived. The king's head was sighted in Britain after the war. The stone slab at the base of the statue served as a burial stone for a British officer and later as a front step at a New Jersey home. The horse's tail and a few stray bits also survived the dismemberment and now reside in the collection of the New-York Historical Society. Eno Collection, Miriam and Ira D. Wallach Division of Art, Prints and Photographs, The New York Public Library, Astor, Lenox and Tilden Foundations.

were advertised in the city papers as enemies of the people, making them fair game for the mob.[26]

While movement and great confusion reigned in New York, some citizens sized up the situation and decided to take their chances in familiar surroundings, electing not to join the general exodus. Some poor people, for instance, had no kin outside the city and opted to stay. Others saw opportunities. Mary Airey, for example, was a widow of Loyalist persuasion who kept a public house and busied herself in acquiring provisions that would most appeal to soldiers. Rachel Ogden, undaunted by the banishment of her husband to Connecticut, evaded the Revolutionary committees' notice to run a lively underground network out of her house for those Loyalists "from distant parts." Some of the enslaved population made themselves scarce in the hopes that the British would come soon and liberate them from bondage, drawing encouragement from the British actions in other areas of America. The Whig authorities were aware of such hopes and tried to dash them by reminding New Yorkers that blacks in Boston who had departed for Canada with the British were subsequently forced to work in the coal mines of Louisbourg.[27]

While some had their reasons for staying, most civilians departed the city by the summer of 1776. In April, William Livingston noted that all of his friends had left. By July, Lieutenant Isaac Bangs reported that the inhabitants in general were "removing from the city" when some British ships moved up the bay and closer to town. The number of Quakers who requested removal certificates to more distant meetings climbed significantly in the summer of 1776. Women, children, and the elderly were ordered out of town in mid-August. Before the blast of battle, one witness estimated that ninety-five percent of the city's population had left town. Some neutral and Loyalist men departed to avoid military service in the Continental forces. Some high-profile Loyalists fled from sure incarceration, and rumors were flying that the Americans would burn the city if they could not hold it. Most departing New Yorkers, however, simply wanted to avoid the battle. With various motivations, outgoing civilians mingled with incoming military personnel to clog the streets. Philip Fithian, an army chaplain, attested to the throbbing quality of a city on the move. In mid-July, he sat in an empty room, vacated by one of the departing New Yorkers. Scribbling at a sermon, he found he made little progress as "half my time cannot even be still for the rattling streets."[28]

By August 1776, the rattling streets echoed distantly. The newly configured New York community, now largely military in nature, waited in nervous expectation for the next move by British forces. On August 12, the city's inhabitants heard a roar of firing from the fleet below town. The city's rooftop balconies filled with gazers, and spectators lined any available viewing space along the batteries. New Yorkers were later to learn that the British were saluting the arrival of the Hessian mercenaries hired by the King to fight in America. Now it seemed inevitable that the battle was imminent. The next ten days dragged on for the citizens and soldiers of New York who lived next to the most impressive assemblage of power ever mustered in their part of the world. The sum total of such might was ominously aimed at them, and they could do little more than wait.

Providence was not kind to the American army in the weeks ahead. On August 22, the mighty fleet began to disgorge 15,000 soldiers onto Long Island. According to one British witness, they "seemed as merry as in a holiday," regaling themselves with the island's fine apples as they advanced. Those few civilians remaining in the fortified city witnessed the battle first with their ears and then with their eyes. The armada in the harbor unleashed shuddering cannon shot onto the battlements so carefully built by the Americans. Philip Fithian's superior education and wide travels had not prepared him for the roaring cannon and the "crack crack, crack" of British guns. "Such a dreadful din my ears never before heard!" he exclaimed. In eight days' time, the British swept the Americans off western Long Island, and after a critical pause to negotiate, steadily advanced up Manhattan. At the island's northern tip, Fithian again noted that "every gun roars and echoes and reechoes among the rocks with great majesty." The few remaining citizens in town lay low among the explosions, the smoke, and the deafening din. Bricks flew and cannon balls hissed through the streets, bounced off buildings, and careened back into cellars. Even more city residents managed to get across the river in the middle of the battle. Those who stayed saw the first representatives from the British ships—Loyalist operatives who were sent to town to urge people to stay. A small group of citizens elected to remain and, to their delight or dismay, witnessed the arrival of their new neighbors.[29]

The tables had turned. Those who formerly had to lie low and swallow the directives of the American Revolutionary government could now let loose and cheer the changing of the guard. The Reverend Mr. Schaukirk, the Moravian minister, saw "a universal joy . . . spread over all Countenances," and "persons that never had taken notice of one another shook hands together and were quite loving." An Englishman saw citizens carrying soldiers on their shoulders, noting that the New Yorkers who remained "behaved in all respects, women as well as men, like overjoyed Bedlamites." While this celebration reigned below, a woman up at the Fort pulled down "the rebel standard . . . and . . . hoisted up in its stead His Majesty's flag, after trampling the other under Foot with the most contemptuous indignation." Thirty-two thousand soldiers formed an inexorable stream of red and dark blue coats as they fanned out across the city in mid-September. New York City was to remain a military camp for seven long years with new major players and new rules.[30]

After the last round of huzzahs had echoed through the littered streets, the British army settled in, allocating housing, obtaining supplies, and securing their positions on the islands that would now comprise their new headquarters. In accomplishing these tasks, they paid short shrift to the thousands of Loyalist citizens who now streamed into town. These refugees annoyed the British with their demands for fairness and a return to civilian government. Civilians and soldiers experienced more opportunities for friction when a fire broke out just six days after the British arrival, reducing the number of habitations in town by one-third. Residents would now have to live in close quarters with the arrogant behavior of their European guests who increasingly viewed Loyalist civilians as tiresome, complaining ingrates. When quick victory proved illusory, these two wary partners realized that their tightly packed haven would be a highly contentious place. His Majesty's army had no intention of allowing civilian government to interfere with its affairs. And so for the duration of the occupation, civilians had little recourse against eviction, assault, phony receipts, and unfair requisitions.[31]

[margin note: Fire in NY limited # places to house Brits]

The plight of those who fled town was no less challenging than that of their city counterparts. The refugees in the American-occupied zone lived on the sufferance of others, whether family, friends, or strangers. Although not eyeball to eyeball with Washington's forces, they were still subject to the demands of armies and the whims of individual soldiers. When circumstances demanded sacrifice, civilians were often forced to move their lodging, to part with blankets, and to see their grain head down the road on their own carts requisitioned by the army. The Patriot authorities monitored speech, severely limited trade, and even on occasion restricted an individual's movement to one's county of residence. That a civilian government composed of elected representatives were the authors of such strictures did not provide much comfort for those who parted company with their property or their liberty. On the whole, a farmer would have preferred to have his grain back in the silos rather than hold a piece of paper endorsed by a newly-formed Congress. Civilian government also meant numerous committees charged with incredible power over local affairs. These neighborhood bodies were not above settling old scores or redistributing wealth.

Abraham Brasher, a refugee who fled to Connecticut, claimed that no one endured as much as the New Yorkers who were deprived of their own hearths for so many years. While Whigs in the city's periphery and Loyalists in New York City would probably lay the blame for their predicament on their foes, they found that the most intrusive force in their daily lives was not the enemy but their own army and government. In the face of such hardship, these people under tremendous stress looked for comfort

where they could find it. And they often found relief with their counterparts on the other side of the lines—individuals contending with similar
challenges, but facing uniforms of a different color. It is useful, then, to examine more closely the conditions confronting both communities, for the
crisis they faced inspired lively networks that would blunt the ravages of
war and relieve the everyday strain of added toil and shortages.[32]

The new soldier in town was a stranger. He was well-dressed, had a
superior attitude, and in some cases spoke a different language. With little
to engage him on the military front, he was apt to seek out new pursuits,
not always wholesome, with which to pass the time. Civilian disapproval
of his rowdy behavior was of no concern to him. His community was the
military family of regiment and so he cared little for the feelings of the
defeated foreigners even if they did claim allegiance to King and Parliament. Throughout the war, he threw his weight around, was occasionally
chastised by his superiors for such behavior, and then continued on in the
same vein.[33]

Throughout the seven-year occupation of New York, unruly soldiers
invaded New Yorkers' homes to take what articles they wanted. An Anglican minister and refugee wrote to his superiors in London that the extent of
"plundering and destruction in the city of New York" was so extensive that
he could not hire or buy a bed on any terms. Not only the victims of theft
lamented the sad situation, but also certain sensitive British soldiers like
John André, an aide-de-camp to British General Henry Clinton. "I have
seen Soldiers loaded with household utensils," claimed André, "which they
have taken for the wanton pleasure of spoil and which they have thrown
aside an hour afterwards." Military authorities tried to limit the damage by
issuing proclamations circumscribing the movement of their men. In January 1777, General Howe dictated that public houses had to stop serving
all soldiers and sailors by 8 P.M. By 9 P.M., all lights and fires had to be
put out in barracks and public houses. The problems that plagued Howe
continued to plague his successors. In December 1779, General Pattison
forbade all seamen in the Wallaback Bay from going ashore on Long Island
because their plundering deprived New York City markets of produce. The
battle for control of their own troops continued into the 1780s for frustrated British officials.[34]

When the army was not busy soldiering, the men became restless, and
with no civil government and little church interference, prostitution assumed new importance with an army in town. The red light district ex-

St. Paul's Church, Broadway, New York. Drawn by C. Burton; engraved by H. Fossette, 1830. This Georgian-style gem sits on Broadway, the only remaining building from the Revolutionary city. It survived the great fire of 1776 as well as the collapse of the World Trade Towers (which would later be built across the street) in 2001. I. N. Phelps Stokes Collection, Miriam and Ira D. Wallach Division of Art, Prints and Photographs, The New York Public Library, Astor, Lenox and Tilden Foundations.

panded around St. Paul's chapel, an area which burned in the great fire in
the first week of occupation and thus acquired the ironic name "The Holy
Ground." In some soldiers' accounts, these women were hardboiled "soldiers' trulls"; in others, they were kindhearted girls who took pity on prisoners of war. One English soldier noted that at services at St. Paul's, he
saw "some of the handsomest and best dressed ladies I have ever seen in
America. I believe most of them was W[hore]s."[35]

Unfortunately for the women of the occupied city, the taverns and
prostitutes did not exhaust the soldiers' energies. Major John Peebles, a
Scots officer in the British army who kept a diary during the occupation, noted that two courtmartials (of three soldiers) for rape in the first
three months of occupation both ended in convictions and eventual pardons allegedly "at the intercession of the injured party." In the first case,
the Commander-in-Chief granted a pardon in the hope that "an act of
mercy will have the proper effect." Such acts of mercy were quite common
throughout the war as soldiers were consistently convicted and consistently
pardoned. Peebles noted that there were many more instances of sexual
abuse "that have not come to the public notice."[36]

Peebles waged the battle against boredom by a dizzying round of concerts, dances, theater, horse races, and impromptu parties. At times, the
gusto with which he pursued these amusements led him to long walks "to
work off the fumes" of the night before. He blamed the venues at which
he caroused rather than himself. "These clubs exceed all rules of moderation," he complained. As the war dragged on, Peebles's drinking bouts increased. By 1781, he related that dinner parties inevitably led to too much
drink. "Above two bottles of Madeira or Port," he estimated, "is generally the quantity that most people carry off." Soldiers like Peebles indulged
in these well-lubricated festivities yet realized that this kind of life was far
from admirable. Still, the men failed to take personal responsibility for their
actions, blaming the city or the city taverns for their dismal decline into
drunken stupors. Peebles wrote that officers returning to Long Island from
New York were "cussing the stupidity of the place, yet all agree that there's
nothing going on there but Luxury and dissipation of all kinds." The lure
of such debauch would bring Peebles and his fellows back to Manhattan
Island in short order.[37]

While the soldiers sank into dissipation, another part of the community watched the frivolities of the city's British defenders in horror and disgust. The military were not the only newcomers in town. Thousands of
Tory refugees risked their lives to cross the armies' lines. They left their

families and livelihoods behind to live under British rule only to find *Lex Britannia* absent or in sharp decline. The flow of refugees to the occupied islands continued throughout the war, with surges of new Tories arriving whenever the British army withdrew its protection from an area: New Jersey in 1777; Philadelphia in 1778; Rhode Island in 1779; Virginia in 1779, 1780, and 1781; South Carolina in 1781. Few refugees could transport whole households to Manhattan. Some were lucky to get away with the clothes on their backs. Others were permitted to carry a few bedticks and some household articles and clothing. Fresh from the devastating experience of losing all that was familiar and comfortable, these people arrived in New York, relieved to be away from their persecutors.

But for many, New York turned out to be a foreign place, far different from their home towns. Rebecca Shoemaker, the wife of a Tory collaborator who fled from her native Philadelphia, was struck by the profusion of goods in New York shops when she arrived in 1780. Her life in New York was studded with contradictions. While she could procure the latest in English fashion, splendid Wedgewood dinnerware, and tea to her heart's content, she could not display such elegant articles in a comparable setting. She described her lodgings in her diary as fronting a narrow street, with a low ceiling which in summer made it unbelievably hot. To her daughters in Philadelphia, Mrs. Shoemaker put on a brave face and cheerily related that she lived "in the modern style, up one pair of stairs," with good-sized rooms and a convenient kitchen. However she viewed her living arrangements, Rebecca Shoemaker experienced the novelty of sharing a house and a kitchen, a far cry from her elegant home in Philadelphia, now occupied by the French ambassador.[38]

Even in a strange land like New York, the refugees strove to duplicate their former lives as best they could. They attempted to set up the businesses and professions of their homes with varying degrees of success. Mrs. Treville, formerly of New England, had the good fortune to be in the entertainment line. In a city filled with military men, there was always room for another tavern. She accordingly opened one in the autumn of 1777 with enough seats in the dining room for fifty gentlemen. Business must have been brisk because one month later, encouraged by patrons of the army and navy, the enterprising New Englander furnished an assembly room for dancing every Wednesday night. The proprietress would provide the music until 10 P.M., after which time, the guests would have to pay.[39]

But not all newcomers were as lucky as Mrs. Treville. As the city filled and new waves of refugees arrived, the opportunities of pursuing one's former work lessened. Daniel Humphreys, a refugee and attorney from New Haven, found no niche in which to practice his profession and so opened a school. When Rhode Island refugees swelled the number of civil servants in November 1779, General Pattison called them "superfluous persons" and moved to cut them from the payroll.[40]

The military was an ongoing option for male refugees who could not find work. The English always needed bodies to operate their ships, fill their Loyalist regiments, and people their battalions. Such employment did not always include a salary, however. The Loyalist regiments of the New Jersey Volunteers, for example, made their bread through plundering raids in their old neighborhoods. They also shouldered the thankless task of supplying the city with wood.

For some refugees, neither old employments nor new opportunities were enough to sustain them through the profound losses prompted by their political choices. Escape was an option for refugees who departed for Europe. Suicide was an option for a few hopeless individuals. It is not hard to imagine that uprooting oneself from all that was familiar caused depression and loneliness.[41]

Other refugees found ways to occupy their time and thus battle the depression that was certainly intensified by the lack of meaningful employment. William Rawle, a young man from Philadelphia, passed many an hour in literary pursuits. He had accompanied his stepfather, Samuel Shoemaker, to New York in the summer of 1778. Rawle enjoyed the advantage of belonging to the Society of Friends, and so stepped into a ready-made circle of support. There, the nineteen-year-old Philadelphian latched on to a literary circle composed primarily of young Quaker women. Headed by twenty-year-old Hannah Lawrence, the high priestess of romantic melancholy, the group wrote poetry and essays, some of which were published in New York newspapers.[42] Using romantic sobriquets, William (Horatio) and Hannah (Mathilda) shared their innermost thoughts by exchanging their journals. (On one occasion, William was miffed that Mathilda had misplaced his diary.) The members of the society also circulated worthwhile books. Rawle waxed lyrical over all the young women in the circle and decided that his sisters in Philadelphia should correspond with them. This correspondence, however innocent, was illegal, a technicality that only seemed to add a sense of tingling adventure to the exchange of creative outpourings between New York and Philadelphia.[43]

As William described it, New York was "overstocked with allurements." Distanced from the Quaker community in Philadelphia while confronting new sources of temptation, the youthful Rawle chafed somewhat under the strict Quaker injunctions not to participate in worldly fripperies. He avoided the "dancing ladies" because he was forced to be a dour figure in the midst of much gaiety. "Nothing can be more distressing," claimed Rawle, "then the pensive silence a young friend must keep when they are talking of balls and [frolicks?], or the patient, placid negative one must return when asked to go to the next play or assembly." It was not easy to obey Quaker strictures in a city with entertainments rare in Philadelphia. In one 1779 gathering, a group of young friends, "mutually condoling and lamenting the strictures of our discipline that prevented our going to plays with other young persons," let off steam by creating a petition to be presented to the meeting. In it, they asked to be allowed to attend entertainments, a request so "ludicrous" that they knew they could never present it to their elders.[44]

Rawle soon grew tired of the vigorous round of socializing among the young female literati of New York. "I am a little ashamed of being near twenty years old," he confessed to his sister, Peggy, in Philadelphia, "without having done anything but talk about sweet girls." There were not enough divine Mathildas and Lavinias to divert his attention from buckling down and choosing a profession. "I have been . . . blowing bubbles in society," lamented Rawle, "wanting the most precious of possessions and enervating at once application and capacity."[45] In the summer of 1781, without obtaining the consent of the Quaker meeting, William went to England to learn the legal trade, returning to Philadelphia in January 1783.

William Rawle's letters from New York City constitute the one sustained account written by a man in which the writer stuck to his own experiences instead of chronicling the political and military developments in the revolutionary city. It is also striking that he barely mentioned the war in his missives home. Except for a few references to soldiers who competed for the girls' affections, one would never know that Rawle walked out of his lodgings every day and saw battlements, military parades, and warships. Indeed, like Rawle, many people in the occupied city strove to continue life in as normal a fashion as possible. But the occupation was a perpetual encroachment on daily life. While Rawle's letters seem like perfectly normal narratives of the life of a young man, the paper on which they were written was folded into one-inch squares for easy concealment as they made their way from the British garrison to Philadelphia. So while the content of Rawle's letters highlight everyday matters in the life of a young man, the folded paper reminds us of the dramatic setting in which Rawle's visits and literary endeavors occurred.

William Rawle eyed the smartly dressed soldiers with envy and disapproval, envy because they attracted the ladies' attention and disapproval because these elegantly attired men did precious little to fulfill the expectations that their uniforms promised. The refugee community was perplexed that so many soldiers dallied in town while reports filtered in at various times that Washington's forces, numbering only a few thousand just across the river, could be taken. They were also exasperated at the fact that these do-nothing military men had the last word on everything that went on in the city. On Long Island, a faithful Loyalist Anglican minister, Leonard Cutting, informed his superiors in England that he and his flock were living a nightmare, as the rapacity of the English officers knew no bounds. It did not escape the clergyman that these persecutors spent the war facing down weaker civilians rather than confronting rebel soldiers. This "worse than useless regiment," Cutting complained, "has scarce been out of the smoke of Hempstead since its first arrival." The outraged and bitter clergyman went on to explain that Englishmen at home could not conceive of the tyranny reigning in America, where "the door of Redress is inaccessible."[46]

The military regime regulated all aspects of life in the city, attempting to insure order and to guarantee that the needs of the army came first. Among other rules, it required farmers on Long Island to deposit two-thirds of their hay in the public magazine; slapped pricing controls on wood, wheat, and flour; and rationed salt. To carry away a maximum of three bushels per family, city residents had to procure a paper from an army officer attesting to their loyalty to the Crown.[47] The British regulated the transportation of goods as well. With considerable movement in, out, and around the city, carts were in high demand, allowing their owners to name their price. British authorities again put a stop to the free flow of supply and demand by imposing carting rates and specifying prices down to the hogshead of sugar and pipe of wine.[48] On the surface, proclamations regulating scarce commodities seem entirely reasonable. But as the civilian community quickly learned, such proclamations usually meant that a few well-placed individuals received the lion's share of profit at the expense of the general population.

In addition to controlling what the city residents could eat and at what price, the British military authorities also arbitrarily moved residents about town to accommodate new waves of soldiers and refugees. It was common knowledge that certain well-connected individuals always seemed to end up on top, displacing less fortunate refugees. When General Cornwallis needed a country seat, for example, refugee John Marston had to make way. The following year, Marston had to vacate for Major General Riedesal. General Henry Clinton circulated among five country properties in addition to his fine town residence, once the palatial home of Captain Kennedy at Number 1 Broadway.[49]

Those lower in the military organization took inspiration from their betters and lorded over civilians. Although this behavior was frowned upon, it could never quite be kept in check. When the inspector of the Brooklyn Ferry decided that he was going to share the house of a Loyalist farmer, he seized every room containing a fireplace, effectively ejecting the owners from their own home. His aggressive bid for roomier quarters was thwarted on this occasion by his superiors. When a number of women connected with the 37th regiment took possession of a house belonging to a prominent Anglican family, they were summarily removed. With few means of redress, the average residents had to be ready to pick up and leave. A Philadelphia refugee, for instance, was allotted a run-down tavern into which he invested three hundred pounds on repairs. As soon as it was restored, the Tally-Ho tavern was seized by the army for a barracks. The tavern's rejuvenator had only one option and that was to beg the British command to reconsider—an exercise in futility.[50]

The refugees had a lot to swallow. The British army, which was their only hope of being restored to their homes, was generally thought to be maddeningly indolent and brazenly oppressive. To add insult to injury, they watched as the British tried to woo the rebels back into the fold. Logical expectations went unfulfilled in this unnatural war.

Such behavior did not endear the leaders of the British war effort to their American allies. William Smith, of more liberal Loyalist persuasion, sarcastically referred to the Commander-in-Chief of the British forces, Sir Henry Clinton, as "The Knight" because of the general's many excursions to the country for fox hunting and riding. He reported that many referred to General Cornwallis as a "blockhead" and found General James Pattison to be "warm, vain, and weak." Thomas Jones, a vitriolic Loyalist who had nothing good to say about William Smith, could at least agree with him on the character of British leaders of the army. Jones related that General James Robertson spent his days "running after little missess . . . lavishing away the city funds upon every well-dressed little female." Howe, according to Jones, was always too busy for military matters, as he was involved in a constant round of "feasting, gunning, [and] banqueting." Jones concluded that the British Commanders-in-Chief were marked by "a fatality, a kind of absurdity or rather stupidity."

The leadership of the British army inspired little respect or affection in the civilian population. They seemed to possess no inclination to face the guns of the Continental army, and they made poor work of keeping law and order in town. The British did not even bother to gloss over such inactivity and ineptitude with soft words. They rarely praised the civilians for their forbearance or cajoled them with heartening promises. The extent of public relations on the part of Clinton or Robertson was to issue proclamations with attendant penalties for noncompliance. Such behavior won few hearts.[51]

Loyalist civilians in New York lived in a military headquarters and so might have expected some of this friction. Occupying armies regularly move into civilians' homes, requisition supplies, and rarely prosecute their own soldiers who attack the people they are supposed to defend. But the Loyalists had looked forward to a happier rapport with the English army on the cultural front as the soldiers had come from the home country and spoke their own language. Such hopes went unmet, since soldiers brought with them customs and principles that were different from the Americans' culture. England was not America, nor was the military culture synonymous with civilian ways. Some Americans strove to emulate Europe, but this hankering after things European was always tempered by American institutions and customs. So, while Loyalist Americans bristled at situations where the military imposed its will, their collective eyes narrowed at the activities created to keep up the spirit of the soldiers.[52]

The British army brought cosmopolitan entertainments that had not hitherto found complete acceptance in the American colonies. In the first winter of occupation, for example, some gentlemen of the army and navy filled their many idle hours by opening a theater company with a lively repertory that ranged from Shakespeare to bawdy farces. The John Street Theater performances were certainly a novelty for many of the native-born Americans in town, as theater had been barely tolerated in a number of colonial communities before the war. Indeed, it was thought to be an entity promoting immorality at its worst and a waste of time and money at its best. In 1776, there were no resident theater companies in Philadelphia,

Boston, or New York. In 1778, the Continental Congress moved to suppress "playhouses and theatrical entertainments" as having a "fatal tendency to divert the minds of the people" away from the Revolutionary struggle.[53] The John Street Theater was not beholden to such regulation and had no formidable adversaries. The Presbyterian and Lutheran ministers were not there to rail against the institution, and while the Quaker meeting continued to chastise members who frequented theatrical entertainments, they made no public pronouncements against them. Not that the British soldiers would have heeded such criticism. "Modesty's no virtue in this place," boasted one soldier in a prologue to a 1779 performance. Such a statement found no quarter among the more rigid Americans.[54]

The British complemented regularly held events by disporting themselves with added gusto on certain traditional days. Although Saint George's Day or the King's and Queen's birthdays were not new holidays to the American subjects of the King, if the extent of the celebration is a hint as to a holiday's importance, these days were far more significant to the English. Before the war, the Queen's Birthday received no press attention whatsoever in America. The extent of celebration consisted of a gun salute at the fort. The British greatly expanded on this holiday, noting its observance in the newspapers and instituting a grand entertainment, fireworks, and an elegant ball and supper. One English observer noted with amusement the reactions of the Americans. "To most of them it seemed a most wonderful phenomenon," he wrote. For the first of these celebrations, the Moravian minister in town, Reverend Schaukirk, lent several wagonloads of benches for the entertainment in honor of the Queen's Birthday. By 1780, the minister felt that the festivities on the Queen's Day were inappropriate given the level of distress in the city. "It is said the ball cost above 2,000 guineas and they had over 300 dishes for supper," the disgusted minister wrote.[55]

British officers might have atoned for the gusto with which they pursued their entertainments had they paid attention to religious matters as well. But the British army requisitioned most of the city's places of worship for its own use and did not encourage religious devotion among its men. When high-profile British officers did attend Sunday services, their actions were often interpreted in a negative way by civilian observers. Reverend Schaukirk noted that the only time that General Henry Clinton walked into a functioning church was to accompany Prince William during his visit to New York in 1781. Admiral Gambier and General Pattison, according

Ruins of Trinity Church After the Memorable Conflagration of Septr. 21st. 1776, ca. 1841. A few days after the British arrival in New York City, a fire broke out that destroyed a large part of town including the Anglicans' church on Broadway. During the occupation, the dismal scene shown here was transformed into a controversial entertainment center. Trinity's current building was constructed in 1846. I. N. Phelps Stokes Collection, Miriam and Ira D. Wallach Division of Art, Prints and Photographs, The New York Public Library, Astor, Lenox and Tilden Foundations.

to another witness, were two old coxcombs whose behavior outside the church disgraced their years, but who, every Sunday, practiced high hypocrisy by praying at church and then later that night, violating the sanctity of the day by hosting Sunday night concerts. The two old lady-chasers further aggravated their offense by wearing satin waistcoats to services, an extravagance that even New York Anglicans thought inappropriate within the sacred confines of St. Paul's chapel.[56]

While the civilians gawked and tsked at British frivolity, their disapproval escalated into discernible anger when the British took their amusements to sacred ground. In August 1777, the military government established an entertainment center on the property of the fire-gutted Trinity Church. The government painted the church walk green, railed it in, and posted guards there to keep common people out. They erected benches along the way, hung lanterns in the trees, and sponsored bands to serenade the soldiers and their ladies as they promenaded on a summer's evening. The British named this promenade "The Mall" in honor of its namesake in London. Many New Yorkers took great offense at what they considered to be a violation of hallowed ground. "A paltry affair," snorted a clergyman who took added offense at the presence of a house directly opposite the church used by the promenading ladies and officers' women. He could not square the existence of such a house when "honest people," both inhabitants and refugees, could not find a place to live. William Smith, another critic of the church walk, exclaimed at the unlikely mixture of people congregating about the site. "What a medley assemble there!" he wrote, "A horrible Contrast! Ladies in the Walk, the Mob in the street, and funerals crossing the company to the Church Yard, the parson there officiating at the grave."[57]

New Yorkers had nearly a year to get used to this situation when the Commandant ordered new alterations to the site. He erected an orchestra stand on the north side of the church's chancel, and widened the walk inwards, occasioning the removal of some tombstones, the flattening of certain graves, and the covering of a family vault's mouth. William Smith shook his head, reminding the Governor that although this change might be thought "trifling" to the army, there was a "tenderness of Mankind respecting the rites of Sepulchre" that would probably prompt the House of Commons to revoke such a "Breach of Decorum." Smith also pointed out that it might convert warm churchmen to the rebel cause. The only good Smith saw coming out of the British gaffe was that it might provide an additional argument for the erection of civil government.[58]

Smith waited in vain for the House of Commons to thunder about this violation of sacred space. The only British criticism of the Trinity site development appeared a month later when a British officer wrote a letter to Rivington's newspaper, chastising the gentlemen for taking all the seats on the Mall "as this must be very disagreeable to the fair sex in general, whose tender delicate limbs may be tired with the fatigues of walking."[59]

A less appreciative witness of the church walk site was the Quaker teenager who headed William Rawle's literary circle. Hannah Lawrence (alias Mathilda) also noted the presence of women at the Mall, suggesting that the women's broader skirts necessitated the wider walk:

Enlarge the walk to which the fair
In shining nightly throngs repair.
The female Size, by hoops increased
Demands a tomb or two at least.

By the poem's end, Lawrence summoned thunder and lightning to avenge the dishonor of hallowed ground. Nineteenth-century family papers maintain that she posted the poem at the offending site and at other places in the city, creating a stir and further feeding the controversy.[60]

Hannah Lawrence, William Smith, and Thomas Jones all considered themselves to be "English" before the war—in all likelihood reflecting New Yorkers' attitudes in general. When substantial numbers of English soldiers came to them, however, they found the English to be a different breed. As the war dragged on, and humiliation exacerbated privation, the British soldiers' seemingly harmless pursuit of pleasure grated on the sensibilities of refugees who had sacrificed their lives and fortunes to support a king whose army seemed bent on violating their sense of what was right and appropriate. Disenchantment grew with every eviction, impressment, and confiscation—and with every parade, fancy ball, and pleasure walk.

While the Loyalist refugees in British-occupied New York had to cope with their own army, the civilian population of the American-controlled periphery were no less challenged by the authorities charged with making independence a reality. The Continental army never left the vicinity. While encamped at Morristown, New Jersey, Washington's 13,000 men consumed thousands of pounds of beef per day in addition to bread, corn meal or rice, peas or beans when available, and spruce beer or cider. During the brutal winter of 1780, the men were so desperate for food that they were "compelled to maraud and rob from the inhabitants," activities that Washington told the Continental Congress he could not punish or repress.[61] At times, foraging parties, operating under the eye of local magistrates, confiscated grain, meat, flour, blankets, and carts. The hapless civilian received a receipt that did nothing to alleviate his pain, being redeemable at no government facility in the foreseeable future.

In addition to army mouths to feed, the civilians in the American-occupied zone had to contend with the refugees who fled from New York City. These people swelled the population of the counties surrounding the city. Some were fortunate enough to have welcoming friends and relatives; others were affluent enough to rent a farm, a house, or part of a house; and still others worked as servants or laborers to earn their keep. The increase in population put a further strain on the resources of the area. With the Continental army headquartered in northern New Jersey and later in the Hudson Highlands, the competition for basic necessities became intense. Resources also found their way to the New York City markets, as British hard currency proved irresistible to certain enterprising Whigs. Refugees had to contend with high prices and depreciating paper currency in procuring items once taken for granted, now precious. Even George Washington, the most powerful individual in New York State, complained about prices. "A rat in the shape of a horse," he quipped in 1778, "is not to be bought at this time for less than two hundred pounds."[62]

While New York City residents worried about the availability of foodstuffs, the refugees on the periphery found few available manufactured goods. Even the well-off had to make do with what they had in hand. Evert Byvanck, a wealthy New York merchant, wrote in January 1778 that he wore the same pair of shoes in which he had fled in August 1776. William Smith reported that the Livingston children on the manor were "literally barefoot." The ladies of the manor requisitioned newspapers to use as outside coverings for their hats, preferring the insulating qualities of paper to any inside linings.[63]

If affluent refugees wanted for basic necessities, what must the poor have experienced during the war? William Smith, while confined in upstate New York, witnessed the poverty in the surrounding countryside as early as 1776. He concluded that the fight for independence would surely collapse under the weight of people fed up with the "tedious impoverishing war." Smith could not fathom that the promises of the Continental Congress could sustain a people who lost so much in the conflict. "If we have no other luxury than that of being free as a counterbalance for cleanness of teeth and the Plague," surmised Smith, "[then] I trust we shall be bad subjects to the Congress a Year or two hence." Indeed, poor men in Smith's neighborhood reported to the Committee to Defeat Conspiracies that they were enticed into Loyalist regiments by the prospect of three square meals a day. The Committee understood their predicament and typically let off first offenders with a warning.[64]

The scarcity that refugees experienced throughout the war included not only provisions but also housing. As early as July 1776, a resident of German Flatts reported that people pouring out of New York could find no available houses in the surrounding area. Refugees were forced to impose on relations and friends or rent rooms in area homes. The odyssey of

[handwritten margin note: Even wealthy had to make do with what they had]

Helen Brasher of New York City, for example, started in Hackensack, then took her to Esopus and on to Paramus. There, she shared a Mr. Hopper's house with twenty-four other people before it was raided in the summer of 1781. Helen's husband later wrote in his new refuge in Morristown that his family was like "birds of passage perched on a tree full of thorns, not knowing what course to take to arrive at some fixed abode."[65]

The movements of the enemy were not the only sources of disruption for citizens in the area around New York City. American authorities too pushed people around when they felt that circumstances warranted it. Mary Hay Burn, the wife of an American soldier in New Hackensack, was ordered by a local American official to vacate her house to make way for others. "Why should I not have liberty," reasoned Mrs. Burn, "whilst you strive for liberty?" Others complained of sharing their quarters with soldiers. Even Susannah French Livingston, the wife of New Jersey's Whig governor, characterized her temporary refuge at a friend's house in Basking Ridge as "less than agreeable" because of the number of soldiers billeted at the house. Anna Zabriskie, originally of Hackensack, but living in Kingston, New York, demonstrated more tolerance of the officers who passed through her lodgings, enjoying the attention and "civility" extended her way. Unfortunately, the sublime uniforms of gentlemen-officers could also be worn by low-born yokels whom Anna could barely tolerate. "One must always bear with the insolence of the lower sort," she wrote to her officer-cousin in Washington's army, although unfortunately, "they have the most to say."[66]

Refugee communities in both Whig- and British-controlled areas suffered the loss of loved ones, expulsion from their homes, and the everyday hardships of the war. But those in the Whig-controlled area faced different challenges from their counterparts in British-held territory. For one thing, the community in American control was much more fractured. There was certainly a contingent of secret Whig supporters in the city, but they had to lie low in a confined area controlled by 25,000 Hessian and British soldiers. The city's periphery, on the other hand, was a much larger area containing forests, swamps, and mountains in which active Loyalists could operate. It has been estimated that between a fifth and a quarter of the lower Hudson valley population, and a third of the New Jersey population, was Loyalist.[67] The more active British partisans roamed the countryside trying to enlist promising candidates for His Majesty's service. They also scoped out rich caches of supplies for possible expropriation once larger contingents penetrated the territory. Armed with tips from informants on site,

British and Loyalist corps from New York periodically raided the country-side, seizing individuals, cattle, and grain. Two such raiders from the De Lancey family were so assiduous in these sorties that they became known as "cow jockeys."[68] Areas closer to New York City were prone to attack, and the no-man's-land between army lines experienced ongoing plundering, kidnapping, and skirmishes. But even communities farther afield were acutely aware of the enemies in their midst. One could never, after all, rule out the possibility of a general uprising of disgruntled "inimicals" who appeared dormant one day, and then erupted the next. Vigilant local committees therefore kept an alert eye cocked on any sour faces, be they critics of the new government or neutrals who balked at signing a loyalty oath to the Convention of New York or the Continental Congress.

One such person under suspicion was a French immigrant and writer who settled on a farm in Orange County, just northwest of New York City. Hector St. John de Crèvecoeur wrote loving sketches of his travels in America and of the daily routine on his farm that brought him much acclaim in the last two decades of the eighteenth century. To read his famous work, *Letters from an American Farmer*, one would hardly know that he had lived through the American Revolution and that he had had serious doubts about the new Revolutionary regime. His controversial essays on the American Revolution would remain in the Crèvecoeur family for 140 years, published only in 1925 under the title *Sketches of Eighteenth Century America*. Crèvecoeur depicted Loyalists as victims and Whigs as immoral opportunists, characterizations with limited appeal in the Age of Revolution.

Unlike Loyalist petitions that tell the bare outline of Loyalist war experiences, Crèvecoeur's stories, particularly one called "Landscapes," provide a lively narrative, replete with dialogue, about the methods used by Whigs to transform Loyalists from long-established neighbors to refugees on the run. The central characters of Crèvecoeur's story include the local deacon, a consummate priggish hypocrite, and his crafty, shrewish wife. Crèvecoeur associated the Patriot cause with hectoring females and empty religious cant. The deacon's wife, who later takes on the character of "Chairwoman," was in the habit of constantly interrupting her husband, correcting him, and dreaming up enriching schemes at the expense of innocuous neighbors whose wealth is the reason that they suffer as Tories. At each step on their road to new riches, the deacon and his wife offer feeble attempts at religious vindication. They justify the horrific imprisonment of a local squire by remarking, "Tis a bleeding cause, as our minister says of it; therefore sufferings must come of it."

In Crèvecoeur's story, the low-born buffoons compose the Committee of Safety while their victims are noble and upright. The deacon and his wife lick their chops over "these rich fellows" who, in refusing to fight, "leave plaguy good fleeces behind." Another ardent committeeman exclaims, "Oh, how it pleases me to bring the pride of these quondam gentry down! This is fulfilling the Bible to a tittle; this is lowering the high and rewarding the low." The Loyalist victims demonstrate more horror at the "low illiterate little tyrants" of their community than any love of King George. The hunted Tories have no choice but to leave their homes and families. One such unfortunate character laments that "we should be thus suspended between poverty, neglect, and contempt if we go to New York, and fines, imprisonment, and exile if we stay!" His story featured skittish authorities on both sides who experienced difficulty in ascertaining allegiance.

Crèvecoeur uttered very similar words when he wrote about his own situation to British authorities in 1779. Under suspicion of inimical tendencies, Crèvecoeur was driven from his home by local enforcers of civic virtue. But he fared no better in New York City where the British imprisoned him as a suspicious character. Like thousands of other refugees, he fled to New York City and there faced new scenes of deprivation and arbitrary rule. Through the intercession of highly placed Tory friends, he eventually succeeded in securing a passage on a ship bound for Europe.[69]

The Revolution at times served as a convenient pretext for settling scores between groups and individuals that had nothing to do with the struggle. Religious differences sundered the Hackensack, New Jersey, community before the war, resulting in discernible political hostilities that had more to do with religion than with the transatlantic power struggle. In the Hudson Valley as well, Crèvecoeur highlighted the friction between rich and poor that resulted in harassment of affluent landowners by recently empowered yokels. Local vendettas culminating in a person's arrest often found their way to the "Commissioners for Detecting and Defeating Conspiracies." Although an organization with a redoubtable-sounding name, the Commissioners decided more often than not to pardon people "seduced" by British agents. They also liberated individuals because of flimsy, unsubstantiated evidence produced by their local accusers.[70] Some of the accused did not wait for their cases to wind their way through the bewildering array of new Whig institutions, opting to flee rather than submit to such fledgling creations in which they had no faith.

With more enemies in their midst, the Americans exercised greater vigilance, but power was more diffused on their side. On the occupied islands, by contrast, the British military ruled supreme. Even when General Howe established a police court staffed by Americans, everyone knew who was pulling the strings. The Whigs, on the other hand, had erected not only a national Congress and state legislatures but also a galaxy of committees to complement the local militias and the Continental army. And occasionally an impromptu assemblage of citizens rose up to correct whatever deficiencies had to be speedily addressed. That this structure might have been confusing to the average citizen is not surprising given that the organizations themselves were not clear as to areas of responsibility. One of Crèvecoeur's characters summed up the situation: We have so many more masters than we used to have. There is the high and mighty Congress, and there is our Governor, and our Senators, and our Assemblymen, and there is our captain of Light Horse . . . and there is you sir, our worthy colonel; and there are the honorable committee. And there are, let me see, one, two, three, four, five commissaries who want nothing but our horses, grain, hay, etc."[71]

To some citizens, such a confusing array of structures was a weakness that could potentially bring down the Revolutionary movement. "Too many rulers," claimed William Smith, "no uniform policy." To others, the multiplicity of ruling powers created too many entrees for grasping amoral individuals who sacrificed justice for greed. Crèvecoeur noted the numerous "givers of passes and pretenders to power and control."[72] There was also an upside to the confusion in the Revolution's ruling bodies. If a citizen could not exact what he wanted from the local committee of safety, he could try other avenues like an officer in the military, or the governor of the state. Despite the seemingly random nature of power in the Revolutionary government, the assemblage of committees, conventions, and congresses managed to "ride the whirlwind" and "direct the storm," to use William Smith's imagery.[73] The fact that civilian government retained its power in American-held territory did not go unnoticed by civilians on both sides of the line. At times, this government enacted harsh measures like property confiscation for the most conspicuous Loyalists and expulsion for those women whose husbands had fled to occupied New York. But this same government was remarkably indulgent when it came to leaving the way open to repentant Tories who wanted to return or to provide a way for suspected Tories to clear themselves. The Committee to Detect Con-

spiracies often resorted to a simple oath in disposing of the cases of suspected Loyalists. A member of a local committee complained to Governor Clinton of New York that a Tory who had actually been in and out of
New York City three times had been given the opportunity of taking the
oath and returning home.[74] For those who officially requested to return,
Governor Clinton decided that incarcerating these people would discourage future desertions, while exacting no punishment would anger faithful
Whigs. So Clinton decided that a short stint in a work detail at one of
the forts would be appropriate. The Commissioners for Detecting Conspiracies further sweetened Clinton's solution by giving the first qualifier
the option of either going to Fort Arnold for a turn at manual labor or
of hiring a substitute to go for him. Provided one was not an egregious
Tory, the path back to reconciliation was not a difficult one. If Whig civilians had taken their cue from Revolutionary organizations concerning the
treatment of Loyalists in their communities, they would have received a
mixed message.[75]

Under considerable strain, the two refugee communities sat facing
one another for seven long years. Both Whig and Loyalist, in temporary,
cramped quarters, experienced the isolation and discomfort of being in a
house they did not consider home and in a community that belonged to
someone else. Both American and British leaders played up these tensions
by launching rhetorical volleys in the press that characterized the other side
as the enemy, pure and simple, imbued with cruelty and even savagery. The
Americans described their enemies as slavemasters, devoid of generosity
and justice, dispensers of rape and devastation. No accusation was too extravagant. If not for the logistical nightmares, the Whig *New York Packet*
claimed, the British merchants would have exported the American community to the "sickly baneful climes of India." The Americans also played
up the alliance between the Indians and the British. They reported with
great relish the atrocities committed by the Indians under British employ,
implying that the British were equally cruel.[76]

The British, for their part, regularly described atrocities committed by
the Americans, particularly on those Loyalists caught in enemy territory.
The more horrific the rumor, the better. In May 1778, the New York City
newspapers reported that two men were crucified in Dutchess County for
attempting to join the British forces. In another story, a Loyalist ventured
into the country in order to bring his family back to New York. En route,
a party of rebels stopped him, strapped him to a tree, and unloaded their
muskets into his body.[77]

Just as the Americans condemned the British alliance with the Hessians and the Indians, so also did the British take aim at the American alliance with France. One satire proclaimed that Louis XVI would soon be proclaimed King throughout America. Linking the Americans with Catholicism and the decadence of French culture and religion, the article went on to say that a French vessel had recently brought a cargo of "50,000 mass books; 200 racks and wheels; 3,000,000 consecrated wafers; 70,000 rosaries" and five chests of "paint for the ladies' faces."[78]

Such propaganda rallied public opinion and explained in a simplistic way why people were suffering. The degree of suffering, particularly in the refugee communities, was intense. George Clinton, the Governor of New York, wrote that New York State "has suffered more by the Enemy than any other on the Continent . . . being the principal Seat of War." Hector St. John de Crèvecoeur told the British authorities in New York that he had borne years of insults, fines, and imprisonment. Yet he realized that his story was no different from that of other refugees, and realized too that the British might become inured to people's pain. "Yet they are not less felt by each sufferer," he reminded those officials responsible for issuing rations. The degree of suffering was not only apparent to those in the midst of it, but also to outside parties. A Hessian officer, Major Baurmeister, saw a devastated America in 1780: "Everybody is disillusioned, and a disastrous indecision undermines all the American provinces. No matter how this war may end, as long as this mess continues, the people suffer at the hands of both friend and foe. The Americans rob them of their earnings and cattle, and we burn their empty houses; and in moments of sensitiveness, it is difficult to decide which party is more cruel. These cruelties have begotton enough misery to last an entire generation.[79]

There certainly were sufferings enough to induce each side to see the other as an enemy, pure and simple. And after reading the newspapers and the leaders' public pronouncements, one is left with the impression that the Revolution was a war between two thoroughly hostile parties—British versus American, or Loyalist versus Whig. But if we delve beneath the rhetoric to examine the revolution at ground level, from the perspective of individual participants, a more ambiguous and complex conflict emerges. Whigs or Tories, undoubtedly attributed their troubles to the enemy. But the most intrusive force in an individual's daily life was not the other side but the army charged with championing the cause. "People suffer at the hands of both friend and foe," wrote the Hessian officer. It is no wonder, then, that an individual could identify with either the Revolutionary or the British side of the conflict and still look for relief wherever one could find it, even if that meant dealing with similarly stressed people on the other side of the political fence. Individuals had to get through each day. One refugee from New York City who lived out the war in New Jersey kept a diary in which the war was barely mentioned. The writer stuck to everyday chores. At least they had not changed. The fireplaces still had to be swept, the animals tended to, and the meadows mowed.[80] The individual farmer, laborer, or innkeeper eked out an existence that oftentimes called for maverick action with respect to the demands made by the men in power. To those individuals, political and military issues were subordinate to concerns about family, earning a living, and basic survival. A family member within enemy lines still needed help, and an illegal shipment of flour from a relative outside those lines could be arranged. Such basic human concerns solidified into networks that throughout the war operated actively across no-man's-land and into the heart of enemy territory.

2

The Web of Family

IN AUGUST OF 1778, Sarah Alexander and her daughter Catherine, both confirmed Whigs, received permission from the American and British armies to cross the military lines around occupied New York. The women wanted to pay a social call on family and friends. Sarah and Catherine stayed in the city for a little over three weeks in the house of Sarah's second daughter, Mary, who had married Robert Watts of the prominent Loyalist merchant family. Their "jaunt," as Catherine called it, consisted of a busy round of social calls with the likes of William Smith, Lord Dunmore, and Andrew Elliot, all Loyalist luminaries in the city. The women were treated with every civility by the British except, Catherine complained, that a lowly sergeant had conducted them to town instead of an officer. Still, Catherine reported in a letter to her father, she had such "an agreeable time" that she hoped to return to town in a few months.[1]

Sarah and Catherine were sipping their tea in Loyalist New York in the summer of 1778; the summer of the Battle of Monmouth; the summer of Tom Paine's "American Crisis #5." It struck neither woman as extraordinary that, as known Whigs, they were given permission to enter the British lines and circulate quite freely there for three weeks. Neither did Catherine and Sarah wonder that as the daughter and wife, respectively, of a Major General in the Continental Army, they were allowed the run of the town. This remarkable forbearance on the part of the British, as well as the sociability of these Whig women, hardly characterize the behavior of enemies. At best, they seem at this juncture to be friends in disagreement.

The Alexander family, like so many others in the Revolution, contained members on the Whig side and the Tory side. But, as we see in this case, political delineations did not necessarily make for definitive splits when it came to bonds of affection. The Alexanders continued to act like a family despite the obstacles thrown up by the war. Their story is further complicated by the nature of Mary and Robert Watts's political beliefs.

Lady Catherine Duer. This picture of Lady Catherine Duer as a sedate, married lady belies her high adventures as a young woman in the Revolution. As Kitty Alexander, the daughter of a Continental army General, she made "jaunts" to British-occupied New York City, where she enjoyed the hospitality of her sister, married to a Loyalist, as well as other high-profile Tories. Negative number 74955. © Collection of the New-York Historical Society.

Were they closet Whigs or disillusioned Loyalists or committed supporters of the King's cause? Did husband and wife see eye to eye on the war? This seemingly simple vignette demonstrates the complexities of life in wartime New York.

Long years of familial connection can often prevail over political differences. But in the New York City area, another factor figured prominently in the creation of family networks that bridged the political divide. New York was different from Boston, Philadelphia, or Charleston in that two major armies planted themselves in and around the city for the duration of the war, giving support to their adherents. Unlike anywhere else in America, Tories and Whigs had plenty of time to eye one another in relatively close quarters. No matter how many loyalty oaths they made their citizens sign, the leaders of both sides had to deal with the disturbing reality that a very powerful enemy loomed in the neighborhood. The armies' presence emboldened partisans to raid enemy territory. Counties between the two armies suffered the most from this violence. But even if not regularly plagued by cattle rustlers or soldier sorties, the civilians in and around the occupied islands lived at a tense, fearful pitch. Unlike the privileged Alexanders, many of them were refugees whose worlds were shattered by the war. Their secure physical base was gone as was the familiar and comforting daily routine of their prewar lives. Residents of these areas saw their neighborhoods inundated with desperate people carrying their belongings on the roads in and out of town. Adding to this influx were the untold numbers of military personnel. Americans had never seen the like of 30,000 soldiers packing Manhattan, Staten Island, and western Long Island. Nor had they imagined another 20,000 troops whose base of operation ranged from New Jersey to the Hudson Highlands. Such raw power made its insatiable demands on civilians and also fed the rumor mill. Even after the major battles of 1776 and 1777, enough military activity occurred to keep civilians alert to the latest reports and frightening hearsay. The demands made on the people affected by the British occupation of New York were enormous and they did not go away.[2]

Such pressure sometimes fractured families, particularly in the early years of the Revolution when war fever induced citizens to sort out each side's partisans and punish them. But the conflict wore out people, most of whom could not sustain political fervor when the logistics of their everyday lives presented such difficulties. This is not to say that the war made the civilian population indifferent to the outcome of the conflict, as much as it encouraged people to distinguish between the private and public demands of the war. In their effort to achieve as much security and stability as possible in time of war, civilians resorted to the conventional networks that had worked so well in the past. The politically fractured community, particularly after 1776, often put family concerns over the demands of congresses, committees, and generals. They leaned on family members and old friends of long standing, it mattering little that armies divided them.

The most dramatic manifestation of this pattern was the movement that took place between the military lines. Civilians crossed the terrain of the two armies ringing New York City on a continuous basis, electing to pursue their private concerns with or without the permission of authorities. And though the authorities tried to regulate movement in and out of town with varying degrees of success, they could never adequately interdict it.

Families could maintain ties in a relatively private and discreet fashion by sending letters across military boundaries. They also engaged in riskier, more public displays of support by aiding incarcerated relatives under the arched eyebrows of the authorities or by crossing the lines to aid kin, often circumventing the authorities' line of vision altogether. Women, in particular, were on the move during the war because they were accorded greater freedom to move around in their role as nurture providers and caregivers. They figured prominently, for example, in the networks of information and kinship that operated in and out of Livingston Manor, where former residents of Manhattan—of various political stripes—lived side by side. Thanks to a particularly informative diary, we can enter this world of complicated allegiances and examine the role of mobile women in wartime New York. The authorities responded to this lively intercourse by passing laws and proclamations against communication with the enemy. We will look at these laws and then at their subjects, Whigs and Tories, who broke the rules and yet still felt that they were members in good standing with respect to their causes. And finally, we will examine the plight of a public servant charged with enforcing these laws. While devising strategies with General Washington and the legislature, Governor William Livingston of New Jersey experienced the mortification of seeing family members join other maverick citizens of the state who found good reason to cross the lines into British-occupied New York City.

Maria De Peyster Bancker Ogden worried about her boys, even though they were men in their thirties, married and settled. She had heard the news of Lexington and Concord, witnessed the increasingly bellicose activity of committees and congresses, and grew ever more fearful that the irresistible momentum to take sides might sweep up her sons, leaving her a grieving mother. She believed that the great events of this world were not for her loved ones to solve, but rather for the Lord to settle who had "the harts of Kings in his hands and rules them as he pleaseth." On May 16, 1775, Maria sat down to pen a letter of advice to one of her sons in her large, careful hand. "I am afraid," she wrote, "[that] New England will set all the continent in blase. I hope," she added, "[that] you and your brothers will not show yourselves too warm the one side or the other." Trust in God, Maria advised, rather than lean too much upon "the arm of flesh."[3]

In this epistolary gesture of maternal affection, Maria Ogden counseled discretion, caution, and a blessed passivity based on the faith that God would chastise where he would. She, like other mothers, did not want to see her children hurt. Her children, however, like many other mothers' sons, ignored the protective admonitions of maternal love. Maria's youngest son, Gerard Bancker, threw himself into the Whig movement with great enthusiasm, becoming the Treasurer of New York under the Provincial Congress. Her middle son, Johannes, joined the Continental army. While her two youngest sons declared their decided warmth for the Whiggish side, Maria's eldest son, Evert Bancker, Jr., stayed in New York City, signed Loyalist petitions, joined the city militia, and carried on his business affairs, which included an appointment as surveyor of the City of New York. He was a model Loyalist citizen of the occupied city yet Maria Ogden did not cut him off. Evert, in turn, did favors for his family, such as sending various purchases to his sister in Albany. She responded in a November 1777 letter by reminding her brother that "many joins in desiring to be remembered to all Friends at New York." Evert conducted business transactions for his Whiggish relatives, including his cousin Adrian for whom he collected rents on city property.[4]

Such family devotion, manifested in an exchange of letters, prevailed in high-profile military clans as well. Daughters of a British officer in Canada, Elizabeth and Ann Phillips married men in the 1750s who would eventually fight on opposite sides during the Revolution. Ann married Robert Fenwick, while Elizabeth married Horatio Gates, both careerists in the British army. Elizabeth and Ann traveled with their husbands and maintained a loving correspondence that no revolution could stop. The Fenwicks, who stayed in the British army, found themselves besieged in Boston in 1775, while Horatio Gates came out of retirement in the same year to become an Adjutant General in the Continental army. With both women on the move in the middle of a theater of war, they did not know where to write and so their correspondence did not resume until 1778, when Elizabeth managed to get a letter to her sister in occupied New York. Ann was jubilant to receive such an "affectionate remembrance." She brought her sister up to date on her husband's illness, the health of her six sons, and her string of tragic pregnancies.

After her husband's death and an unpleasant run-in with the city's housing office, Ann dismantled her Broadway household to move her family of seven children (she finally gave birth to a girl) to England, "there to rest the remainder of my unhappy days," she wrote. Although sorely challenged by the war's circumstances, Ann betrayed no hint that she bore a grudge against those on the other side of the military lines, no intimation that she was jealous of her solidly settled and well-off sister, no hatred of her brother-in-law who proved to be the nemesis of the British army in the New York military theater. On the contrary, Ann poured out her affection for her sister and her family, even to the point of asking to be remembered to "General Gates." Elizabeth Gates, for her part, offered to take one of Ann's sons (Elizabeth and Horatio's godson) into her own household. For all the hardships that Ann Fenwick suffered during the war, she did not lack the emotional sustenance provided by a sister and friend who not only empathized with her illnesses and losses, but also offered to help in more concrete ways. Ann squared the war and her relationship with her sister in a 1778 letter when she wrote, "In my breast and I most sincerely believe in yours, there has never been the smallest interruption (of friendship and affection) and tho Accidents, Fate, and Opinions may have thrown us into different Walks, yet nothing could shake or diminish our loves and esteems." For Ann Fenwick, there was a realm of "loves and esteems" alongside the jarring world of "Accidents and Opinions." The sisters' discreet correspondence did not cause a ripple in that harder, public place where their husbands had invested themselves. They were thus able to maintain their positions in the wider society while sustaining one another in their roles as loving sisters.[5]

While it is readily acknowledged that civil wars can produce fractured families, it is less understood that intense conflict and suffering can make individuals resort more than ever to the intimate bonds forged through a lifetime. Adversity can rearrange one's perspective so that what one once thought to be of primary importance, such as issues like British taxation, takes second place to family welfare. Folded pieces of paper artfully hidden in a bundle or a piece of clothing often overcame the formidable obstacles thrown up by the war.

Family reassurances went beyond the relatively low risk private letters and aid packages to public acts that put the participants in greater peril. In January 1777, John Varick, Jr., a resident of New York City, learned that his father was taken in a raid on Kingston, New York, and confined in one of the city's prisons. John obtained a pass to visit his father every day of his one-year captivity, and was able to report back to his family in the New York countryside that their father enjoyed good health. Mr. Varick, Sr., was spared the dispiriting isolation of incarceration by the daily visits of his son, who likely brought him extra provisions from town and news from the family.[6]

A Mr. Hadden, an ardent Whig and Tory prosecutor from Newark, New Jersey, also suffered imprisonment after his home was raided. In his case, the Loyalist raiders had to make haste, and so Hadden had no time to don his shoes. By the time he reached New York, the prisoner's feet were frozen and "as black as his hat." But while languishing in the prison hospital, Hadden's Tory son, a Lieutenant in a New Jersey refugee corps, visited his father on a regular basis. The fact that the elder Hadden was a Tory persecutor back home did not prevent his Tory-soldier son from supporting his father in the very public act of entering a prison.[7]

Men were not the only individuals bold enough to extend a helping hand to actively belligerent relatives. Women too helped family members from the other side when they were incarcerated in their neighborhood. Vincent Pearse Ashfield, a Loyalist merchant in New York City, suffered for seven weeks in American captivity until "some relations on the rebel side" arranged for a parole. Those relations turned out to be "his wife's friends," particularly "her brother being in the Provincial Congress."[8] On the other side of the lines, Lydia Robbins saw her two brothers, both slightly wounded, incarcerated in the city jail (called the Provost) and then the Sugar House. She had lived outside the city for most of the war but then joined her husband in New York for the last three years of the conflict. (We have no idea if she was compelled to join her husband). Lydia did not have the connections to get her brothers out of jail, but she did bring them provisions and did their wash throughout their captivity.[9]

A similar shock visited Susannah Leggett, who, while standing on her brother-in-law's stoop at his shoemaker's shop in the city, glimpsed her brother, Abraham, straggling down the street in a group of rebel prisoners. "As soon as she espide me," recollected her brother, "she dropp'd." Although unable to visit her brother in the Provost, Susannah managed to send bedding and provisions. Abraham did not mention in his memoirs his other sister, Mary, who had married the shoemaker, Mr. Norwood. The Norwoods decided to stay in New York City and were likely Loyalist (three Norwoods did sign the Loyalist Petition to the Howes). Later on in the war, Susannah married an American prisoner of war on Long Island but still spent the last months of her first pregnancy in the New York City home of her sister and her ostensibly Loyalist husband. So at the Norwood's shoemaker shop at #12 Princess Street, lived the Norwoods, in good standing with the British, along with a female relation married to an American officer-prisoner who visited the house from time to time to check on his wife and baby.[10]

That women were the ones at the city's prison windows is an indication of the greater leeway that women enjoyed with respect to their movements during the war. Considered weak and childlike, females could go where few males dared because they were considered no threat. And since women were supposed to succor the distressed, it struck the British as natural that they should supply the unfortunates in prison with food and clothing. A man hanging around the city's prisons was usually suspect; a woman was not. But no matter what her motivation or personal stance, a woman confronted with a relative in trouble would most often brush aside the political "unpleasantness" to lend a hand.[11]

And so too did women who had to cross the military lines to aid family members. Mary Allen, for instance, a New Jersey resident who was one of the disaffected, heard that her son in New York was ill with consumption. Anxious to see her son before he died, she also wanted to take care of her house in the city and "the little Estate she has in the world."[12] While Mary Allen wanted in, Elizabeth Jarvis wanted a pass to go out of the city. She obtained one simply for the pleasure of seeing her father.[13] When the prospect of failure confronted them, resourceful women scrambled to find some likely individual who would issue a pass. A Miss Romine of New Jersey bypassed the British Commandant's office by applying to a captain of a refugee post instead. She was found in the city visiting her father in one of the city's Sugar House prisons.[14] Wives of officer-prisoners could join their husbands in captivity. Susannah Everitt ran errands to Manhattan for her husband who was paroled to a restricted area on Long Island. Individual acts of kindness to vulnerable relatives might seem harmless enough to the grand men directing the larger affairs of a major war. But in negotiating their way through soldiers and cannon and bulwarks, women formed an impressive information network that operated continuously throughout the war. The news they brought back home and disseminated far exceeded the contribution of famous spies like Nathan Hale or the few well-known female spies under Washington's employ.[15] Yet the hundreds of women who crossed the military lines did not think of themselves as professional information gatherers. Most crossed the military lines with a set agenda that had to do with relatives and friends. But while in enemy territory, their eyes and ears were at work, taking in what was happening around them, and returning home with the latest news from town or country. Whether through personal visits or letter writing or conveying letters, women functioned as purveyors of information who kept the communication flowing between British New York and the Whig-controlled periphery.[16]

Lively female networks provided reams of military information, political rumors, and personal news throughout the war. One such network comes to us from an unlikely source. William Smith, Jr., one of New York's most prominent political leaders before the war, found himself confined by the Revolutionary authorities to his in-laws' manor house up the Hudson Valley because he did not approve of American independence. This former resident of Manhattan, so accustomed to the world of male power, found himself at Livingston Manor, dependent on the women in his life to obtain the smallest bit of information. The scene at the manor throws into bold relief an anomaly produced by war: women on the move and men confined. While the women of the family traveled the Hudson Valley and crossed the military lines into New York City, their influential husbands stayed behind, either confined like Smith or kept to one side of the military lines because of their prominence, like John Jay and James Duane. The family circle at Livingston Manor also provides a striking picture of genteel family life where the conviviality of the refined played out against the tensions produced by political crisis.

For a man used to operating in the heady realm of male-dominated politics, it is striking that the clear majority of Smith's informants during his stay on the manor were women. The constant stream of female visitors provided ample grist for Smith's speculative and analytical faculties. Female family members, friends, acquaintances, "negro wenches," tenant wives, and men whose information sources were women kept Smith apprised of events like the great fire of 1776 in New York City, of ongoing topics of interest like troop strength, and of the daily political temperature

William Smith, Chief Justice of New York and Canada, engraved by H. B. Hall. A leader in the anti-taxation movement before the war, William Smith could not bring himself to accept independence. After a period of house arrest at Livingston Manor, Smith was permitted to go to New York City, where he advised the British commanders there until the end of the conflict. After futile attempts to remain in America, he moved to England and thence to Canada, where he became the Chief Justice. Glass negative number 21278. © Collection of the New-York Historical Society.

of important Livingston connections. Sarah Livingston Alexander, for example, informed Smith of a one-hour conversation between General Philip Schuyler and Colonel Livingston. As the wife of a prominent American general, Lord Stirling, Sarah showed no compunction about sharing this information with her politically suspect relative. The Livingston women were full of news because they were out and about, not confined to the domestic scene. Mrs. Cochran, another Livingston relation, traveled from the manor to Albany in 1778 with a sensitive political message for General Schuyler. Smith acknowledged that the ladies could get a message through faster than could the post. In a letter to P. R. Livingston in January of 1777, Smith reported that Livingston's "great secret was known . . . and was communicated here by the Ladies from Fishkill before your letter arrived." [17]

Smith's sources covered a wide spectrum politically because he lived at a prominent family seat where filial connections proved more important than political ties. The manor lord embraced his Loyalist relatives like Catherine Livingston Patterson, who lived on the manor with her Loyalist husband, as well as Sarah and Janet Livingston who married American generals, and Mary Livingston, who married Whig political leader James Duane.[18] This eclectic assortment of political opinions dined with one another on a regular basis, and from each table setting spread an impressive network of outside connections which culminated in the dinner conversation every night. Although a certain amount of information was shared, family members did not unburden their hearts with abandon. The manor residents used guile and aggressiveness to obtain what they wanted to know. Smith paid special attention to the ladies when it came to gleaning what his male relations were hesitant to share with him. His wife, no shy wallflower, often pumped prominent visitors for information. When Continental army officers came to call, she would ask about American army troop strength and although she sometimes received no more than a smile and a vague answer, she remained undeterred in her quest for information. On another occasion, Mrs. Smith saw her brother-in-law pull out a list of the people accused by the local Committee of inimical behavior. "My wife reached for the Paper to count them," recounted Smith, but his brother-in-law snatched it back. When James Duane came to visit, Mrs. Smith formed part of a group of women who pressed the Congressman to expand on his opinion about the imminent end of the war. Smith wrote on July 23, 1778, "The ladies rallied him a little for his opinion that we should all be soon in New York and pressed him with their Questions. How Mr. Duane? How? The war he said is near its end." Mrs. Smith found the prospect of peace hard to believe since at the Battle of Monmouth, "our people [the Americans] were beaten in Jersey."[19]

Smith soon learned that the Patriot leaders were much more likely to let their guard down to the ladies. What he could not glean from overhearing these mixed-sex exchanges, his wife filled in for him. In February 1777, James Duane, Robert R. Livingston, and Gouverneur Morris (all prominent Whig politicians) came to call. "I listened most to what these Delegates dropped to the Ladies to still their fears by their Hopes from France." Smith's wife peppered Morris with questions on the subject of Patriot recruitment. Learning that it went "slow enough," Mrs. Smith pressed on by asking why the 6,000 men lately in Westchester did not descend to New York. Gouverneur Morris "whispered that the General (Heath) was a Coward"—a confidence that Mrs. Smith directly imparted to her husband.[20]

Paying attention to the women yielded dividends in other ways. Smith believed that if one could not engage the men in an informative conversation, he could tease out their views by listening to the women in their lives. In July 1777, Janet Montgomery took General Schuyler to task for a troop movement he had recently ordered. Smith figured that Mrs. Montgomery was mimicking her brother's sentiments. In April of 1778, when the news arrived that Parliament would swear off the right to tax America in return for peace, Smith tried to glean the opinions of the closed-mouth Whig leaders by listening to their women. "We find their sentiments by the women—Mrs. Duane called this a contrivance of that wicked fellow Tryon to divide the people." Smith had no success in trying to draw out Robert R. Livingston on the subject of peace overtures until Livingston's wife provided a hint. Smith wrote, "RRL will not declare himself yet upon the peace overtures. Nor says he have I to any person, but his wife says to his face, I am sure you are for Peace because you are a good man."[21]

The fact that Mrs. Livingston could have her own opinion of the matter, one very distinct from that of her husband, did not occur to Smith. The assumption that women did not come accoutered with the independence or rationality necessary to hold a serious political belief, nor endowed with the power to act on it, encouraged men to talk more freely with the ladies and to ascribe any political utterance from their mouths as being put there by their husbands, fathers, or brothers. Even though Smith's wife was a consummate political operator, her husband's world view differed little from his male cohorts in this regard.

This manoeuvering for information created an underlying tension that sometimes erupted in discord. According to Smith's diary, tempers flared most often among the women. In April 1777, he recorded some "sharpness" among the ladies at the manor over a letter that the lord of the manor's son, Peter Livingston, had sent to his father, expressing doubts about the success of the Americans in the current campaign. Peter's sister, Mary Duane, turned on her brother's wife, Margaret (who was also a sister of Smith's wife), and "with some Indelicacy to Mrs. PRL expressed her surprise that her brother could write such a letter to his Father, and said it was no wonder Mr. W [Washington] was so weak since Gentlemen did not order their sons into the army." Mrs. Duane then advised one of Peter and Margaret's sons, who was present in the room, to sign up with the army "whether his Parents consented or not." Smith was obliged to retire with a furious Margaret Livingston, as "this occasioned a little sharpness among the Ladies."[22]

In Smith's diary, these emotionally charged scenes are always sparked by a woman of Whiggish proclivities. At Christmas dinner in 1777, Mrs. Robert R. Livingston put a damper on the festive spirit reigning at the table when at one point she "instantly took fire" and declared that Governor Tryon, the Royal Governor of New York, "deserved to be hanged and quartered." No riposte from the Loyalist quarter is recorded in Smith's diary. One can only imagine lowered eyelids and a greater concentration on the food in front of them.[23]

The women in Smith's life regaled him with concrete information like troop movements and served as windows to the political opinions of their husbands. They also kept him amused with rumors of little import like the fact that General Schuyler slept with a blunderbuss at his side every night.[24] But we would be largely unaware of this activity on the part of women if Smith had not been confined to the manor. There he was deprived of the normal male circles of discourse. The men of the American cause did not quite trust the obviously disaffected Smith. Before Mrs. Robert R. Livingston exploded at the Christmas dinner in 1777, Smith recorded that James Duane sent Smith "upstairs to the Ladies . . . and the gentlemen continued for some time."[25] When Smith moved to New York City in August 1778, his world became one of male power figures once again. The women so prominent in the manor years gave way to British generals, high government officials and Loyalist grandees. Even Smith's feisty and articulate wife largely disappeared from her husband's journal. One would think that women played little role at all in the circulation of important news in the occupied city if not for one lone remark buried in Smith's countless recitations of male dialogue. Smith noted that several times a week, he made it a point to attend Mrs. Barrow's tea where he met other prominent Loyalists.[26]

The information humming along female lines of communication was not confined to the high society network. Market women and slaves also conveyed information to the manor—"my wench Jane," "A Negroe of Rose's brother," "Daughter of John Post," "Sally formerly a maidservant of ours," "Peter the Fuller's wife," "Mrs. Campbell the housekeeper," "Dulcinia of Major Johnson," "a woman from Poughkeepsie," "Van Voorhuy's Negroe," "Mrs. Mandeville, a market woman," "my Negroe Caesar, Charlotte's husband," "my Negroe jack," "Dr. Latham's slave," "Miss Clopper," "Mrs. Plaas," "Mrs. Duher," and a parade of anonymous people, mostly women, kept Smith informed. So successful were women in moving about the war zone that male spies sometimes dressed in women's clothing to improve their chances.[27]

While women of a wide spectrum of socioeconomic backgrounds could enter and exit the city, those with connections could cross the military lines for a simple visit to family or friends who were in no dire need of their succor. As we have seen, the Whiggish side of the Alexander family paid a social call on the Tory side with nary a concern or worry in the summer of the battle of Monmouth. Even members of the rebel government did not deem it unthinkable that they could take a jaunt to the city as well. In June 1778, Richard Morris, a Senator in the New York State legislature, expressed the desire to accompany his ailing sister to the city. In that same month, Mrs. Frederick Jay, John Jay's sister-in-law, returned from her jaunt to New York and told Miss Bayard, who told Mrs. William Smith, Jr., who told her husband, that Mrs. Jay's husband, a member of the new assembly, advised her to stay in the city if her health required it and promised to follow her if needs be.[28] In July 1780, another member of the New York Assembly, William Boerum, accompanied his wife to the British post of Paulus Hook to see her off to the other side of the Hudson. In February 1781, Gouverneur Morris, a former member of the Continental Congress and a prominent official in the rebel government, put out feelers for a pass to visit his ill mother behind enemy lines. The pass was given to Morris's sister in town who managed to have it sent out to her brother. Morris chose not to use it.[29] The Morrises, Boerum, and Jay played prominent roles in the new American government and yet had access to British headquarters on Manhattan Island. What might well have deterred both

Richard Morris and Gouverneur Morris from acting on their personal desires was the appearance such a trip would make to the general public. They were too prominent to conduct a discreet visit.

The British also allowed American soldiers of prominent families to come to town solely for the pleasure of speaking with kin, hoping to induce these individuals to desert. Indeed, they had succeeded in luring two male members of the Livingston family to the British side. But they were not always successful. Lieutenant Colonel Livingston proved himself of solid Patriot mettle, for on his jaunt to town in 1777 he roundly insulted Governor Tryon when he was mistakenly sent to the British Governor's headquarters. "He behaved very rudely," when he reminded the Royal Governor of his past resolution never to bear arms against Americans and of Tryon's boast that he "knew no such Person as King George."[30] For such insolence, the English ordered him off the island before he got the chance to carry out his errand to his sister. On the American side, Governor George Clinton of New York heard complaints of known members of Tory regiments simply returning home as if nothing had happened. Clinton was also distressed to find that Tories of the most notorious name, in this case, Thomas Colden, could come and go to New York City with no disturbance whatsoever.[31]

Clinton's frustration was not an isolated episode. The movement of people in and out of the occupied city was an ongoing headache to the governing elites of both sides, particularly when the locus of war centered on New York. The city had a perpetually operating turnstile. While the governments tried to control movement across the lines by authorizing and even encouraging some jaunts and errands of mercy, they tried in vain to stem the substantial flow of illegal communication. In April 1777, New York Governor George Clinton complained that "the communication between this place and New York is entirely open to the Tories and they, I am afraid, make too much use of it for our good." In December 1778, William Livingston complained of the number of supplicants for passes to the occupied islands. "Not above one in twenty appeared intitled to that indulgence," the New Jersey Governor exclaimed. In December 1779, the British Commandant of the occupied city complained that too many people received passes from officials and officers unauthorized to issue such permissions. In late 1780, the Continental Congress fretted over those citizens who crossed the military lines under the pretext of retrieving property.[32]

The elites of both sides did more than just fuss about the problem. They issued proclamations and passed laws to staunch the flow of illegal communication. This legislative activity indicates that more than just a few elites managed to cross the lines. Illicit movement was so pervasive that legislatures and public officials busied themselves with remedies throughout the war. In October 1778, the State of New Jersey passed an act entitled "An Act to Prevent the Subjects of this State from going into, or coming out of, the Enemy's lines without permissions or Passports, and for other Purposes therein mentioned." The law forbade all movement in and out of the occupied city unless a pass were procured from the Governor, the Commander-in-Chief of the army, or a select group of officers in the Continental army or militia. A person issuing a pass with no authority would be fined. Soldiers could seize goods and provisions en route to or from New York City. The law further stipulated that both males and females were subject to prosecution.[33]

The State of New Jersey either added to or amended this basic law throughout the war, trying, in each instance, to plug up the holes that previous legislation created. The subsequent legislation on movement is the story of how New Jersey's citizens strove to circumvent the directives of their government. In December 1778, the New Jersey government amended this law by reducing the amount of supplies allowed to cross the lines to three days' provisions, and prohibiting people with passes from taking out goods unless given special permission by the Governor, the Commander-in-Chief of the state forces, or the Commander-in-Chief of the Continental army. Six months later, New Jersey acted to restrict the movement of its own citizens within the state because too many "Spies and other disaffected Persons" could travel at large and carry intelligence to the enemy. The law restricted New Jerseyites to their county of residence (and away from the British lines) unless they procured a certificate from one of a small number of state officials. The Americans realized that if they could not stop the flow of people in and out of town, they could at least try to control it. They instituted flag boats that legally transported authorized personnel and supplies from New Jersey into British-controlled New York. In December 1778, the number of official trips effected by these official craft was getting out of hand. Washington and Governor Livingston agreed that it was necessary to restrict the passage of these boats to once a month. Yet, in 1780, Washington still wondered at the number of flag of truce vessels that carried on illegal intercourse "to alarming heights."[34]

In December 1779, the state legislature found the acts thus far passed to be "inadequate." The new legislation tried to put a stop to citizens who arranged for goods to come out of New York City and then "seized them" as illegal contraband. One year later, in December 1780, the assembly restricted the number of people authorized to sign passes. Now only the Governor, the Commander-in-Chief of the state forces, and the Commander-in-Chief of the U.S. army could authorize such movement. In June 1781, the Assembly deemed its December 1779 law to be easily evaded and "in many respects . . . ineffectual." In June 1782, the legislature passed yet another law, clarifying old rules and adding new ones. In December 1782, the state's lawmakers had to admit that despite the law passed six months before, "great quantities of Provisions and Produce are constantly conveyed to the Enemy." Henceforth, a passport had to be obtained to drive cattle through Bergen County.[35]

Illicit movement in and out of New York City claimed a substantial portion of the New Jersey Assembly's time throughout the war. The Assembly churned out two laws in 1778, two in 1779, one in 1780, one in 1781, and two in 1782. Such legislative activity bespeaks the mighty ingenuity of the populace with respect to their assemblymen's labor.

The State of New York moved to restrict movement within its borders as early as November 1776. County commissioners were to appoint two judicious men to handle the issuance of passes. Without this completed printed form, citizens could not travel outside their "district or manor or precinct." Four years later, New York authorities, still concerned about inimical activity spilling out of New York City, declared that any person (whether male or female) coming out of town to lurk about American-held territory would be courtmartialed on the charge of spying. The State of New York did not have as extensive a border with the occupied islands as did New Jersey. Its chief concern was to regulate the flag of truce traffic on the Hudson River. Despite an act passed to prevent abuses with respect to flags of truce, Governor Clinton regularly labored to communicate the content of this law to subordinates who violated its strictures.[36]

The British, on their side, wanted to restrict the American flag boats as well. In October 1779, they stipulated that American flag vessels would go no further than Decker's Ferry on Staten Island. "The sending of Flour etc. to their Prisoners here, we have Reason to believe is only a Pretext for their coming to this town in order to serve other purposes," the British Proclamation read.[37] The British also tried to control the market boats bringing provisions to the city. As of August 1, 1779, all small boats had to have passes in order to go in and out of town. Provisions from the mainland were crucial to the city's wellbeing but such provisioning opened yet another avenue for possible enemy infiltration. To control this essential traffic, the British gave blank passes to Abraham Van Buskirk, a Bergen county Loyalist, who distributed them to old pro-British neighbors in New Jersey.[38] Both sides tried to make perfectly clear who could issue passes and who could not because it seemed that endless numbers of petty officials felt entitled to issue certificates. The British established a central clearinghouse in the Commandant's office to check certificates issued by army officers, civilian police, the Royal Governor, Chief Justices, and Commissaries of prisoners.

In New Jersey, Governor Livingston spelled out in proclamations exactly who could issue passes to the city. Over time, the list shrank to just the Governor and the Council of Safety. At times, the spirit of these proclamations was subverted from unexpected quarters. When a young woman asked General Washington for a pass to New York City, he correctly referred her to Governor Clinton, in keeping with a law passed by Congress. But Washington wrote out a pass on his own authority just in case the woman did not find the Governor at home. Washington did not want the woman to be inconvenienced by waiting.[39]

The subjects of this tireless work in the halls of power, the American citizenry, were not perverse subjects who took pleasure in flouting the laws. Many simply did not see the law's reach as extending into all aspects of their lives. People often distinguished between the public domain of political allegiance and the private realm of family. They could espouse independence, for instance, and still visit an ailing Loyalist relative in New York City. Moving across the lines to aid and abet the loathsome redcoats was treasonous, but transits taken in the interest of close connections merited a more complaisant stance. Such reasoning could sway the authorities of both sides depending on the degree of crisis experienced at any particular junction. The officials who sanctioned the Alexander women's visit to New York City certainly subscribed to this distinction. On another occasion, Washington chided the Executive Council of Pennsylvania for issuing passes to women subsequently arrested for carrying major amounts of merchandise out of the occupied city. It was obvious, noted Washington, that these ladies were involved in illicit trade "under the pretence of visiting their Friends." Washington is here distinguishing between a private visit (no harm done) and the public activity of conducting trade (where the enemy benefited from the exchange).[40]

British officials also made this distinction in the case of Jesse Waln, a resident of New York City accused of carrying on "correspondence with the enemy." When the court learned that Waln had stuffed a chest with chintzes, pepper, tea, needles, two bales of raccoon skins, and "other little nicknacks" on his trip to New Jersey, the Court asked whether this haul sounded more like "traffick than merely . . . presents to a friend." The former activity merited the court's attention; the latter did not. Ultimately, Waln was let off the hook when Loyalist General Cortlandt Skinner testified that he sent medicines to his sister's family in New Jersey through the enterprising trader. The court registered no concern about Skinner's aid package and promptly exonerated Waln.[41]

At times, authorities on both sides opposed personal visits whether they were errands of mercy or purely social calls. When military action was particularly intense, generals and governors turned down requests to pass through the lines. People tending to private matters became a problem as well when their activity became a public issue. By 1779, the Governors of New Jersey and New York were accused of partiality when they issued passes into town. The political heat was so intense that even a Continental army general could not manage a pass for a relative to cross the lines.[42]

Private doings could also become public issues when a high-profile individual took advantage of the authority's complaisance. The length of Mrs. Frederick Jay's jaunt to New York City (four months) became an issue for her husband, a member of the New York Assembly. Her female relatives spelled out the nature of her offense. "It is very natural for her to wish to see her relations," opined Susannah Livingston, "but she ought to consider the reputation of her husband before any gratification." Margaret Jay's visit was fine until it negatively affected her husband, a public official.[43]

As the women of the Jay family attest, a discreet visit to the other side on private matters was deemed acceptable. To many citizens the laws were never meant to control their private affairs, but rather to regulate the public action of individuals. Officials responsible for enforcing the law often acknowledged the distinction between the public and private doings of its citizens. While legislatures churned out statutes defining illicit movement, their constituents interpreted and implemented these laws according to their own sense of right and wrong.

The problem of illegal movement always seemed to overwhelm the harried officials trying to control it. A particularly perplexing issue in this regard revolved around the movement of women in and out of town. Upper-class women benefited from the gallant behavior and courtly regard owed to a lady by a gentleman. General Howe was certainly prey to such expectations. He made a great show of not opening letters addressed from or to high-society women. In December 1776, William Smith, Jr., reported that his letters were routinely opened by the New York State authorities. Washington's intercepted correspondence, on the other hand, went straight to Howe, whereupon the British General opened the dispatches but sent along unopened a letter addressed to Mrs. Washington. Although totally ignorant of its contents, Smith and Howe assumed that the letter from George Washington to his wife was a private letter. For these men, there could evidently be no other kind of communication between husband and wife. Another year of war had not disabused General Howe of this practice. In November 1777, Howe allowed Mrs. Israel Pemberton's letter to pass unopened to her husband. A correspondent of Mr. Pemberton informed him of Howe's rationale. According to this man, Howe opened a packet of letters and saw "the letter from thy wife to thee, said it was a Letter from thy wife to thee, said it was a letter from a Lady to her Husband, did not read it but clos'd the Packet and sent it to General Washington who did not open it at all but forwarded it here . . ." Pemberton's correspondent did not think that Howe's complaisance would extend to Mrs. Pemberton's husband. He advised his friend to send his letters unsealed "as they will be opened."[44]

That women were nonentities in the political sphere made it possible to laud women attached to male enemies in the public prints. The August 7, 1777, edition of the *Pennsylvania Evening Post* featured a glowing obituary of Elizabeth Franklin, the wife of the high-profile Loyalist, William Franklin. The Whig newspaper praised her qualities, her "peculiar sweetness of manner . . . the virtues of her heart" along with her affability and dignified bearing. No such encomium would accompany her husband's obituary or that of any other Loyalist male. The Whiggish publishers could afford to be generous because Elizabeth Franklin's person was not political, unlike her notorious husband.

The male gatekeepers of the Whig and British camps shared this perception of women and allowed them to cross the lines in numbers significant enough to be noticed by contemporary observers. One such witness was William Livingston, the Governor of New Jersey. While his cohorts issued passports with little compunction, Livingston saw a great hitherto-unrecognized menace in allowing women to pass back and forth so easily. In November 1776, he pleaded with George Washington to counsel his officers to moderate the number of passes they issued to women. He had just examined six or seven women who had recently come from New York City, and although they appeared to be Whigs, Livingston detected in their stories "a natural tendency to discourage the weaker part of our Inhabitants." He described the six women whom he had just interrogated as "Mistresses of infinite craft and Subtlety." Livingston reminded Washington that he had "never heard or read of a great Politician who did not employ petticoats to accomplish his Designs." "Certain it is," continued Livingston, "that the greatest politician on Record, I mean the Devil, apply'd himself to a female Agent to involve mankind in Sin and ruin."[45] Two years later, Livingston picked up the same refrain replete with biblical metaphor. In December 1778, Livingston described supplicants for passes as being possessed of "a vain curiousity (extremely predominant in women)" who are "cloaked with the pretence of securing their debts or effects in which they seldom, if ever, succeed, or for the sake of buying tea and trinkets (for which they would as soon forfeit a second paradise, as Eve did the first, for the forbidden fruit) that they are perpetually prompted to those idle rambles."[46]

Livingston exposed these devious women for what they were and belittled them as foolish devotees of consumer items at the same time. In acknowledging that women did indeed pose a threat, Livingston invested them with attributes that society dictated they were not supposed to have. He made them more nearly equal in abilities to men. He certainly acknowledged more in these potential female spies than did the men who blithely wrote them passes. That Livingston may have felt uncomfortable with such an acknowledgement is manifest in his tendency to make women the butt of his jokes in the same breath that he reveals his respect for their capacity to damage the Whig cause. This is a theme he reprises at various stages of the Revolution. In December 1777, Livingston could not supply the Jersey battalions with winter waistcoats and breeches. Under the penname, Hortentius, Livingston wrote a piece for the *New Jersey Gazette* in which he attacked the women of Bergen county whose slavish accumulation of petticoats could clothe his freezing soldiers. Hortentius explained, "It is well known that the rural ladies . . . pride themselves in an incredible number of petticoats; which like the house furniture, are displayed by way of ostentation, for many years before they decreed to invest the fair bodies of the proprietors." With the tone of a schoolmaster, Livingston continued to display his expertise on the undergarment customs of Bergen County women. "Till that period, they are never worn, but neatly piled up on each side of an immense escrutoire, the top of which is decorated with a most capacious brass-clamped bible, seldom read." Satisfied now that he had exposed their hypocrisy, the essayist came to the point. "What I would, therefore, humbly propose to our superiors, is to make prize of those *future* female habilments, and after proper transformation, *immediately* apply them to screen from the inclemencies of the weather those gallant *males* who are now fighting for the liberties of their country. And to clear this measure from every imputation of injustice, I have only to observe, that the generality of the *women* in that country, having for above a century, *worn the breeches*, it is highly reasonable that the *men* should now, and especially upon so important an occasion, make booty of *the petticoats*."[47]

Despite the ridiculous light in which he painted women, Livingston told Washington that he had been "very sparing in gratifying their requests" for passes to New York City. On several occasions, he told close friends and family members that he could not indulge them in authorizing passports because the court of public opinion would accuse him of partiality. He denied one woman a pass to enter and exit the city because he said it was his policy to authorize only one-way trips. Although Livingston admitted that the supplicant seemed harmless enough, he explained that "to keep a Court of Inquiry upon every particular application and make the odious distinction between who would and who would not injure their country, is what I have neither Inclination nor Leisure to do."[48]

Livingston articulated a similar rationale in refusing General Lord Stirling's 1779 request to allow his daughter from New York City, Lady Mary Watts, to visit her relations in New Jersey. As seen at the beginning of this chapter, Lady Watts's mother and sister had no problem visiting her in the summer of 1778. A year before, Lady Watts herself had visited in New Jersey, sending her best regards to Governor Livingston's wife and daughters in her letter requesting a pass to go back to New York City. But by September 1779, Governor Livingston could not afford "the Charge of Partiality" and denied her request for a pass. The Commander-in-Chief also turned down Stirling and his daughter, citing the same concern about popular clamors. Yet two weeks after this final refusal from the Commander-in-Chief, Lady Mary Watts applied for a pass from British authorities to go to Elizabethtown, New Jersey, with a trunk of clothing. Obviously, she had found a way around the Governor of New Jersey and the Commander-in-Chief of the army.[49]

Livingston's firm policy against permitting Loyalist and Whig relatives to cross the lines sent some supplicants to Governor George Clinton in New York State. But Clinton had no desire to interfere in the affairs of another state. With William Livingston's scrupulous adherence to his principles well established, it was with some wonder that Governor George Clinton read another letter from New Jersey requesting Clinton's help in allowing a woman to go to, and return from, New York City. The supplicant was none other than Governor William Livingston, whose sister, a resident of New York State, was destitute. If allowed to go to New York, she could recover house rents and so alleviate her financial pinch. "I know it is a delicate point to interfere in the policy of other states," admitted Governor Livingston, but he pleaded mercy for "a distressed widow and a good Whig." It is not known whether Clinton obliged his fellow governor (he probably did; he was a much softer touch in general than Livingston). Whatever his decision, he most likely acted with circumspection because one month before, a vigilant state official criticized him for interfering in the arrest of two women who had come out of New York City with no passes. The Governor had the women released and sent on their way before a proper investigation could be conducted. The irate arresting official cautioned the Governor against giving special favors to certain ladies, finding it important "to let the world see we acted impartially with all Rancks." The man acquiesced to the Governor's command, however, ending his letter to Clinton with the plaint, "it's hard to kick against the Pricks."[50]

Unlike Clinton, Livingston was a strict disciplinarian with respect to special favors, but his exceptions were numerous enough to be used as ammunition by his enemies. A Mrs. Chandler softened the Governor with the story of her mortally ill son in New York City. Mrs. Ann Hoit received permission as well but with the stern proviso that she was not to bring any necessities back for her family. Still, he admitted to Washington that he often experienced "the mortification to find that many of those whom I had denied, were notwithstanding successful in their subsequent addresses to the military officers, who from a mistaken complaisance seemed incapable of resisting the solicitations of those eloquent and pernicious vagrants." To put these women in their place, however, Livingston added that men were even more ingenious when it came to devising ways to enter the city. "The men are still more seriously mischievous," wrote Livingston, "and go with commercial motives to secure capital Quantities of British merchandize." In noting men's superior ingenuity over women, Livingston had restored the natural order of things.[51]

Particularly galling to Governor Livingston were instances of female family members flaunting his authority and the laws of the land to make jaunts in and out of the city. In the fall of 1781, the Governor's ailing sister, Alida Livingston Hoffman, sent her son, Philip, to ask that her daughter, a resident of New York City, be allowed to come visit. The sight of young "Philly" did not move his uncle, who stood adamant on this particular request. A year later, in October 1782, Alida requested a pass into the city so that she could collect some money from her husband and buy her son some books for his education. With marked control over his anger, Livingston ticked off one by one the alternate routes by which his sister could accomplish her goals. Mr. Hoffman could send the money out at any time he wished, and Philly's books could be procured in Philadelphia. Then, in an outburst of frustration, Livingston poured out his complaints about family members who made a "play" of flouting the laws. He wrote of his "unspeakable mortification" in having to deny family requests for passports. Undeterred, his kin still managed to cross the lines with passes that the general public assumed came from his pen, thus causing political problems for the governor. "And to be still plainer with you and the family at Basking Ridge," continued the supremely vexed Livingston, "they have in fact done more to injure my reputation and to furnish my personal enemies with weapons against me than perhaps any twenty families in the state." Weary of having to defend himself "hundreds" of times, Livingston called his sister on the carpet, demanding an explanation of the latest family infractions. Alida's daughter (the person Livingston had denied the year before) had visited Basking Ridge "in violation of the laws of this state." A sister-in-law had paid her father "the like illegal visit." And a third female relative took a jaunt to the occupied city "with the same contempt of our Laws." Having delivered the lecture and having unburdened his heart, Livingston signed the letter "your affectionate Brother." Despite a stern gatekeeper and laws on the books, the determined ladies of Basking Ridge managed to maintain family connections throughout the war.[52]

The British, too, acknowledged that women were particularly dangerous in their transits to and from the city. In October 1779, Brigadier General Pattison, commanding on Staten Island, complained to his superiors that too many people passed and repassed the lines through his post, creating a channel of intelligence for the other side. Pattison was particularly upset about a mother and daughter who clandestinely reached Staten Island in a canoe. Although the women in this case turned out to be kinswomen of a Loyalist in New York City, Pattison's superior agreed that the parade of unregulated individuals had to stop. He instituted a flag of truce vessel to make the transit to Elizabethtown on a weekly basis "for the purpose of carrying Persons to and from that place as may be thought expedient to give permission to."[53] Four months later, during the severe winter of 1779–80, when the rivers and bays froze around the occupied islands, General Pattison ordered that no market women be allowed to cross from the Jersey shore. Pattison believed that the women came to town under the pretext of bringing provisions to market while their real intention was to carry out intelligence. The British commander found this movement to be especially alarming at this time because he feared an American invasion over the solid blocks of ice linking islands to mainland.[54]

The men who crafted the laws on both sides had to acknowledge that women were more than mere adjuncts to their husbands. Even if they believed that women were nothing more than lesser versions of men, the lawmakers had to admit the serious threat posed by these hitherto harmless and loveable characters. These concerns were revealed in laws specifically mentioning women's movement and women's property. The demands of war called on women to be physically out and about as never before, while the men in the legislature unwittingly pulled women further into public life by highlighting their movements in the laws of the land.

While generals and legislators struggled with their respective populations, fathers and mothers coped within their own families to maintain order and protect their children. A major challenge for some families concerned their daughters' marriages to British soldiers. As William Rawle noted in his letters from town, soldier marriages were fairly common, even in the Quaker community. Young members of the Society of Friends faced not only parental disapproval and anger for marrying someone outside their religious community, but also disownment from the close-knit congregation of Friends. At the Flushing Quarterly Meeting, which included Manhattan and eastern Long Island, the number of disownments due to young people marrying outside the fold increased significantly during the war despite the fact that many families had moved out to avoid the conflict. Before the Revolution, in the years 1770–74, there were between two and three disownments per year for marriages out of unity recorded in the quarterly meeting records, the overwhelming majority of which were men. Between 1778 and 1782, the average number was between five and six per year. In 1781, fifteen young people married out of unity, seven of whom were women. This independent activity reflected a significant increase in the number of mavericks, particularly women, who defied parents and religious community to follow their own inclination.[55] One such independent soul was a twenty-two-year-old New York City resident, Hannah Lawrence, the leader of William Rawle's literary circle. This feisty character crossed every conceivable boundary in her marriage to a Loyalist soldier: familial, religious, political, and even geographical. In early September 1780, her local Quaker meeting recorded that Hannah "was married to a Person not of our society and by a priest." Two representatives of the meeting were appointed to visit her. At the following monthly meeting, these women reported that Hannah "did not appear to be disposed to condemn her misconduct or desirous to be continued a Member in Unity." The Meeting lost no time in disowning her.[56] Hannah Lawrence exhibited an independent streak well before she defied father and Meeting to marry her heart's desire. She was the daughter of John Lawrence, a prominent merchant in New York City, who opted to remain in town in anticipation of the British arrival. In line with their adherence to the Peace testimony, Quakers were supposed to be neutral, but many Quaker families voted with their feet to leave their local meeting for safer havens. John Lawrence did not exercise that option, an indication that he did not fear the British occupation, and may have been one of the Quaker community disposed to sympathizing with the English cause. Hannah, on the other hand, had no patience with such guarded, conservative behavior. She was pro-Whig and expressed her feelings forthrightly in her poems and letters. Adopting the pen name "Mathilda," Hannah wrote about the unwelcome invaders. "They [the British] fly to crush the blameless son of Freedom and of me," she declaimed in a poem entitled "The Interposition." As mentioned in Chapter 1, she held forth on a variety of topics, gathering about her a literary society of Quaker youth. As Hannah Lawrence, she was simply the daughter of her father; as "Mathilda," she was the standard bearer of righteousness and freedom. In the world of words, under a pseudonym, she found a place to express herself and communicate her feelings to others. Mathilda wrote to friends in the city as well as to correspondents in Philadelphia. Her interest in writing drew her to a brief acquaintance with Crèvecoeur during his sojourn in New York. As a young woman living in an occupied city during the high drama of war, Hannah Lawrence found no dearth of subjects to commit to paper, and no shortage of receptive correspondents with whom to share her musings.[57] While Mathilda's quill filled page upon page, the man of her destiny lived half a continent away. Jacob Schieffelin received his military commission in Detroit, securing a post as Secretary in the Indian department of the British army. Taken prisoner by the Americans on the frontier, Jacob was marched to Williamsburg, Virginia, where he escaped and made his way to New York City. Schieffelin took one look at Hannah Lawrence and contrived to obtain billeting at the Lawrence residence on Queen Street. The rest of the story is in Hannah's words as she wrote, "A Journal of a Lady's Courtship" for her friend, "Lavinia." She assigned the name "Altamont" to her beloved. She agonized over his real character. She seemed not at all distressed that he was in the British camp but expressed some hesitation that he was connected with the military. "The World, the world will indeed condemn me for impudence," she wrote on July 29, 1780. Afraid to confide in her friends and family, Hannah poured out her fears and hopes to a male neighbor whose "cruelty to an amiable wife" could not blot out "a heart open to the claims of compassion." Armed with a confidante who facilitated their meetings, Hannah began to envision a course of action that would "shock those whose esteem is most dear to me, and astonish all those who ever heard the name of Mathilda." By August 9, "Altamont" was quartered in the Lawrence home. At close hand, Hannah could now "have opportunity almost hourly of discovering new merits." She did not need many more hours to plumb her Jacob's character because two days later, she informed her father of her intention to marry the British soldier and move to Detroit. John Lawrence opposed the match, asking his daughter why she could not marry someone they knew and settle in town. He threatened to inform the Quaker meeting of her plans. "Mathilda in love" completely subsumed "Hannah the dutiful daughter." She began to "dissemble." Four days later, Hannah and Jacob were married in the home of her male confidante. Their honeymoon consisted of an overland trek to Canada, where their adventures included the successful negotiation of the military lines and a meeting with the Iroquois leader, Molly Brandt.[58] With very little effort, Hannah Lawrence leapt over her political convictions to marry one of the soldiers whom she earlier characterized as crushing freedom-loving peoples.

Be it the verve of young love or the quiet confidence of years of close association, family ties often prevailed over the demands of congresses and committees. These ties were made of strong yet pliable stuff. The pull of the private and public created an incredibly complex situation in the New York area, resulting in countless combinations of kinship and political leanings. One has only to look at Norwood the shoemaker's house in New York City or at Livingston Manor on the Hudson to see that political and private mix in an accommodating fashion.

To read the public prints of the day, one would think that Whigs and Tories were on opposite sides of an unbridgeable divide. But even the creators of such polarizing rhetoric, the leaders of the Revolutionary movement in New York, often found themselves in complicated family situations: John Jay's vacillating brother; General Gates's sister-in-law; Gouverneur Morris's half-brothers; General Lord Stirling's daughter; and

LIEUT. JACOB SCHIEFFELIN   HANNAH (LAWRENCE) SCHIEFFELIN

Jacob Schieffelin and Hannah Lawrence Schieffelin as pictured in Lawrence Bulkley Thomas, *The Thomas Book*, following p. 488. In their youth, they were on opposite sides of the political fence: he, a soldier in His Majesty's service; she, an anti-British poet. But once they met, a secret courtship developed, followed by elopement and a dramatic trek through Iroquois country to Canada. After the war, the couple returned to New York and became the upright, staid characters of these miniatures. Negative number 53181. © Collection of the New-York Historical Society.

the hopeless jumble of the politically-variegated Livingston family. These highly influential men did not cut off their relatives because they lived in a place characterized by the Whig press as full of treasonous weaklings. Many made a distinction between their own relatives and friends, on the one hand, and the rest of the population behind British lines.

While this evidence of family interconnectedness is overwhelming in the extant sources, the existence of seriously fractured families cannot be discounted. The Revolution was a civil war and, in some areas around New York, a consistently virulent one. Family members who considered one another as enemies would hardly leave a convenient paper trail for future historians by writing letters to one another. But even in the sources left by the most bitter losers of the Revolution, that is, the Loyalists who left

New York in 1783, the evidence suggests that family members remaining in America were largely supportive of their expatriate relatives. They helped them gather the documentary evidence required by the British Claims Commission; in a few cases, they bought back attainted lands; a few even prognosticated when their relatives might return. The Loyalist son who declared that he never would talk to his rebel father again is an exceptional case in the New York loyalist claims.

It might surprise no one that civilians with overriding family concerns would circumvent the laws and the armies in crossing the military lines. But there was another group of individuals crossing and recrossing the city's portals who hailed from a totally unexpected quarter. The warriors themselves formed a lively network in and out of the occupied city. Under the steady, unperturbed gaze of the sentinels of both sides, enemy officers crisscrossed the lines from 1776 to 1783.

3

Gentlemen at War

WHILE CONFINED AT his in-laws' manor house in upstate New York, William Smith had little else to do but listen to the latest war rumors and write in his diary. One January day in 1778, a woman who had recently returned from New York City broke the monotony of the miserable mid-winter gloom at the manor. Mrs. Watkins regaled her news-starved hosts with the sights and sounds of their former hometown, including an account of the captured rebel General, Charles Lee. She did not glimpse Lee in a prison window nor did she encounter him surrounded by guards. The American Major General was discovered simply strolling down one of New York's streets. Smith's spirits soared on hearing this story because he figured that such liberty of movement surely meant that Lee had switched sides, or as Smith put it, "changed his sentiments." Smith reasoned that the British "would not have suffered him to procure information and inspect their conditions if they were not confident of his conversion."[1]

Smith could not fathom the possibility that Lee might be allowed to amble down the Broad Way, inspect the Battery, take in the condition of the city's slips, chat with the soldiers and civilians, or examine the battlements on Pearl Street if he had not changed sides. But while William Smith puzzled through situations he could only hazily comprehend from Albany County, Charles Lee, the American General, was indeed enjoying the notoriety of his position in an occupied city which was wide-open to his inspection. The city authorities accorded Lee such liberty not because he was English-born, or because he had been an old colleague in the British army, or because he ranked in the highest echelons of the American forces, but because he was an officer and hence a gentleman. Lee could well have run into fellow American captives on his strolls through the occupied city because the British accorded such liberties to colonels, majors, captains, and lieutenants as well. Even as prisoners, the officers of both armies belonged to an international confraternity of gentlemen, whose members extended certain courtesies even to those they deemed politically misguided or who appeared at the head of an opposing army. Such courtesies overrode concerns about security in the British army's headquarters. In other words, the code of the gentleman trumped what we would consider standard military wisdom today. Captured American officers were allowed the liberty of the city or, if quartered on Long Island, the liberty of a certain zone. Captured British officers enjoyed the same liberties in American-held territory. The officer class had formulated a set of rules that muted war's deadening blows, extending privileges to one another that made the conflict reminiscent of a fight among friends. Through paroles, enlarged areas of confinement, and permission to bring supplies and servants into the city, the gentlemanly "rules of war" worked to ease the plight of captured officers.

This entrenched system of favors did not jibe with the political rhetoric that cast one's opponents as wicked enemies operating against God's providence. Men of "parts and understanding" stood above the fray once the heat of battle subsided. On their word of honor alone, officers moved back and forth across the lines with the full blessing of both sides. This military smudging of boundaries may appear more perplexing than civilian movement across the lines because officers were professionals of war whose trained eyes knew where to look for valuable information. Their word of honor carried them to places that mere privates and noncommissioned officers could not tread.

The enlisted men's experience of war differed significantly from that of their superior officers. The lower-sort prisoners languished in the sugar houses, converted churches, and prison ships which served as the city's places of incarceration. Unlike their betters, these men enjoyed no opportunity to shop for rare British goods in town, nor could they slake their thirst with a tankard of flip at Scotts' tavern. Mention of Rhinelander's Sugar House or His Majesty's ship *Jersey* struck up lurid images of filth and misery for all participants in the conflict. These dreaded places provided accommodation to those American soldiers and sailors whose prime misfortune was the rank of private or seaman. Yet, though confined in miserable conditions, these prisoners were far from isolated, benefiting from a network of supporters who managed to get the latest family and war news to them behind their thick walls and iron bars. Thus, the occupied city's porosity extended even to those whose movement was most restricted.

To understand the movement of army personnel across the lines, it is necessary to explore the notion of civility in the military, how it worked, and how it was perceived by all ranks. There was one Revolution for the well-placed and the wealthy, and another Revolution for the plain and the poor. For the most part, everyone accepted these social discriminations. Just as in civilian life, the upper echelons of the military hierarchy included the more educated and honorable leaders whose comportment was expected to be different from that of the working people. Yet while the American privates did not rise up in massive protest or mutiny against the civilities accorded the officer group, some nonetheless questioned a system which accorded better treatment to enemy prisoners than to the backbone of the American army. Occasionally these two perceptions of war, and the expectations born of them, butted up against each other.

The John André spy controversy provides the most dramatic example of the disputed notion of generous enemies. André, Benedict Arnold's English contact and Adjutant General in the British army, was captured in the no-man's-land between the armies by shadowy figures whose movement between the military lines was also questionable. In this case, lowly soldiers, aspiring gentlemen-officers, British professionals, and angry civilians all had their say about the place of the code in the disposition of a "man of parts" caught in the act of spying.[2]

The convention which permitted gentlemen in the War of the Revolution automatically to acknowledge their counterparts on the other side was of long vintage. For centuries gentlemen could see themselves in their opponents and so tended to adopt the enlightened notion of treating others as they themselves would want to be treated. The medieval "law of arms" applied only to knights, not to peasants; it set out the rules of the game concerning proper treatment to be accorded to soldiers of noble birth.[3]

The hierarchy of the battlefield reflected the hierarchy of civil society. Like the princes who ruled them, the European gentry were born into their high stations. They felt themselves to be naturally endowed with superior abilities and so naturally entitled to wealth and social position. The men who formed the European officer class hailed from this group. One of their number, British General John Burgoyne, summarized the noblesse oblige embraced by this group when he wrote to a Continental army general in 1777, "Duty and Principle, Sir, make me a public enemy to the Americans who have taken up arms; but I seek to be a generous one." Burgoyne was confident that his Continental counterpart saw eye to eye on this issue as "all men of honour think alike."[4]

But Americans did not think exactly like Europeans. They upheld this system in their own way. While the hierarchical British army, officered by undisputed gentlemen, had operated under the code's auspices for centuries, the more democratically constituted American army was not as fluent in such civilities. As erstwhile Europeans, the Americans were not totally ignorant of the military code; they were simply out of practice. One hundred and fifty years of warfare with Indians did not make for bred-in-the-bone understanding of decorous behavior. While Washington had read Castiglione, and had himself been paroled in the French and Indian War, his subordinates in the officer group often sprang from less-than-genteel origins. Such individuals, inculcated with the liberating rhetoric of the Revolution, might have disregarded a code that sprang from medieval kings and high knights. But they strove to play the game nonetheless. Artisan-officers were not about to repudiate a system that carried them a notch higher on the social scale. American officers strained to take on the mantle of honor and gentility. In fact, they often tried to "out-gentleman" the gentlemen, exhibiting a high level of sensitivity over slights to their honor. But these Americans were not career soldiers steeped in this tradition. They had to learn the script.

Officers in the American army learned the rules of military civility from English soldiers who had fought alongside them in previous wars. Americans were equally familiar with the prerogatives of gentlemen in their own society and so had no trouble translating civilian rules to the military. In the plethora of classic military textbooks hurriedly published by the Americans in 1776, not one dealt with officer comportment and the privileges accruing to rank or with the courtesies to be tendered to enemy gentlemen. The English published no such tracts and the Americans had no time to write any of their own. For those American officers not groomed in the gentry, the example of upper-class models led the way. The only books to be read on the subject of military civility were biographies, the most popular being the history of King Gustavus Adolphus of Sweden. This solidly Protestant King shone as a paragon of honor, magnanimity, and morality in the middle of the particularly brutal Thirty Years' War. He was strict but fair and treated the enemy with respect. A master of mathematics, he spoke Latin "with uncommon energy and persuasion" and could hold his own in French, Italian, and German. He had the common touch when it came to humble soldiers and civilians. In the barrage of military books published and reprinted by Americans in 1776, Gustavus's biography figured prominently.[5]

Whiggish Americans admired the qualities so magnificently embodied in the Swedish King. Yet honor and gentlemanly reciprocity were not the only foundations on which the officer class relied. There was also the fear that the enemy would respond in kind if either side broke the code. Both British and Americans monitored the situation. In March of 1778, the Congress in Philadelphia complained that American officers were incarcerated in "loathsome gaols" and treated with "unparalled rigour." The Congress then gave Washington the green light to "order a number of the enemy's officers, as nearly equal in rank and condition of life as possible, to the persons so confined without just cause forthwith to be imprisoned, subsisted and treated in the same manner." State governors did not wait for Congress's approval to right inequities on the local level. In New Jersey, Captain John Simcoe, commander of the hated Tory regiment called the Queen's Rangers, found himself in rebel custody after an unsuccessful raid. His initial incarceration went according to formula. He signed a parole and promised to stay in the neighborhood. But when Governor William Livingston of New Jersey heard that the British in New York had slapped two influential American adherents into jail, chaining one of them to the floor, he ordered Simcoe in irons, although he still allowed a doctor out of New York and Simcoe's servant to come to prison and tend him. Two months later, the English Captain received the long-expected letter from Elias Boudinot, the American Commissary of Prisoners, in which Boudinot announced Simcoe's imminent release. But Boudinot added that "security [monetary payment] for the performance of your parole" would be demanded. "This, I assure you," wrote Boudinot, "is not because your honor is at all questioned, but to follow a late cruel example" in New York City.[6]

The system of military civility was thus tempered by the other side's willingness to play the game. At times, it is apparent that Americans understood the quid pro quo element of the system better than the gentility aspect of it. George Clinton, the Governor of New York State, for instance, found himself in a bind when a woman from his state was kept behind British lines against her will. Mrs. Hatfield had obtained passes from both sides to visit her prisoner-of-war husband, an American officer, on Long Island. On her way back, Mrs. Hatfield lost her English pass. The British refused to issue her another, advising her to return to her husband on Long Island. Governor Clinton wrote to George Washington for help. Of Mrs. Hatfield's husband, Clinton pointed out that as an officer, his station "entitles him to good treatment from a generous enemy and his Family to every indulgence from his Country." While the Governor could speak the language of civility, he was stymied on how to proceed along these lines in actual negotiations with the British. Clinton explained to Washington, "I am a stranger to the steps proper to be taken on this Occasion." He asked for the commander-in-chief's help in negotiating with the British. While at a loss as to how to negotiate the fine points of civility with the British, Clinton demonstrated that he could handle the situation if necessary because he could simply incarcerate the wife of a Loyalist until Mrs. Hatfield was returned. Clinton clearly understood the quid pro quo aspect of the code of civility better than he grasped the intricacies of gentlemanly reciprocity.[7]

Each side kept an ear cocked for the doings of the other party. The quid pro quo element was most obvious when officer-prisoners were involved. At times, British officers had to swallow hard when according special incarceration privileges to their American counterparts because many American officers did not strike them as equals, having been shoemakers and blacksmiths in their civilian days. To the skeptical British officer, these so-called American officers rose to a military status far above their rough social standing. But if the English winnowed out the true gentlemen from the offending upstarts, the Americans would respond by reducing the privileges of the British officers. Both sides, then, maintained a carefully calibrated balance when it came to the treatment of their imprisoned men.[8]

The handling of the imprisoned officer class could encompass a range of possibilities. Lieutenant Angus McDonnell, for example, a British prisoner of war taken at Saratoga, signed a standard parole in June of 1778: "I pledge my Word and Honor to Major General Gates, Commander-in-Chief of the army of the United States of North America, in the Northern Department, that I will return to his Headquarters in two months after my arrival in the city of New York, unless I can procure my exchange for an officer of equal rank of the American Army Prisoner of War in said city." McDonnell's contract rested on his honor and the good faith between captured and captor. In the two months he was allotted to effect an equal prisoner exchange, he could not resume his old duties in the army; he was still a prisoner even though residing at the headquarters of his army. Once the exchange was made, he could then pick up a musket with no nagging conscience. At times, honor and good faith did not quite suffice, as in the case of two English captains whose parole to New York City had to be insured by two respected Americans. The Americans put up bail money, feeling certain that the English prisoners were true gentlemen who would conform to the stipulations of their parole.[9]

Paroles could encompass another mode of expanded incarceration in that some officers were released from prison but confined to a certain geographic area. General Lee, for example, enjoyed the liberty of Manhattan Island. An officer kept on Long Island might have the liberty of moving wherever he wanted within eight miles of his lodging. American prisoners in these cases promised in their paroles not to endanger the British war effort by proselytizing others or aiding fellow Americans in any way.

When Angus McDonnell signed his parole and promised to return to captivity, was it really expected that he would live up to his promise? The evidence suggests that the expectation was real in the minds of the officers who participated in this system of exchange. Moreover, there is evidence that men actually returned to their captors in the rare instances when no exchange could be made. Charles Willson Peale bemoaned the fact that his brother-in-law had to return to New York City based on the terms of his parole. Another American officer, who was paroled to his home indefinitely, pleaded with Congress to arrange a prisoner exchange so he could get back to the business of soldiering. The languishing quality of his life in limbo is readily apparent in his letter to Congress: "Altho the Enemy have . . . suffered me to return to my Family and Friends, I am still subject to their power and Controul, liable to be called upon by them to surrender myself a prisoner whenever they please; and restrained by the sacred Ties of Honor, from drawing my Sword again in defence of My Country, till exchanged for some Officer of theirs." Those prisoners restored to their homes largely respected the injunctions to remain militarily inactive while on parole.[10]

Officers adhered to parole restrictions even when clearly free to break them. At times, however, the men were not sure about how to proceed. In such instances, there is evidence that officers made good-faith efforts to find the honorable solution, not the one most expedient to themselves in the short term. American officer-prisoners on Long Island, for instance, formed a Board to decide whether certain other American officers had the right to escape from their captivity. It seems that a captain and two lieutenants, captured by the British and on parole, had stopped some fishmongers on their way to the New York City market. The tradesmen refused to sell to rebels. "This produced reproachful language on both sides, when the officers laying hold of the fish, began to bandy them about the jaws of the ragamuffins that had insulted them." A complaint was lodged and the American officers taken up. When the Americans refused to acknowledge their "aggression," the British deposited them in the Provost until they saw the error of their ways. After two weeks, the British released the unrepentant Americans and returned them to Long Island without exacting new paroles. The freshly sprung prisoners claimed that any close confinement of officers annulled the terms of their old parole, and since no new parole was signed, they now had the right to escape. Instead of immediately acting on this belief, they submitted their case to a Board of American officers (themselves prisoners on Long Island) led by Colonel Ethan Allen. The Board held that while confined in the Provost, the officer-prisoners had the right to escape. But now released from prison, the terms of their old parole had to be honored. The men complied and waited to be properly exchanged.[11]

The repercussions of a parole violation and the care with which officials on both sides monitored the situation is also evident in the case of Lieutenant Andrew Lee. This American officer escaped from his captivity in New York and found no open arms when he returned home; instead he lived under a cloud for having broken his parole. As an American Commissary of Prisoners described his predicament, "Andrew Lee's honour has been impeached and his general character suffered on account of his late escape from the enemy." The American Commissary of Prisoners corresponded with his equivalent on the British side and obtained a letter from the British official exonerating Lee because he was unjustly confined in jail. The Americans had this letter published in the newspaper in order to clear Lee's name.[12]

Officials on both sides had a vested interest in paying strict attention to the details of the parole system while the individual officer felt a strong compunction to comply. His identity as a man depended on the perception that he conducted his life in an honorable way, and breaking one's parole was breaking one's word. If the soldier did not subscribe to this ideal, he would soon find to his chagrin that other people did take it seriously. The transgressor would pay for his disregard of the system in the disapproving looks and darting glances of a community who found his behavior reprehensible. High military and civilian officials, for their part, also had an interest in enforcing the code of gentlemanly soldier behavior, as such rules invested them with power to temper the fury of war.

While most American prisoners firmly obeyed the parole's stipulations, some others used the system more creatively by adhering to the letter of their paroles while clearly violating its spirit. An American captain, captured by the British on the retreat from Ticonderoga and en route back to New England on a parole, refused appropriately an American colonel's questions about the strength of General Burgoyne's force. He did, however, tell the colonel of certain others who had escaped and had not taken a parole. While some used inventive interpretation to clearly violate the spirit of the contract, others used the parole as an excuse to stay out of the fighting altogether.[13]

American authorities pursued parole violators and returned them to captivity if they could not prove sufficient and honorable cause for their escape. In June 1779, a General Board of Officers, headed by Nathanael Greene, Lord Sterling, and General von Steuben, reviewed a list of parole violators provided by the British. They summoned the suspects, heard their respective cases, and passed judgment on each. In some cases, the man in question was a private and so not expected to honor a parole; in other cases, the Board found that the British violated the parole agreement by confining American officers to prison cells. In yet other instances, the Board could find no excuse for the officer's behavior and returned him to British custody.[14]

The issue even concerned George Washington, who wrote letters and issued circulars about parole violators. In explaining to his American brethren why it was important to round up the accused, Washington employed the language of civility, emphasizing the ignominy, dishonor, and ungentlemanly behavior of these men. But just in case this flowery rhetoric did not hit the mark, the Commander-in-Chief ended his circular with the practical reasons for returning violators, which included the future smooth operation of the system of prisoner exchange.[15]

A Hessian officer, just released by the Americans, "pleasantly entertained" his comrades "with stories of his captivity." Making his experience sound more like a vacation than imprisonment, he related his visit to the Moravian community in Bethlehem while on parole. How do we account for Heldring's experience in captivity? We will never be sure about this case because evidence is lacking, but we can make a judicious guess based on the experiences of detained officers in the New York City area. It is likely that Heldring was moving about in a fairly comfortable situation. We already know that officer paroles entailed "enlargement," that is, they could move within a certain area "from sun to sun." At the end of the day, most officers returned to private lodgings that they shared with their civilian owners. In many instances, they probably had more amenities while prisoners than they had in the peripatetic army—better lodging and more consistency at mealtime. Both sides provided supplies to their imprisoned soldiers and both sides permitted certain officers, through paroles, to return to their camps and homes in order to collect "necessities." The Americans allowed two British officers taken at Stony Point to return to New York City to collect what they needed. An American captain detained on Long Island was permitted to return to Maryland to "collect some small supplies for myself and those poor dogs who remain with me from that state." If a prisoner could not obtain a parole to get home, he might write to a friend or family member to send money and supplies. Captain James Heron, while a prisoner in New York, asked his correspondent to send a "little silver or Gold" and his "chest and chests and cloaths." In the aftermath of the battle of Saratoga, a flurry of activity ensued as servants of officers crossed military lines to carry supplies to their imprisoned masters. Ironically, some New Yorkers opined that the British defeat at Saratoga was due in part to the officers' baggage, which "greatly incumbred the Army."[16]

With their physical comforts in place, many officers spent an enjoyable time socializing with one another and with the enemy. British officer John McNamara Hayes was downright effusive in thanking General Gates for such a lovely time during his incarceration. "I shall ever acknowledge with gratitude your attention to me while a prisoner," he gushed, "and shall ever consider it the Greatest happiness of my life to have an opportunity of testifying it." Hayes obviously knew Gates's wife, as he sent his compliments to her and ended his letter by asking his good friend Gates to allow a woman and her children to go to Canada to be reunited with her husband. Obviously not all officers enjoyed this kind of intimacy with their opponents. Such friendships were likely to prevail among the higher officers in the army; such careerists might have known one another before the Revolution. (Gates was born in Britain and may have known Hayes there.) And the higher an officer's rank, the more visible were the respect and gentlemanly treatment accorded to an enemy. After the battle of Saratoga, the defeated British General, John Burgoyne, stayed in the mansion house of the American General, Philip Schuyler. One week after the battle, some American officers attended a dinner at General Burgoyne's table in the Schuyler house. Amid much mirth and laughter, a British Major commented on the irony of their situation. It was "an odd world" they lived in, mused the Englishman, that they now were "the best of friends, drinking your [American] wine and the day before trying to put one another to death." An American Captain replied that this was "very true and that if he had met me, he [the Englishman] would have killed me if he could . . . This brought on a laugh all in good humour."[17]

In British-occupied New York, officer-prisoners were generally assigned lodgings in Manhattan or on Long Island. John Adlum, a young American soldier taken in the fall of Fort Washington, provides a lively picture of officer life in the occupied city. After a few days in jail, Private Adlum was paroled because of family connections. Liberated from Bridewell Prison, he roamed the city in search of work—literally a man with no place to go, no lodging, and no job. At the end of a fruitless day of searching, he discovered the lodgings of his regimental officer and was taken on as an errand boy and messenger. His employers were two American Colonels who shared a room at a Mrs. Carroll's house on Queen Street. Their landlady, whose husband was then in the American army, boarded several officers who thought it below their station to do "small jobs" like shopping for food. Adlum proved to be a very savvy shopper, so much so that he was soon doing the marketing for Mrs. Carroll as well. Adlum's brown coat with white facings signaled to the city's merchants that he was a prisoner, and as such Adlum benefited from substantial discounts (up to 20 pecent off the price Mrs. Carroll would have paid) given by closet-Whig retailers. On holidays, the American officers often dined out at the lodgings of fellow American officers. The "large company" who often came to dine at Mrs. Carroll's was sometimes regaled with the amusing tales of Adlum's favorite dinner guest, Colonel Ethan Allen, also at the time a prisoner in New York. The famous man from Vermont held center stage. "His manner of telling a story, his fund of anecdotes, his flashes of wit, and the force of his observations," noted Adlum, "never failed of having an attentive and amused audience." One night, Colonel Allen shone with such particular brilliance that the company stayed unusually late and ran out of wine. Adlum was summoned to go out after curfew and fetch some more. The reader of Adlum's narrative can almost feel the warmth of the room, see the wine-flushed faces, and hear the festive atmosphere of these gatherings. Adlum's wine run resulted in a series of adventures topped off by his hearing the news of Washington's victory at Trenton. This provided a perfect excuse to celebrate with yet another dinner, and since the party goers had never left Mrs. Carroll's, they plunged into another round of festivities. The officers dispatched Adlum to the market to procure "plenty of wine, rum, fruit etc. so that there might be no want nor chance to run out of other things." Adlum's employers no doubt rued their absence from the glorious victory, but Washington's soldiers at Trenton probably feasted no better on the remains of the Hessian's Christmas dinner than did their incarcerated countrymen behind enemy lines.[18]

Adequate food and lodging did not make for contentment among these officers, however. There were long stretches of time between the convivial dinners when the officers were "gloomy and thoughtful." The mo-

notony of a life without vocation hung heavily on these otherwise fortunate prisoners. Adlum noted that they rarely went out on the streets as
"it was not very pleasant for gentlemen of any sensibility to hear from the
mouths of blackguards 'There goes a rebel' with a 'damn' frequently attached to it." Adlum deemed these blackguards to be of the lower sort who
did not know how to behave when faced with men of quality, and he distinguished between these yokels and the "more respectable citizens" who
would "pass on . . . taking little or no notice of us."[19]

Officer-prisoners on Long Island experienced more isolation and less
comfortable quarters than did their compatriots in Manhattan, but they
still enjoyed the hospitality, however grudgingly given, of the island's farm
houses and circumscribed movement about the island. They could not
entertain on the scale of their city counterparts but evidence exists of lighter
moments that one would not expect in the prisoner state. Abner Everett
got married while a prisoner on Long Island and celebrated the occasion
with "Wedding Cheer." He recorded in his diary various jaunts to neighboring towns where he drank and conversed until the wee hours of the
morning. On one occasion, he dined with thirty fellow officer-prisoners
on wild fowl and drink. Everett also mentioned the receipt of letters from
home as well as newspapers from as far away as Georgia. Another Long
Island detainee, Captain James Morris, found comfortable accommodations with a Dutch family in King's County and struck up a friendship
with a Flatbush resident whom Morris identified as "a man of science." For
the next two and one-half years, Morris read "through a course of ancient
and modern history" from Mr. Clarkson's "most extensive private library."
When not reading, Morris made a little extra cash by farming small plots.
On the whole, he "felt no disposition to murmur and repine." Yet another
prisoner, Alexander Graydon, found his "low Dutch hosts" barely civil
and complained of a "fatiguing sameness in our occupations." Despite such
drawbacks, the sprightly American Captain "took the full latitude of our
parole traversing the streets in all directions, with a good deal of assurance."
Graydon's stay on Long Island included dinners with other soldiers, island
residents, and Loyalist refugees, where he rarely left the table "unexhiler-
ated." Another American prisoner on Long Island kept an account book
in which the largest entries related to the purchase of Continental lottery
tickets. On both Manhattan and Long Island, letters, newspapers, lottery
tickets, and paroled officers flowed freely behind and across British lines.[20]

Officers like Everett, Graydon, and Adlum's masters all eventually returned to the American lines. Once there, they served as potentially in-

valuable sources about logistics, morale, and troop movements in occupied New York. British prisoners in American hands could carry the same information back to their home base. Close incarceration would have lessened considerably their value as information gatherers, as well as their ability to influence the community around them during their imprisonment. But neither side considered close confinement an option for the gentleman prisoners of war. The British were particularly casual when it came to allowing enemy officers the run of their headquarters. Unlike the Americans, who could send enemy soldiers to obscure, faraway spots like western Pennsylvania or the interior of Virginia, the British controlled only very limited areas of New York and so tolerated a high degree of enemy infiltration in continuing to honor the system of gentlemanly civilities. A British officer reported the arrival of two rebel officer-messengers in camp who "staid all night and took a look of our parade this morning after which they sett off." Such laxity on the part of the British might be ascribed to overconfidence. Firmly entrenched in their island headquarters, they were surrounded by enough navy ships that only the arrival of the French fleet put them on their guard. But while the British navy could protect the occupied islands from direct attack, it could do nothing to protect the city from arson. Yet despite a devastating fire which destroyed a large part of the city in the first week of the occupation and a second major fire in 1778, the British betrayed little uneasiness about the possibility that, at any time, American officers could conspire to burn down the city of New York. Notwithstanding such strategic risks, the British continued to issue paroles and enlargements, confident that American gentlemen would keep their word.[21]

For most fighting men in the Revolutionary War, the code of civility was beyond reach. Privates and noncommissioned officers experienced the wretched conditions one would expect of incarceration during wartime. One of the first exercises performed at the close of a battle was to separate the officers from the rest. After the British victory at Fort Washington, Private John Adlum of the American army had barely marched a mile on his way to imprisonment in New York City when his English guards called out that officer-prisoners should move to the front of the line. The British stationed their own men between officers and privates to maintain strict segregation so that when Adlum attempted to move up the line, he was stopped by the British guard. On arriving at New York City, Adlum reported that the line was "halted near the East River to dispose of the officers." The privates moved on to Bridewell Prison, the French Church and the Dutch Church, and "a large sugarhouse several stories high." Adlum and 130 men of his regiment found themselves in the southwest corner room of Bride-well. During the first night of imprisonment, they received their rations of broken biscuit. Adlum kept some biscuit for the next morning and in the light of day, he winced at the "yellow and green streaks of mold" in his rations, pronouncing it "unsound biscuit." The next day, Adlum's group received a paltry amount of pork. This alternating diet of biscuit and pork continued until the news of the Hessian defeat at Trenton, when for the first time, the prisoners received greater portions of bread and meat on the same day, and "sound biscuit" too. After the Battle of Princeton in January, the prisoners saw for the first time peas, butter, and rice as well as pork and bread. With British and Hessian soldiers now in American custody, the British began to treat American prisoners as they hoped their imprisoned comrades would be treated by the Americans.

Adlum's understandable fixation on food ended when he received a parole, but he continued to drop by the prison to bring news and provisions to his "schoolmates, playmates and companions." As he ran errands for his American officer-employers, Adlum was reminded of his high fortune by his visits to Bridewell's windows. The men kept him informed of the mortality within. Adlum noted that several companies lost half their men in New York's prisons. He estimated that of the 1,660 American prisoners taken at Fort Washington, approximately 1,100 died in the first two months, while a full third of the rest never recovered from their prison experience and died at home. Adlum added that mortality was particularly high in the churches and sugarhouses. On one occasion in January, he saw a heap of dead, naked bodies dumped on a dungcart, which, Adlum surmised, were stripped of clothes and blankets by "their living friends" still within. One of the soldiers who survived the worst conditions, John Heller of Pennsylvania, could "well recollect" fifty years later the men who did not wake up in the morning and were carted off to some unknown destination. Heller marched from Fort Washington with John Adlum but had the misfortune of being confined in one of the city's meeting houses, where the men trembled for want of fire and were provided with questionable biscuit. Heller could count his blessings that he remained one step away from a more fearful prison. If he had become ill, he would have been sent to the Quaker Meeting House which served as the American hospital in New York. After one too many horrible stories, the Americans were allowed to employ their own matrons and nurses in the hospital, leading to improved care. But the young surgeons were a different matter. To amuse themselves, these allegedly sadistic doctors were said to "take hold of a clotted bandage and make a poor prisoner spin round like a top."[22]

Word of such miserable conditions reached the Americans, who sent their Commissary of Prisoners, Elias Boudinot, to investigate. Boudinot steeled himself for what he called harsh treatment, expecting to be blind-folded or otherwise restrained in the garrisoned city. Instead, to his amaze-ment, he joined General Robertson at tea for a pleasant two-hour chat, at the end of which Boudinot, as a gentleman, was given carte blanche to go wherever he wished in New York. The American insisted, however, that he be accompanied by a British officer at all times since he wanted to avoid any future accusations of "improper behaviour unworthy of my character." On his tour, he found that 300 to 400 men were so crammed into the French church that they could not all lie down at once. After the American vic-tory at Saratoga, the men told Boudinot that conditions improved, with fewer inmates, more wood, and better food. He heard similar stories at the one sugar house he visited. At the Provost, New York's major prison, he found a small group of officers who were incarcerated for reasons that Boudinot found specious. He procured their release. Boudinot's concern centered around the officer-prisoners. Incensed over the flimsy reasons for his officers' incarceration in the Provost, Boudinot barely mentioned the privates in the sugar house, and he never visited any of the prison ships.[23]

After 1777, the disease-ridden prison ships were reserved for naval personnel, and Boudinot was an army appointee. Survivors of the ships docked off Long Island remembered the filth, the vermin, the inedible rations, and the walking skeletons within. One survivor described the firmly entrenched worms in the bread rations. "It required considerable rapping upon the deck," a sailor recalled, "before the worms could be dis-lodged from their lurking places in a biscuit." Included in the litany of hor-rifying conditions mentioned by the survivors was the outrage that no dis-tinction was made between officers and enlisted men, though the prisoners themselves enforced a separation by reserving a large room in the ship for officers only. American prisoners counted their blessings that they were not consigned to the lower dungeon whence the French prisoners emerged from time to time with hollow, unworldly eyes.[24]

Despite the wretched conditions in New York City's prisons, a net-work reached into the various places of confinement and kept the American prisoners connected with well-wishers in Whig-occupied New York state. There were many paths into the prisons. Prisoners on parole could talk to

their brethren at the jail's windows. In exchange for a simple favor to a
British soldier, John Adlum gained access to the Provost and to Bridewell,
two of the larger prisons of New York. Other conduits included the New
York City–resident relatives of American veterans who brought provisions
and news to the incarcerated men. Samuel Mott recalled that as a fifteen-
year-old resident of New York he had carried provisions to his Uncle Jesse
Coles in the Old Jail. Samuel's father later procured Coles's release, acting as security that the American soldier would not leave town. Another
similar case involved an American drummer boy whose mother had remained in the city and had several British officers billeted at her residence.
She used her influence with these men to spring her son, who immediately

broke his parole by leaving town with "dispatches for General Washington." Mother may have abetted her son's decision to flee, as she remained in
town throughout the war keeping "General Washington informed of the
intended movement of the enemy."[25]

When John Adlum made the nocturnal wine run for his superior officers on Christmas Night, 1776, he received word of Washington's victory
at Trenton from a city wine dealer. On blurting out the news to his employers and their company, the elated Adlum was greeted with a certain
skepticism since some officers could not conceive that news could travel
so fast. The following day found Adlum at the Bridewell prison windows
informing his buddies of the victory and reminding them that 900 Hessian
prisoners meant the possibility of an exchange for all of them. In the fall of
1777, New York City learned of the outcome of the Battle of Saratoga by
the roaring cheer issuing from the Provost prison. Through a piece of paper
inserted in a loaf of bread, the American prisoners learned of Burgoyne's
defeat before the handbills and newspapers officially confirmed it.[26]

But though news and support networks reached into New York City's
prisons, the everyday reality experienced by privates and noncommissioned
officers was vastly different from that of their superiors. The officers took
for granted and enjoyed their privileges. They ate venison, not "offal cakes"
or moldy bread crumbs. They were the first to be exchanged. They could
stroll about town with impunity. The enlisted men were of course aware
of the prerogatives inherent in officer status. One might expect them to
protest the more civilized treatment of enemy officers or to use the egalitar-
ian rhetoric of the time to attack the privileges of rank. Yet they posed no
major challenge to this traditional system of hierarchy and honor. The election of militia officers and the increased opportunity to replace unpopular
men in the American army may account in part for their acquiescence. Sol-

diers did petition to remove themselves from regiments where offensive superiors held sway, and the American soldiers clearly had more choice in the matter of officer selection than did their European counterparts.[27]

While not mutinying over this issue, the men in the ranks eyed these genteel goings-on with begrudging skepticism. Early in the war, there are examples of challenges by the lower sort who did not understand the rules and had to be educated. After the fall of St. John's in the Canadian campaign of 1775, the American General Richard Montgomery allowed British quartermasters to collect their officers' baggage in Montreal. The poorly clad American soldiers watched as twenty-two batteaux were loaded with clothing and supplies that they could have used to alleviate their desperate situation. Murmurs began, and finally the shivering New Yorkers stopped the British quartermasters at bayonet point. General Montgomery had to intervene and educate his men about honor and privilege. He reported the lesson to fellow General Philip Schuyler. "I wish some method could be fallen upon," wrote the exasperated General, "to engage *gentlemen* to serve: a point of honor and more knowledge of the world, to be found in that class of men, would greatly reform discipline, and render the troops much more tractable." Montgomery went on to say that the New York militia, "were very near a mutiny the other day because I would not stop the clothing of the garrison of St. Johns. I would not have sullied my own reputation," continued Montgomery, "nor disgraced the Continental arms, by such a breach of capitulation for the universe. There was no driving it into their noodles that the clothing was really the property of the soldier; that he paid for it; and that every regiment . . . saved a year's clothing to have decent clothes to wear on particular occasions." Montgomery finally persuaded his troops to let the quartermasters go.[28]

Such instances of near mutiny within the American army over the disposition of enemy prisoners were few in number and generally found at the beginning of the conflict. An educational process, much like Montgomery's explanations to his men, could well have reconciled the lower sorts to the rules of war. Still, while no mutinies occurred over this issue, the rank and file occasionally grumbled about the gentlemen's code, particularly with respect to their own officers. They might especially resent the airs assumed by officers, who were parvenus to positions of power in the American army. Samuel Tenny, an unhappy but faithful soldier, expressed his frustration in a letter to a friend. "In the army at present, merit is measured only by rank. Those who are high in rank are clever fellows. The Low are small Folks—and those who have none at all, like us, are poor Devils—

We are Nobodys. We are Nothing." Tenny looked forward to the day when, back in civilian life, he would "have the opportunity to convince the *Lordly Insignificances* who now take the advantage of being mounted on stilts to look down upon [me], how sincerely I despise them."[29]

This well-documented tension in the army, exacerbated by poor provisions and erratic pay, did not translate into a general condemnation of the code of civility. Even for those prisoners of war incarcerated in New York City, the difference in treatment between officers and the rank and file did not provoke a hue and cry against the system. The prisons in New York should have been seedbeds of class consciousness, yet no known survivor denounced the system of military civility or pointed to his prison experience as a turning point in his perception of the justice of social distinctions. Though enlisted men seemed to accept that a private would find himself in a prison while his officers walked the streets, they exhibited sharp discomfort about any fraternization between their officers and enemy prisoners. Madame Van Riedesal, the wife of a Hessian general, witnessed an instance of just such edginess. She and her husband found themselves part of the captured contingent of Hessian soldiers from the Battle of Saratoga. At one point after the battle, the Marquis de Lafayette rode up to them and paid his compliments. The aristocratic Van Riedesals and the French Marquis laughed and chatted most cordially in French. While they thus amused themselves, "Lady Fritz," as she was known among the Hessians, noticed that Lafayette "had many Americans in his train who were ready to leap out of their skins for vexation at hearing us speak constantly in French." Delighted with this situation, Madame mused that "perhaps they feared on seeing us on such a friendly footing with him, that we would be able to alienate him from their cause." The perceptive Baroness might also have noted that the Americans saw this easy conviviality between aristocrats as an uncomfortable reminder that their hero, Lafayette, had more in common with enemy Hessians than he had with his own men.[30]

The complex tensions generated by these distinct experiences of war, along with issues of civility, wounded honor, sanctioned and unsanctioned movement, revolutionary virtue, and the need in America to consider public opinion, formed the dynamic elements of one of the most famous episodes of the revolution—the Benedict Arnold–John André spy case. In the disposition of Arnold's English contact, Major André, one sees the clash of two different notions about war and the treatment of one's enemy. Washington, on whose shoulders the decision about how to deal with the captured André rested, had to grapple with his own inclinations as a man weaned on southern civility and the European military code, as well as with considerations of what he called "policy." And when Washington wrote of "policy," he meant the necessity to placate the public, a public which in this case included the backbone of the Revolutionary force—the enlisted soldiers who had little appreciation for André's genteel wit and ingratiating bonhomie.

Benedict Arnold's treason was an explosive story in the autumn of 1780. Soldiers expected that a war would include battles, late pay, and miserable victuals, but they never expected the heroic Field Commander of the American army, who had permanently injured a leg while turning the tide at the Battle of Saratoga, to betray his country. When the unthinkable happened, it shook the army's confidence in its leaders. Decisions made by their officers meant life or death to every soldier. Enlisted men expected a certain level of ineptitude from some officers, about whom they often spoke disparagingly, but they could not accept a leader whose heart was in the wrong place. The treason sparked outrage everywhere, but it also brought on a high level of anxiety in the army about the reliability of the high command. If Arnold could sell his honor for pounds sterling, how vulnerable were the other military leaders?

Few soldiers could say that they were present at West Point when Arnold fled downstream to the British. In marked contrast, thousands of men could claim they were at Tappan for André's execution because Tappan was the site of the main army encampment in October 1780. The Benedict Arnold–John André affair was the second most often cited event of the Revolution by New York City–area veterans, roughly one in three soldiers from the New York City region mentioning it in their pension applications.[31] Few of the pensioners asserted that they actually saw the execution. Indeed, only a few hundred of them were close enough to see André's noble face and proud beauty. But the soldiers' mere presence at Tappan put them in proximity to the great event. Moreover, the André story placed a lowly soldier in emotional proximity to the events of September-October 1780 because the heroes of the day were not generals, but three of the plainest members of the military establishment—privates in a militia company.

At least, this is how the captors were defined in the wake of Arnold's treason. But like so many other characters circulating between the lines, the captors' motivation was ambiguous at best. Many men in the no-man's-land between the armies were little more than brigands masquerading as virtuous militiamen. Were John Paulding, David Williams, and Isaac Van Wart serving the cause or serving themselves? This is a question that becomes pertinent when Americans assess the episode in later generations.

Questionable identity also characterized the person of John André. As an officer, the British Adjutant General should have been treated as a generous enemy. His actions behind the lines, however, bespoke the machinations of a spy—an activity deserving the hangman's noose. But a spy was defined in the eighteenth century not only by his actions but also in terms of identity. A spy was a low, venal character solely motivated by money. André's captors fit that description better than the impeccably mannered British officer. With the life of such a paragon of officerly comportment at stake, both British and Americans argued the fine points of the code of military civility that permitted certain types of movement between the lines.

The Arnold-André episode thus provides a useful perspective from which to examine the code that made permeable boundaries possible among the war's combatants, as well as the view of that code from above and below. Officers and foot soldiers saw events differently in the dispostion of "the unfortunate André," as officers would have it, or simply of "the spy," as the rank and file dismissively identified André.[32]

Benedict Arnold was one of the few American generals to inflict pain on the British during the early years of the war. This former apothecary from New Haven distinguished himself in the Canadian campaign, on Lake Champlain, and at the Battle of Saratoga, where his heroism turned the tide for the Americans. He never got what he considered to be his due, however, particularly for his bravery at Saratoga, and ended up under a cloud in 1778 when the civil authorities of Philadelphia charged him with improprieties while he commanded in that city. It was in Philadelphia that a disgruntled Arnold, whose honor had been impugned, started a correspondence with the British in New York.

The astounded recipient of Benedict Arnold's secret letters was General Henry Clinton's chief aide, John André. After only a scant six years in active service, this thirty-year-old officer had become Clinton's eyes and ears. Son of a wealthy merchant, André had forsaken the counting house for a military career after his father's death. His continental education included two stints at the military school of Göttingen before his regiment was called to America, where he arrived in September 1774. André's first engagement with American fighting men came at the siege of St. John's

in Canada, where a force under Richard Montgomery defeated the British and captured the garrison, including John André. As a first lieutenant, André signed a parole and spent nearly ten months in Lancaster and later in Carlisle, Pennsylvania. Through an exchange of prisoners, André found himself in British-occupied Philadelphia, where he circulated brilliantly in the high society of the rebel's former capital. His talent for theatricals, his powers of inventiveness, and his great charm were put to good use during a dreary winter in an occupied city where the military had very little to do in the martial line. Buoyed by his high profile in the Philadelphia campaign, including a prominent role in the Paoli massacre, he returned to New York and found a spot on Henry Clinton's staff.

Using code books and invisible ink, Arnold and André corresponded for sixteen months through a Philadelphia crockery merchant and a refugee Anglican minister at New York. André wondered at first whether the notes delivered to him were really from the most celebrated Field Commander of the American army. And if this were so, it was surely a trick to lure the English army out of New York City and into a vulnerable field position where the Americans could pick the soldiers off. Arnold, for his part, wanted a king's ransom in pounds sterling, not for his own enjoyment, he explained, but to secure a satisfactory competency for his wife and child. To reinforce this selfless role, Arnold cast himself as a model military figure of his time, by using the code name "Gustavus" to correspond with his new allies. After months of haggling about money and plumbing the hidden meanings of notes disguised as merchants' correspondence, it was time for Arnold and André to meet face to face.

On the night of September 21, 1780, Arnold, now stationed at West Point, delegated Joshua Hett Smith, brother of the prominent New York Loyalist William Smith, to pick up a Mr. Anderson (André) from the British ship *Vulture*. Claiming no knowledge about Arnold's true intentions, Smith, along with two of his tenants rowed out to the warship and brought Mr. Anderson to a meeting place on the river south of West Point.[33] The length of Arnold and André's conversation, coupled with an exchange of fire between American batteries and the British ship, forced the ship's removal further downstream and weakened the tenants' resolve to participate any further in this murky and increasingly perilous business. Not able to retreat to the *Vulture*, André accompanied Arnold to Hett Smith's house within the American lines to await nightfall on the 22nd. At Arnold's strong suggestion, André exchanged his regimental uniform for civilian clothing. Armed with a pass from Arnold, André rode through

Westchester County toward the British lines. He had passed the American outposts and was in no-man's-land once again when three underlings of indeterminate allegiance stopped André's steaming horse. Instead of immediately producing his pass from Arnold, André, who probably felt elated to have crossed beyond the American lines, began a chummy conversation which ended in arousing the suspicions of the three men. John Paulding, Isaac Van Wart, and David Williams conducted the British Adjutant General to the bushes, where they made him disrobe and found tucked in his stockings the plans and troop dispositions of the American fortress upriver at West Point. Still using his alias, André found himself conducted back to the American lines where the commanding Lieutenant Colonel decided to send the incriminating papers to Washington while dispatching Mr. Anderson's person to Arnold at West Point. En route, André fell into the custody of Lieutenant Joshua King at Salem. King's eyes alighted on the "somewhat thread-bare" purple coat with gold lace in which the bedraggled, unshaven man was clothed. King brought his own barber to his prisoner's place of confinement in order to spruce up this "reduced gentleman." Observing that when the ribbon was taken off, his prisoner's hair was full of powder, King knew that he had "no ordinary person in charge." Later that day, André divulged his true identity to the sympathetic and friendly fellow officer and promptly penned a letter to General Washington.[34]

Prefacing his remarks with the statement that he wrote the American Commander-in-Chief in order to "vindicate my fame" rather than solicit any security for his person, André explained that his intention on the night of the 21st was to meet an informant between the military lines of the two sides. As the meeting dragged on until daybreak, André was conducted within the American posts. In an attempt to put Washington in his shoes, André exclaimed, "your excellency may conceive my sensation" when his American contacts refused to conduct him back to his ship. This refusal was tantamount in André's mind to actual imprisonment, and so André felt he had a reason to attempt an escape. Involuntarily put into the position of a prisoner, André exchanged his regimentals for civilian clothing in a futile attempt to get away. Now with nothing left but his honor as an officer and a gentleman, he reminded Washington that "though unfortunate, I am branded with nothing dishonorable." André logically suggested that his case be handled in a manner typical for high-ranking prisoners—a timely exchange. André reminded Washington of the South Carolina spies who were in English custody and whose fate might reflect the treatment André received. After this veiled threat, he closed with a reminder of why

A Representation of John André, 1780. This engraving, based on a drawing made by John André on the day before his execution, shows the British officer being rowed to shore for his fateful meeting with General Benedict Arnold. Emmet Collection, Miriam and Ira D. Wallach Division of Art, Prints and Photographs, The New York Public Library, Astor, Lenox and Tilden Foundations.

Washington should empathize with his situation and grant his requests. The "generosity of [Washington's] mind" and his "superior station," André reasoned, would lead the American General to comply with his wishes. Clearly André was confident that he was speaking a language Washington understood. It was as coded a message as any he had ever sent to Arnold and potentially just as effective, for André fully expected that the sensibility and empathy of a gentleman of high rank would result in the customary exchange.[35]

Washington did indeed understand the latent content of the captive's letter, but he also had learned by the time he received it that André's informant was Benedict Arnold, the man whom Washington had entrusted with the command of West Point. On the morning of September 25 Washington had intended to breakfast with Arnold but found instead that his man at the fort had fled downriver to British shipping.[36]

The army learned of Arnold's treachery the day after it was uncovered. "Treason of the blackest dye," the general orders of September 26 read, "was yesterday discovered." The report went on to describe Arnold's perfidy and the mortal blow his plan would have inflicted had he been successful, adding that God had certainly intervened to foil such a "fatal misfortune." The orders also noted that a Mr. André, Adjutant General of the British army, had been taken prisoner.[37]

In the days after the discovery, army men looked at one another and wondered. If the hero of Saratoga could so utterly betray the cause, then everyone was suspect. Washington assumed that Arnold did not act alone and so began an official investigation into possible accomplices, more than likely casting his unofficial eye on all the officer corps. The General's marquee tent was so packed with people in the days after the discovery of the treason that it was difficult for even the likes of General Nathanael Greene to get more than a few minutes with the harried Commander-in-Chief. The stock of gentleman-officers was at an all-time low. The first newspaper account of September 28 called the affair a plot involving Arnold and other persons. Public opinion, as reflected in the same story, had already passed judgment on André, labeling him a "spy."[38]

Into this supercharged atmosphere entered the affable English officer who had already charmed his American guards on his progress toward Tappan. The American officer escort, Major Tallmadge, had found André "a very genteel, sensible man." Alexander Hamilton noted André's candor, modest firmness, liberality, politeness, manliness, selflessness, courage, fortitude, elegance of mind and manners, and excellent understanding. The besotted Hamilton further rhapsodized that André's "sentiments were elevated . . . his elocution handsome and his address easy, polite and insinuating." André did not press these sterling qualities on anyone but assumed a diffidence which Hamilton found positively fetching. In the hours before the court martial, General Greene noted the British officer's "apparent cheerfulness," an indication that "he little suspects his approaching fate."[39]

Such a paragon belied the very definition of a spy. According to the military dictionaries of the day, spies were venal characters who had to be well paid for their work. They were grubby, untrustworthy, plebian men. André could not be so described even in a thread-bare costume. Yet he was Arnold's accomplice, caught in disguise with incriminating papers. Washington made a conscious decision to avoid any meeting with André, so that his disposition of the case could not be seen as prejudiced in any way. According to the military code, Washington had the right to order an immediate execution. He could also intervene and shelter the accused from the ultimate penalty as had happened in the past with other capital cases.[40]

But this was no ordinary case; the traitor was the hero of Saratoga and the spy was the very embodiment of gentlemanly grace. Although Washington held the ultimate power regarding André's case, he claimed he would be guided by the decision of a fourteen-member panel of generals called the Board of General Officers, a star-studded group which convened on September 29 in the full heat of shock and outrage generated by the affair.[41] By that date, the news of Arnold's treason and André's capture had spread well beyond the Hudson Valley. Philadelphia heard of it on the 27th, the day after the army did. On the 29th, Philadelphians paraded about "in Derision" an effigy of Arnold made by the artist Charles Willson Peale. They repeated this performance the following night "with lights" as spectators were treated to the sight of Arnold "with the Devil on his Back offering him a Purse of Gold." The crowd consigned the Devil back whence he came by hurling him and his minion into a bonfire "amidst thousands of spectators and loud huzzahs and acclamations and rejoicing to think that his traitorous Plot was discovered so soon and thousands of lives saved." From Morristown, a refugee New Yorker, Abraham Brasher, wrote that "the common topic of conversation here" was the astonishing, unaccountable treachery of Arnold. "This is a loud call," opined Brasher, "upon the vigilance of those who hold the public trusts."[42]

The officers at Tappan could not but have heard this "loud call." All eyes seemed to be focused on their recommendation to Washington. The head of the court martial, General Nathanael Greene, feared "mischievious consequences" from an American populace now suspicious of the army. In such a crisis, the men who held the public trust may well have felt compelled to show an extra dose of patriotism. Given this golden opportunity to reinforce their Patriot credentials, the hypersensitive Board of Officers was not about to work out a prisoner exchange for the elegant André, no matter what their personal inclinations. Still, André was smothered with courtesies as his fate was weighed. Hamilton recorded that "when brought before the Board of Officers, he met with every mark of indulgence, was required to answer no interrogatory which could even embarras his feeling." During the inquiry, André stuck to the story he recounted in his first letter to Washington. He was under no flag of truce. He came, he said, in secret to the no-man's-land between the armies, met an informant, and was unexpectedly conducted behind the American lines. In his attempt to escape, he shed his uniform. The Board needed no further statements. André admitted that he was disguised and within the American lines on his way back to New York City. Had André's actions been covered by a flag, his surreptitious behavior (feigned name, night meeting, change of clothing) would have been unnecessary. The Board concluded that André was indeed a spy and "that agreeable to the law and usage of nations . . . he ought to suffer death." Washington promptly set a date for the execution.[43]

A chorus of British voices rose to André's defense. They urged observance of "the custom and usage of all nations," as an American Loyalist, Beverly Robinson, put it in his letter to Washington on September 25, 1780. André, he wrote, "went up with a flag at the request of General Arnold . . . and every step Major André took was by the advice and direction of General Arnold even that of taking a feigned name." Henry Clinton, André's superior in New York, threw his weight behind Robinson's argument by laying whatever blame there was on his own shoulders. He wrote to Washington, "I have the honor to inform you, Sir, that I permitted Major André to go to Major General Arnold at the particular request of that general officer." Writing as one supreme commander to another, Clinton cast André as a dutiful officer who acted on the wishes and orders of those above him. Arnold himself invoked his "undoubted right" to issue André a flag of truce in his letter to Washington dated September 26, because technically, at the time of his meeting with André, Arnold was "in actual service of America, under the orders of General Washington, and commanding General at West Point." (Arnold did not formally tender his resignation from the American forces until October 1.) Lieutenant General James Robertson's letter to Washington took on a sermon-like tone when he reminded the American Commander that as an enlightened, compassionate gentleman, he should want "to promote [rather] than prevent the civilities and acts of humanity which the rules of war permit between civilized nations." Robertson felt that Washington's only honorable course was to send André back to New York. To the British, at least in this case, the sanctity of a flag of truce overruled any lesser infractions of conduct taken under its auspices. The "form" of things, argued the British, was honored in André's every action from the time he left New York to the moment he was captured.[44]

The Board of Officers took these arguments seriously. Far from ignoring the British contentions, they adopted the terms of debate created by the other side. The Americans risked little in doing this since they had André's letter of September 24 in which the prisoner admitted to a set of circumstances quite different from that presented by his friends in New York. To put the issue to rest, the Board of Officers asked André pointblank whether he operated under a flag of truce. André could make only one answer consistent with his honor, and that answer was to adhere to his original story. As the Board recorded André's words, it concluded that "it was impossible for him to suppose he came on shore under that sanction." In so directly addressing the nub of the British argument, the Board of Officers showed they were well aware that political fencesitters and pro-British supporters were part of the American audience closely following the case. Only after the Board's decision to convict André as a spy did Washington reply to Clinton that the British commander knew as well as he that flags "were never meant to authorize or countenance" actions such as André and Arnold engaged in that night.[45]

Undeterred by the Board's decision and André's impending execution, Clinton asked Washington for a face-to-face meeting where British representatives could better present their case to Washington's representative. Washington, who could hardly have been comfortable about the potential execution of such a highly placed officer readily acceded to Clinton's request and postponed the execution. "Anxious to procure the means of saving the life of André and at the same time to make an example of a traitor," wrote a member of Washington's staff, Washington had sent an American soldier to New York City posing as a deserter. The soldier's mission was to abduct Arnold and bring him back to justice. As the American operative easily entered the city, Washington sent official messengers to the British who unofficially let drop that if Clinton would deliver Arnold, then André would be returned. Washington may also have hoped that such an exchange would be worked out during the face-to-face meeting between General Greene and the British General, James Robertson.[46]

At that meeting, Robertson pounded once again on the "flag of truce" defense, but finding Greene unimpressed, suggested that two European generals whose military educations were impeccable should decide the issue. As Robertson put it, "I wished that disinterested gentlemen of knowledge of the law of war and nations, might be asked their opinion on the subject, and mentioned Monsieur Knyphausen [Hessian general] and General Rochambault." Pushing for an exchange, Robertson reached for language that would appeal to his fellow gentleman-officer. "I wished that an intercourse of such civilities as the rules of war admit of," he explained, "might take off many of its horrors." Robertson then reminded the American that "Sir Henry Clinton had never put to death any person for a breach of the rules of war though he had, and now has, many in his power." Specifics of the case aside, Robertson argued that gentlemen did not act in the manner then being exhibited by Washington and his generals. Indeed, if André were executed, the whole system of civil treatment which had thus far blunted the ravages of war would be in jeopardy.[47]

Undoubtedly, Washington did not appreciate the lecture, yet he was familiar with and understood the logic behind it. Washington had other things to worry about, however. His order to delay the execution had provoked disquieting murmurs "from tent to tent." It was common knowledge in the army camp at Tappan that "some compassionate minds" wished for André's release, and André's reprieve from execution seemed to bolster the rumor. The arrival of André's personal servant from New York City, who brought his master "some necessaries," exacerbated the soldiers' uneasiness. Now, if a glimpse of André could be had, he appeared in gleaming regimentals, not in the seedy suit and beaver hat in which he had been arrested. The men of the camp could also see wildly sympathetic officers paying homage to André in prison. They may also have heard that, although the decision of the Board of Officers was unanimous, there was dissension during the Board's deliberations. The American soldiers' perceptions may not have been far off the mark. A close friend of André's, Captain John Simcoe of the Queen's Rangers, appealed to his old friend, "Light Horse Harry" Lee, in support of André's case. Lee, who was stationed at the American camp at Tappan, replied that André would probably be saved; but before Lee finished the letter, he obviously had heard news that led him to add a postscript which negated his initial optimism. By the time Lee had penned his post script, rumblings from the ranks had obviously registered at headquarters. Lower-ranked officers were threatening to quit, since they considered their lives to be at risk when the machinations of spies went unpunished. A French volunteer at the American camp later claimed that "the least indulgence shown to him [André] would, in the circumstances in which we were placed, have been followed by a mutiny in the army."[48]

Obviously the army took the entire episode personally. Arnold had played with their lives. A British attack meant their blood. American soldiers had swung from the gallows for much less than spying. Two weeks before the treason crisis, a soldier had been hung for plundering. American troops could also recall the recent execution of a soldier who had forged officers' handwriting in passing out discharges and furloughs to his buddies. He suffered the ultimate penalty for doing favors for his friends. It seemed inconceivable that a key player in the planned fall of America's most strategic fortress should walk away. "The defection of Arnold had excited such a general suspicion that no one dared trust another," noted one witness at the American encampment, "and nothing but execrations were heard from hut to hut."[49]

Washington had no doubt heard as well the reports of civilian reaction to the Arnold affair in the American capital of Philadelphia. The military and civilian communities were aroused at a time when each group distrusted the other. Washington was involved at the time of the crisis in urging Congress, already anxious over the growth of military power, to authorize longer terms of enlistment in the army. The crisis amplified the distrust between civilian and military powers, as duly noted by one Loyalist observer. "The Civil at present greatly dread the Military," wrote Andrew Elliot to William Eden in London. "They call Gates an Arnold . . . their distrust of themselves makes them still more distrustfull of their Great and Good Ally [France] so that although the great point has failed [the seizure of West Point], yet consequences will be highly favorable."[50]

The emotional outpourings that Arnold's treason and André's spying engendered had to be satisfied. George Washington, though a gentleman-officer to the bone, refused to answer Robertson's arguments or Arnold's threats, and ordered André's execution to proceed. He also rejected André's flowery request to be shot like a man of honor rather than being hanged like a common criminal. Alexander Hamilton observed that either Arnold or André had to be sacrificed, and "the former was out of our power." While Washington claimed that the actual circumstances of the case justified his decision, he also realized that "policy required a sacrifice." So while he permitted André to have his manservant and sent breakfast from his table to the condemned officer, Washington also ordered the gibbet raised and denied André's request to be shot. The military command could afford no ambiguity in the stance it adopted at this critical juncture. Perhaps only in Revolutionary America would Washington have had to bow to the wishes of the public over his anxiety about executing a kindred soul.[51]

On October 2, ten days after his capture, John André linked arms with two American officers and walked to the place of execution with "a most agreeable smile" on his face. That smile disappeared when he saw a gibbet at the end of his path and not a firing squad. Still, he hoisted himself upon the cart and performed all the necessary preliminaries like blindfolding himself and placing the noose around his neck. Hamilton admired André's fortitude and composure. Major Tallmadge, the head of American intelligence, was moved to tears at the "affecting spectacle," as was the Board of Officers who had condemned André. In these officers' world of refinement and

Major John André, *Self-Portrait*, 1780. While imprisoned by the Americans shortly before his execution, André drew this self-portrait. Yale University Art Gallery. Gift of Ebenezer Baldwin, B.A. 1808.

courage, André was destined by act and legend to become the embodiment of the gentlemanly ideal.[52]

There were other spectators of more lowly rank at André's execution. Andrew Kettel, for instance, a Sergeant in the Massachusetts line, tersely mentioned André's last day in his diary, offering no encomiums to the British officer's stellar qualities. Kettel wrote, "I went to see Major Andrée who was executed for coming out from the enemy as a spy to negotiate the business with Genl. Arnold." In Kettel's matter-of-fact version, there are no tears or lamentations, suggesting that the rank and file had little appreciation for André's winning ways and stylish grace. Another soldier wrote to his wife, "Major André we have got [who is] to be hanged in an hours time which will be 5 in the afternoon as a spy. this is the way we keep the sabbath, I wish we could employ every day to as good advantage." John Shreve, an eighteen-year-old freshly minted Lieutenant at the time of André's execution, repeatedly described the condemned man simply as "the spy." What was most striking to Shreve was the figure André cut in hanging from the rope. "I have seen several men hung," noted Shreve, "but he flounced about more than any one I ever saw." In contrast, the officers who subsequently wrote about André, always exhibited the deepest empathy for "the unfortunate" young man.[53]

The Arnold-André episode included dramatic elements that would haunt veterans' memories and spark imaginations for years to come. The story was one of treacherous villainy, divine intervention on the brink of disaster, and an expiation of sorts in the execution of André. The villain of the piece was never in doubt. The heroes, however, varied depending on who was narrating the story and when it was told. In October 1780, the undisputed heroes of the hour, at least according to the Americans, were the three captors of André. John Paulding, Isaac Van Wart, and David Williams formed part of a band of seven men who operated in the no-man's-land between the armies. Whether members of the American militia or independent operators (one could be both in those days), the men who roamed this lawless area had a reputation for being greedy opportunists who waylaid individuals and stole their property. These three, having found the incriminating papers on André's person and listened to the gentleman's attempt to bribe them, had decided to turn the spy back to the American army.

The three militiamen's decision on the morning of September 23 foiled the plot, exposed a traitor, and saved the army from a devastating blow. The three men had accomplished more than the army and several generals could get done on a good day of battle. Nor was this the full extent of their contribution. They tendered another service to their country by exemplifying the virtuous soldier at a time when such paragons were sorely needed. Paulding, Van Wart, and Williams were feted, praised, and given substantial financial rewards for their selfless devotion to duty. Washington called them "men of great virtue" and invited them to sup at his table. The army orders of September 26 praised them as "bright ornaments" who resisted "the arts and seductions of an insidious enemy." Congress awarded each man an annual life pension of $200 in specie and a silver medal engraved with the words "Fidelity" and "Vincit Amor Patriae." The State of New York gave each a farm, confiscated from area Loyalists. Thus did the power structure strain to convey that virtue did indeed pay.[54]

When the news of André's execution reached Britain, the howls of outrage were universal. The London press gave an object lesson on the intricacies of the military code that was promptly published in the Loyalist press of New York. There was a difference, claimed the British, "between spies and spies." Men of the highest rank could spy and retain their honor. The laws of war decreed that such men were never hanged. On the other hand, those spies deserving summary execution were "peasants, or of the very lowest class of men." The article hastily added that one life was not inherently more valuable than another, but that "a peasant, a low lifed mercenary taken as a spy, is currently supposed to be actuated merely by the promise or prospect of a sordid fee or reward for the mischief implied by his errand. He is looked upon as having gone out of his line of life for a vile hire, without a spark of principle or of honor [and] is accordingly treated and executed with very little ceremony." The article then punched the point home by claiming that generals or commissioned officers were gentlemen, hence not material for the gibbet.[55]

In later years, the three heroes disappeared from public view and went back to living and working in their communities. And in the cooler aftermath of the Revolution, the dead Major grew in stature. André's personal beauty further bloomed; the range of his talents expanded; the delicacy of André's honorable behavior grew ever more fabled. He was lionized in poetry and plays as a tragic hero, becoming prime fodder for the romantic literature of the time. As André's stock went up, the three militiamen who foiled his ambitions lived on in obscurity.

In 1817, one of the captors, John Paulding, resurfaced to apply for a pension increase. Congress voted, however, to deny André's captors anything more in the way of remuneration, having been swayed by the moving words of Congressman Benjamin Tallmadge, who had shared André's last days and was emotionally devastated at the execution. This former American officer told his colleagues that André was certain his captors were no more than free-wheeling cowboys who would surely have let André go had he possessed enough money with which to bribe them. This was not a farfetched assertion as those characters who operated between the military lines during the war were shadowy figures whose actions were questionable. Many opportunistic men preyed on defenseless civilians in the no-man's-land between the armies, using the term "militia" to mask their nefarious dealings. This is the version that prevailed in 1817. The word of a dead enemy officer and gentleman prevailed over that of a now obscure farmer.[56]

Although the gentlemen of the national government seemed convinced of the militiamen's venality (they had adopted the British point of view) in 1817, the local power structure in post-Jacksonian New York demonstrated sympathy and support for the local heroes. In 1853, the "young men of Westchester county" erected a monument in honor of the then-dead militiamen. At the unveiling of the captors' monument, the keynote speaker marveled at the incredible train of events leading to the capture of André: that the correspondence between Arnold and André should have gone on for over a year; that a meeting between the two principals, planned at Dobb's Ferry on September 11, should have been set up "by the most open means, through a third party and he an American officer"; that André remained within the American lines "for a day and a night without detection"; that André should afterwards have "openly crossed the ferry and met and conversed with various persons" on his way back to the British lines. And after all that astounding activity, that he should be taken "at the very border of the British camp" seemed to the speaker "the most marvelous of the incidents of this strange history." But what the speaker in 1853 did not understand was that there was nothing unusual in the movement he described. American officers under the protection of a flag climbed on board British warships as a matter of course; enemy officers regularly crossed the military lines on parole; officers conversed with civilians behind enemy lines in the light of day. Americans in 1853 were as perplexed with these actions as was William Smith during the war.[57]

In the most hotly contested terrain of the Revolution—the New York metropolitan region—the sanctioned flow of enemy military professionals in and out of the city had gone on unabated. Though these officers' seasoned eyes could size up a redoubt, watch for unusual action in the disposition of horses and wagons, and monitor the movement of prominent Loyalists, both sides nonetheless assumed such risks in the interest of upholding the conventions of civilized nations. The permeable lines between the British and American officer corps and the widely respected traditions of military civility suggest a more complicated view of the Revolutionary War—at least as it unfolded in the vital theater around New York City.

4

The Eagle Eye of Profit

ONE OF THE most eagerly anticipated events in occupied New York was the periodic arrival of the Cork Fleet. Delighting the eye and raising expectations of the city's residents, the fleet was a dazzling display of white sails that engorged the Narrows and burst out into New York Bay. The great fleet brought grain, flour, wine, candles, cloth, crockery, and news from home. It was the lifeline of the occupied city, furnishing provisions enough to feed 36,000 men for twelve months. Its late arrival unleashed high anxiety on the part of a population largely reliant on its cargo. In 1779, when the fleet had not arrived by New Year's Day, the city's commandant lamented that not one barrel of flour could be found in the public stores, and the oatmeal used in its stead to make bread was but "a trifling quantity."[1]

Complicated planning went into the coordination of the city's needs and the ships' cargo because there was no reliable, secure alternative to the products from Ireland. The smallest item could not be taken for granted. On the subject of candles, for instance, a British general estimated the army's requirements over the winter months by figuring the number of men per regiment (612 plus officers) and the number of rooms they inhabited (75 rooms). Applying this fraction to 40,000 men, he estimated that the army filled 4,900 rooms, requiring 127,400 pounds of candles over the twenty-six weeks of winter, "one-third part of which to be mold candles for the use of the Officers, the Remainder to be dipt Candles." As the fleet sometimes did not arrive before the end of October "when the Season for issuing them commences," the British general suggested that the army order three-fourths of their needs from Ireland, and one-fourth from the American market in the summer months when candles were particularly cheap. The detail and care that went into the provisioning of the city bespoke the vulnerable position of the British in New York. During the seven years of war, they never succeeded in controlling enough territory to feed themselves, hence requiring a 3,000-mile supply line over the high seas. Had the fleet tarried a couple of weeks more in 1779, Washington might have marched into New York City four years sooner.[2]

The Americans, for their part, experienced provisioning problems as well. At the time of the Arnold-André crisis in October of 1780, for instance, the army had only a few days' provision in its stockpile at Tappan. Washington's time was consumed with urging or cajoling the Continental Congress and state legislatures into providing enough sustenance for his men. Yet the American supply line was infinitesimal compared to that of the British, at least where food was concerned. While self-sufficient in food and fuel, the Americans hungered to satisfy the more sophisticated tastes they had developed during the colonial years, from Bohea tea to mirrors and brocades. As Washington's expense book during the war years indicates, the American Commander-in-Chief himself had an insatiable appetite for imported wines, tea, fine table linens, Russian-leather letter cases, casks of Madeira, silk thread, cut-glass vinegar cruets, and ivory-handled table knives. Europe possessed these items in abundance, and its most busy entrepot in the mid-Atlantic states during the war years was British-occupied New York.[3]

The Americans had what the British wanted; the British had what the Americans wanted. Such a scenario of supply and demand provided one kind of laboratory to test Adam Smith's theories on the market. The "Invisible Hand" loomed over the New York area, effectively quashing the little measures busy legislatures passed to inhibit trade with the enemy. The "Invisible Hand," composed in the New York military theater of armies of individuals with unmet desires, challenged all the grand pronouncements about civic virtue. The outcast Manhattanite in New Jersey, sweltering in leather pants during the summer months, or the city refugee in Connecticut, still possessing in 1778 the same single worn pair of shoes with which he fled the city in 1776, might find ways to justify a little harmless exchange with the other side.

These operators found some justification in Revolutionary rhetoric which, particularly in the commercial centers of the northeast, often conflated liberty and free trade. Elias Boudinot, born to a prosperous Philadelphia family, defined liberty as the allowance to send "our Single free Bottoms to every part of the world." Robert Morris hoped in October 1776 that Britain would "acknowledge our independency and enter into commercial treaties with us." New Yorkers were especially prone to link liberty and free trade, even using business language to talk about freedom.

"Stocks have risen in favor of Liberty," wrote Alexander McDougall to Samuel Adams in 1774. Adam Smith himself argued in 1776 that freedom and equality were linked.[4] There is no evidence to suggest that Boudinot, Morris, or McDougall engaged in illicit trade. Whereas anyone might employ the rhetoric of liberty to justify his actions, the average businessman probably understood that liberty required a sacrifice and that trading with friends was not the same as trading with one's opponent.

To some, however, conducting business with the other side did not seem like trading with the enemy at all. Many circumventers of the law did so with former business colleagues and family members. Others were neutral to begin with, and experienced no conflict. Still others had become disenchanted with both American and British governments, finding little difference in the arbitrary confiscations of both sides. Whether a businessman saw his property "impressed" by the Americans, who issued vouchers for severely depreciated paper curency, or confiscated by the British in a raid, the result was the same—a net loss of wealth. If the authorities of either side ignored basic civil liberties and imposed themselves on peaceable people, then citizens could the more easily justify bending the rules to survive and prosper. For whatever reasons, a number of citizens put the profit motive or family survival above civic virtue, thereby warranting the attention of their governments. Both British and American authorities had to deal with citizens who insisted on conducting business between the lines. A look at the complex movement of goods and people from 1775 to 1782, as well as the two governments' attempts to control a seemingly unstoppable flow of trade, suggests some of the challenges confronted by businessmen in the occupied city.[5]

Controversial business dealings occurred in New York even before the Americans vacated the city. The confusion generated by the transfer of powers—from British colonial government to a bevy of American committees and military personnel—opened the door to more possibilities as the business community of New York City was thrown back on its own devices. There was no consistent line, no rules of the game, acknowledged by New Yorkers in those fast-paced days of 1775 and early 1776. Revolutionary leaders, from whom private citizens might take their cue, provided no clearcut procedures with respect to the enemy. The radical leaders would profess their love of King George on one day, and then send an American expeditionary force to Canada on the next. The Continental Congress banned trade with the Canadian fisheries while supplying the King's ships in the harbor. The Revolutionary leadership was no more consistent with respect to treatment of its own citizens. Liberty was a watchword of the Whig movement, yet the Whig's military wing confiscated houses and supplies in a most arbitrary show of power. Individual businessmen might scratch their heads when looking to the community's leaders for an indication of what was right and what was wrong.

Despite the chaos in a city on the brink of war, many Whigs and Tories remained on friendly terms. In March 1776, when two merchants begged the Revolutionary authorities' forgiveness for violating price regulations, thirty fellow merchants, including future Patriots and Loyalists, signed a petition supporting the two offenders. In the perplexing days after Lexington and Concord, a soon-to-be Tory merchant, Christopher Smith, asked for advice from John Alsop, a friend, business associate, and member of the Continental Congress. Smith, who labeled himself as one of the "tea sufferers," asked Alsop to use his influence to get congressional approval for merchants to sell tea already in inventory. In his letter to Alsop, Smith called the Congress "your house," indicating that Smith did not consider himself connected to Alsop's Congress in Philadelphia. Yet he advised his Whiggish friend on where to deposit money, and re-registered a ship in which both men were invested so that Alsop's name did not appear, "as I did not know how they might like in England to see your Name in the Old One." Alsop was a member of the Congress who had voted to ban trade to England after September 25, 1775. The voyage of which Smith wrote was to start before that date, making this potentially profitable business venture entirely legal and profitable for both a conservative merchant and a member of Congress.

While wealthy businessmen with much to lose looked for ways to extricate themselves from this unstable situation, businessmen of lesser means saw only opportunity in the coming conflict. George Cook, a saddler, offered his services to Congress in the event that any pouches or belts were needed for the army. The musical instrument makers of town petitioned to supply the army with drums and fifes "on most reasonable terms." One savvy merchant, Abraham Beekman, saw the conflict coming and had thirty cannon on hand for a ready buyer. Sitting out on Beekman's pier, the cannon caught the eye of Isaac Sears, who was responsible for confiscating and moving all such stray ordnance up to the northern tip of the island. Helpless to stop this operation, Mr. Beekman watched as his five-hundred-pound investment rumbled up the road towards Kingsbridge.[6] Along with pouches, musical instruments, and cannon, entrepreneurs hawked human beings in the feverish atmosphere of the early days of mobilization. Donald McLeod, an enterprising Scotsman, informed the Provincial Congress that he could provide a boatload of Scots fresh from Europe provided they retained "their own country dress commonly called the Highland habit." McLeod suggested himself as their leader "as some cannot speak the English language."[7]

The opportunity of making hefty profits in high-risk ventures emboldened other merchants to test the will of the Revolutionary authorities. John Hylton managed to procure a certificate from a member of the Provincial Congress, allowing him to load up his ship with beef, pork, flour, and hogsheads. No sooner had he loaded his vessel than he learned that Congress forbade these articles from leaving New York. The state authorities and the national Congress did not always synchronize their activities. Another merchant, Mangle Minthorne, tried to sell tea above the congressional price, and so was ordered to explain himself. Having purchased the tea at a high price immediately before congressional price fixing, Minthorne claimed he was obliged to sell at a higher rate than dictated by Congress; otherwise he would have sustained a loss. Denying that he acted out of any inimical tendencies, he claimed he was just doing what everyone else was doing.[8]

Samuel Burling sent a sloop down to the West Indies in violation of the non-importation Association in 1775. On the ship's return to New York harbor, Burling was called to account by the Committee responsible for enforcing the Association. Years later, Burling recalled no untoward behavior at the Committee hearing but did remember the damage inflicted by a "mob" who stormed his vessel and made off with the sails. Undeterred, Burling sent the ship on another West Indies voyage, but this time instructed its captain to dock in Monmouth County, an area more tolerant of these types of excursions. But here, too, Burling was star-crossed, as a British vessel seized the New Yorker's ship for being in violation of the Prohibitory Act of Parliament, which forbade all trade between rebel colonies and other parts of the British empire. As a major part of New York's trade was with the West Indies, the city's merchants found themselves in a particularly tight bind, violating the laws of both the Continental Congress and Parliament.[9]

Women too braved the disapproval of Committees to make a little money. Margaret Beck landed in jail for having ignored several warnings of the committee concerning her provisioning British ships in the harbor. Mrs. Lawrence, the wife of an American soldier, sold Bohea tea for six shillings per pound when the congressionally regulated price was eight shillings per pound. Lawrence made a pretence of offering her product at the fixed price by selling bags in which to put the tea at two shillings. Tea plus bag equaled eight shillings, but the authorities realized as well as any customer that Mrs. Lawrence's clients had the option of buying the tea without the bag at a discounted and illegal price. The committee called on Mrs. Lawrence at her house "in tenderness for her sex."[10]

In justifying their infractions of new laws, businesspeople maintained that they acted without regard to politics. While they insisted that the realms of business and politics could be separate, the Revolutionary authorities did not see it that way. In New York, one's adherence to the non-importation movement became the issue that separated friends from foes. Prior to 1776, America's most potent weapon against Britain was its refusal to buy British goods; this called for substantial sacrifices, most notably from New York's affluent merchant class. While the revolutionary movement placed merchants trading overseas in a vise, the burgeoning American military establishment opened new opportunities for domestic artisans like saddlers and musical instrument makers.[11]

As hostilities heated up, the American committees, legislatures, and congresses developed a tougher stance with respect to trade with the mother country. The First Continental Congress prohibited all exports to Britain or the Caribbean after September 10, 1775. Still, businessmen petitioned the New York provincial congress for special permission allowing boatloads of wheat, flour, and staves to go to England, Lisbon, and Jamaica. The Congress in Philadelphia put a stop to any exceptions by reiterating the ban on all trade with any area outside the thirteen colonies.[12]

Despite the fact that, for all intents and purposes, the Americans and British were at war around Boston in 1775 and early 1776, the business community strove to maintain regular operations. Even in the war zone itself, indefatigable operators spied a market opportunity and moved to take advantage of it. Such risk takers were found on both sides of the ocean. One New Yorker received a letter from London in which his correspondent expressed amazement at the level of trade still directed at the war zone: "However extraordinary it may appear, yet we find there is now shipping from the place in transports to Boston nearly as much goods as ever for the merchants there."[13]

Enough New Yorkers participated in the victualing of the British army outside Boston to attract the particular attention of a prominent member of the Continental Congress. He noted a nefarious network reaching from Manhattan to Long Island and thence to Boston. "No man can hesitate to say that this is an hostile Invasion of American Liberty," fumed John Adams, "as much as that now made in Boston. Nay," he continued, "those People are guilty of the very Invasion in Boston as they are constantly aiding, abetting, comforting, and assisting the Army there; and that in the most essential manner by supplies of Provisions." The enraged gentleman from Massachusetts, whose family braved many dangers in this war zone, then suggested to George Washington that he secure New York City by rounding up the Tories in town before they could rise up and assist the British when they arrived.[14]

In the following month, John Adams got his wish. In February 1776, General Charles Lee marched into the city and sent a detachment of men onto Long Island to find the most offending Tories for transport to Connecticut. In June 1776, the Committee to Detect Conspiracies printed up one hundred copies of a broadside, listing the names of 119 men in southern New York who were to be arrested or summoned to appear before the Committee. This was the signal for businessmen of Tory sympathies to scatter: Jacob Walton to an old Quaker's barn in New Jersey; Frederick Rhinelander to a rented house in Paramus; Theophilus Hardenbrook to the woods of Bloomingdale. By the summer of 1776, the British sympathizers knew that they would not have long to wait until they were back in their own beds once again.[15]

The British did indeed make quick work of the Americans once they launched their invasion in late summer. With British authority securely in place, the town's merchants looked forward to the prospect of once again making money. But "business as usual" with the mother country was not what the British had in mind. The restrictions in place against the rebels were not about to be lifted. The city's entrepreneurs found themselves confronted with a set of serious roadblocks in their quest to reclaim a level of prosperity in their war-ravaged city.

The most serious obstacle was Parliament's Prohibitory Act. Passed in late 1775 as a response to America's trade embargo with Britain, the act forbade *all* trade between any of the colonies in rebellion and the rest of the British Empire. The act also forbade any trade among the American colonies. The goal of its parliamentary framers was to chastise rebellious subjects. Loyalist businessmen, as obedient subjects, looked forward with good reason to a suspension of the onerous act, at least with respect to themselves. Indeed, a section of this legislation provided for its own demise by according authority to certain persons appointed by the King to proclaim a colony to be at Peace with His Majesty. But the British were in no rush to activate that part of the law. The army's first order of business was to crush Washington. When this goal proved elusive in the 1776 campaign, the British were confident they would make quick work of the rebels in the next round of hostilities. General Howe could argue that except for a small piece of the colony, New York was not "at the King's peace." But that would have been disingenuous. The army had no intention of opening what they considered to be a Pandora's box. Suspension of the Prohibitory Act would only complicate matters for the military. Declaring a region at the King's Peace would diminish the army's hold, allowing back the establishment of meddlesome civilian government. Exhibiting a marked lack of sensitivity toward the civilian community that would characterize its behavior throughout the war, the British army refused to budge on this question, seeing New York as a garrison devoted to military needs, rather than a city with an economic imperative.[16]

Not only did the Prohibitory Act hurt loyal merchants by completely clipping their wings, but it was enforced to the detriment of sometimes innocent Loyalist traders. City merchant Robert Gault found himself and his cargo seized on the high seas by a rebel privateer, only to be retaken by a British ship. On arriving back in New York harbor, Gault saw his entire cargo condemned as part of a rebel prize. He argued in vain for a distinction between Loyalist and Whig property.[17]

In November 1776, General Howe issued a proclamation permitting goods to leave town provided that a permit were procured from the Superintendent of Exports and Imports. "It was soon found necessary," claimed a town resident, "from the number of permits applied for, to grant none," unless the applicant furnished manifold proofs of loyalty and that the trade proposed would bring in goods that would benefit the island.[18]

It was not until the autumn of 1777 that the British agreed to make an exception to the strictures of the Prohibitory Act in the interests of New York's loyal mercantile community. General Clinton lifted restrictions on trade to England only, for a period of one year. But when General Sir William Howe, the supreme Commander-in-Chief, heard of this new development while he was involved in the Philadelphia campaign, he wrote back to Andrew Elliot, the Superintendent of Exports and Imports, that this permission was contrary to the Prohibitory Act and that all exportation from the port of New York should cease. Howe and Clinton apparently uncrossed their wires because one year later the merchants and traders of New York, under the leadership of William Walton, implored

Sir Henry Clinton, the new supreme Commander, to grant an extension of the autumn 1777 proclamation. The merchants and traders took this opportunity to ask for more. Prompted by "recent instances in which loyal faithful subjects have been aggrieved, we fear beyond redress, by the seizure and condemnation of vessels intended for this port," Walton also requested that other British ports in the empire be opened to trade from New York. The British "excellencies" graciously complied with the merchants' request, at least for another year. But they refused to declare New York City at the King's Peace because "a free commerce with England," claimed a high British official, would entail "the Improproety of crowding this Place with Goods till the certainty of Holding it was clearer."[19]

While pouring enormous energy into restraining trade to friendly ports, the British had no problem with trade conducted with the enemy. Their perennial provisioning problems led them to encourage residents to use their ingenuity to procure flour, grain, and wood. But the British wanted to control such traffic for security reasons, and most importantly, for profit. All traffic in and out of New York had to flow, at least in paperwork form, through Andrew Elliot, the Superintendent of Exports and Imports. The British issued licenses to boatmen, requiring them to renew at certain intervals. Money changed hands for these allowances, licenses, and permissions. The "villany, extortion, oppression, peculation, and rapine" of officials like Andrew Elliot became a major theme in the recollections of Loyalists in the occupied city. Judge Thomas Jones, a particularly waspish Tory, described Elliot as a rapacious, dissolute, overbearing fraud:

he became before the end of the war a man of great property, lived in the style of a gentleman, gave what the military called "damned good dinners," wallowed in luxury, and rioted upon plunder *illegally* and *unjustly* extorted from his Majesty's loyal subjects within the lines, to whom upon every occasion he behaved with all the haughty superciliousness of a Turkish Bashaw or a proud overbearing Highland Scottish Laird.[20]

If an enterprising resident chose to go the legal route, and managed to obtain essential foodstuffs and supplies, he still had to cope with additional restrictions leveled by city authorities. In a highly inflationary market, the British regulated prices on all essential items and demanded that residents of the occupied area supply the army with stipulated quantities of hay and wood. They also regulated who could sell at city markets, periodically closing various sites with no explanation. One merchant complained,

"Business is precarious being subject to so many restrictions and new alterations that I am afraid to venture far, and at present I am chiefly imploy'd in looking about me." The enterprising businessman therefore, who assumed all the risk and danger of such trade, could only realize so much profit if he elected to obey the law, a law imposed by people whose greed and excess were apparent to everyone.[21]

In the daily pursuit of earning a living, a citizen behind the lines saw the British interposing themselves between a struggling civilian population and its comforts and happiness. As an institution that seemed to thwart the citizen's every move, the army became a roadblock to get around. When the army demanded a certain percentage of wood and hay from the population behind the lines, just about everyone ignored it. Enough people conducted their trade beyond the purview of legal authorities that the British had to devise new laws and repeat old ones. In 1777, an order from military headquarters declared that all boat traffic between the New York islands and the Jerseys be stopped between gunfiring in the Evening and gunfiring in the morning unless a trader procured a special passport from Headquarters. It appears that too many traders had found comfort and profit under cover of darkness. In June 1778, a proclamation authorized the seizure of any goods lacking proper permits. In 1780, the city's Commandant reiterated the old regulation requiring businessmen conducting trade to get permission from the Superintendent of Exports and Imports.[22]

The one salient advantage of the army's presence in New York was that it swept the Revolutionaries out of the areas it occupied. In the first year and a half of occupation, the British army controlled most of Long Island, permitting a lucrative trade along the island's southern shore. Over 150 schooners and sloops busily plied the extensive coastline to provide the city with fish and wild fowl, a special boon in the tough winter months. They also bartered manufactured items from the city with the country people of Long Island in exchange for hogs, lambs, calves, hams, smoked beef, cheese, butter, poultry, boards, and shingles. In the spring of 1778, the army pulled back its forces to the vicinity of New York City, leaving much of Long Island exposed to the Americans. Enterprising Connecticut men launched whale boats across the Sound to a one-quarter-mile-wide isthmus over which they dragged their boats. Thus attaining Long Island's south shore, they picked off the smaller trading vessels from the city, effectively foiling the lucrative trade between eastern Long Island and the city. When Loyalist traders appealed to Admiral Lord Howe for a few row-galleys to ward off the rebels, the British admiral flatly refused, claiming he had none to spare. While the exigencies of war might have required that the boats be elsewhere, a Loyalist's experience with peculating British officials led him to see greed, not necessity, as Admiral Howe's motivation. Row-galleys in the service of guarding the Long Island coast would reduce the number of privateers in operation, he reasoned, at the same time reducing Admiral Howe's one-eighth share of privateering profits.[23]

At every turn, the war threw up new challenges to the city's business community. How did the city's merchants operate in this morass of regulations and rapidly changing scenarios? Frederick Rhinelander's business records tell the story of one merchant's strategies in the shifting sands of a wartime economy. Rhinelander, a crockery merchant, fled the city of New York with his family after having suffered for four months "many inconveniences and difficulties as great perhaps as you can conceive." On his arrival back in British New York, Rhinelander impressed upon his contacts in Britain his honorable conduct in this "most unnatural and unhappy contest." To allay any nervousness on the part of his suppliers, Rhinelander wrote that he expected the Prohibitory Act to be lifted at any moment. He also assured British firms that he could pay all debts as he had purchased land and produce and had hidden goods worth two thousand pounds sterling "in cellars safe." He spent the next two years eagerly awaiting shipments that never arrived and losing money on items that were marketable when ordered but that arrived in New York at a time when consumer interest for them had fizzled out. To reassure the British merchants who he thought had abandoned him, he sent a letter from the Loyalist Governor of New York attesting to his loyalty. He also mentioned the new opportunities for profit as he explained, "Trade is now carried on upon principles very different that it formerly was—we sell all for cash and have not a doubt of making two thousand pounds by these goods." In the autumn of 1778, Rhinelander sent substantial proof that trade could indeed be a lucrative proposition for his trading partners when he sent a shipment of furs to Britain including 263 minks, 123 red fox, and 25 otters.[24]

Despite a hesitant resumption of trade with his old contacts, the vagaries of the market made an item popular one moment and worthless the next. Rhinelander was stuck on occasion with paintings or looking glasses he could not sell. He also had to compete with a "vast number" of smaller shops whose proprietors cut special consignment deals with ship captains, some of whom were privateers. To continue to compete in this volatile market, Rhinelander had to change his ways. He started a correspondence with a Canadian firm, instructing it to send along any prize goods that might sell in New York. He also joined the privateering craze, investing heavily in ships that plied West Indian waters and hovered around tobacco country in the Chesapeake. By war's end, Rhinelander corresponded with various captains on the most profitable way to proceed depending on the cargo and type of vessel seized. A quick study, Rhinelander had become an old hand in this new world of trade.[25]

Businessmen of all degrees of wealth found privateering as attractive as had Rhinelander. The practice of legitimized piracy is of immense importance in understanding the business networks operating in and out of the occupied city. Both sides recognized the importance of disrupting the enemy's trade. They thus gave "letters of marque" to civilians authorizing them to plunder enemy shipping, with the proceeds to go primarily to investors and crew with a small percentage to be shared with the authorities.

The opportunity to make quick and hefty profits far outweighed the risks involved. Privateering was so lucrative that the navy had a problem keeping seamen. It was so prevalent that merchants had a hard time competing with the auctions of cheap prize goods. One such merchant complained to his friend in Philadelphia, "The sale of goods is very dull, much affected by the great number of prizes that are constantly bringing in and selling off." While complaining about this competition, the city's established merchants were not above benefiting from the trade themselves. When Long Island merchant Christopher Smith wanted to stock his wine cellar, he consulted with the owner of a privateer.[26]

The arrival of a prize ship in New York's harbor precipitated a mad rush as soon as the ship's hull touched the dock. John Greenwood, a rebel prisoner on board one such ship, knew that his best chance for escape would be in the madhouse atmosphere of the ship's arrival at port. He was right. As approximately two hundred people stormed the rebel prize to see what was on board, Greenwood calmly walked off the ship and headed down Water Street to a safe haven.[27]

The Quaker community was not immune to the lure of riches or a good cheap price. In November 1779, the New York Meeting added a query concerning prize goods. Henceforth, the Meeting would have to search any members who indulged in booty of war. Women too were not immune from the financial rewards of privateering. In 1779, Mrs. Ann Bancker expressed interest in buying shares of a certain captain's cruise. Unfortunately, she was too late, and the ship sailed. Once on the high seas, the captain remembered her interest when one of the crew members, despairing of any booty, offered to sell his share "for a chew of tobacca (or some expression to that purpose)," noted the captain. He purchased the man's one and one-half share for Mrs. Bancker, which resulted in some profit to the venture-some lady.[28]

New Yorkers were quick to adapt to the new world of trade wrought by war. But while they confronted the American Revolutionaries in an adversarial way on the high seas, they conducted thoroughly civil, mutually profitable business deals on land. When, in the middle of the occupation, Frederick Rhinelander sent a shipment of furs to England, where did he get such wealth? It was surely not from Hempstead, Staten Island, or Harlem. He obviously had procured the furs from traders on the American mainland, controlled by the rebels. Trade with the states in rebellion proved to be a very lucrative option, allowing merchants like Rhinelander to unload excess looking glasses and landscape prints for hot-selling staple items. The communication between the occupied city and Connecticut was so extensive, wrote a Loyalist observer, that two men in New Jersey had gone into New York to procure deeds for Connecticut land. Bergen County, said the same witness, attended the New York market. Since the British stood to benefit most from these exchanges, there is little evidence of this trade in official records from occupied New York; city authorities rarely complained about it. To find confirmation of such amicable business dealings, one must go to the other side of the lines, where trade with the enemy was a more contentious issue.[29]

Had the people of the occupied city been able to live on rum and molasses, claimed an historian of Revolutionary New York, there would have been no hunger. If diets could have been satisfied with products from the West Indies, there would have been no piles of kegs clogging city warehouses, and hence no impetus to trade with the mainland. But people had to eat. The Americans, for their part, did not need rum, molasses, sugar, fine cloth, or mirrors. This was the point of the anti-importation movement before the war. A virtuous citizenry would spin its own cloth, drink its own cider, and forgo the niceties of life. With the successful prewar precedents, it is no wonder that Revolutionary authorities continued to use trade restrictions as an important part of their arsenal. They pounded and thundered about such trade with the British, labeling it a rank betrayal of the cause.

Enough citizens on the American side found reasons to ignore government dictates to warrant the close attention of state governors and congresses throughout the war. The trade could be as insignificant as one lone adventurer crossing the Kill Van Kull to make a little money. In August

1777, a man living in the home of a Tory sympathizer in Newark, New Jersey, reported that his landlord went to New York with provisions and brought back Bohea Tea and handkerchiefs. In that same summer, Israel Underhill in White Plains, New York, was arrested for his enterprising excursions to New York City, from which he returned with various articles including West Indian sugar. His wife testified on his behalf that her husband brought back sugar at the behest of soldiers in the American army. "O Tempora!" remarked the skeptical Whig official overseeing this affair.[30]

These two instances of illegal trade from states bordering on the occupied zone are not isolated examples. In the fall of 1777, the President Pro Tempore of the New York Council of Safety noted that the sale of flour to Long Island was significant and had to stop. In November 1777, William Livingston, the Governor of New Jersey, wrote an urgent letter to George Washington conveying the complaints of good Whigs in Elizabethtown, New Jersey, respecting the trade carried on from there to Staten Island. This "evil" had grown to such proportions, reported Livingston, that the enemy was "plentifully supplied with Fresh Provisions" while those who conducted the trade had set up shops to retail British manufactures. The cover under which these "Banditti" operated was their work for the army in their capacity as spies. Although Livingston moved to arrest the most egregious offenders, he apparently received little help from the Commander-in-Chief. When, in late 1778, the same set of circumstances occurred at Shrewsbury, the Governor did not write to Washington but to the Continental Congress. This was a much more effective tactic as Congress leaned on Washington who leaned on his subordinate in charge of North Jersey, General Lord Stirling. Washington made a vague request that Stirling look into the matter and, if any officers at Shrewsbury were involved in "improper connivance," punish them.[31]

Washington trod carefully regarding this issue because he and his generals did use spies whose cover was black market trading with New York. When Washington wanted information on sudden British troop movements in November 1778, he depended on Lord Stirling's spies to get that information for him. Still, public opinion induced Washington to write more forcibly to Stirling one month after his vague request to have Stirling investigate. "Inasmuch [as] many of the well affected Inhabitants complain" about the abuses carried on under the name of spying, Washington ordered Stirling to "take proper measures to curb this extravagant passion for gain." Washington was assailed from all quarters about this problem. He replied with exasperation to the plea of those affected in Connecticut to do something about the trade, "We have no authority to punish the persons taken in the act of illicit commerce." The army could only seize merchandize and deliver the culprit to the civil authorities, noted the Commander-in-Chief. When Governor Livingston pleaded with Washington to station troops for the winter in Monmouth County to prevent illicit trade, Washington gently declined the request. Perhaps the Commander-in-Chief had heeded the opinion of an officer on the scene in Monmouth County who opined that "5,000 footmen could not prevent" the trade between the numerous inlets of that part of New Jersey and the British-occupied islands.[32]

But the issue of illegal trade did not relax its grip on the harried Commander-in-Chief. When, in early 1779, he arrived on the scene at Elizabethtown and heard firsthand about the "open and free intercourse" with New York City, he gave very strong and explicit instructions that no one should pass the lines without permission from himself or the Governors of New Jersey or Pennsylvania. In the same month, Washington moved with decisiveness to stop a similarly robust trade between Monmouth County and New York. He sent two hundred and fifty men of the Continental Line to stop the "very Great Amount" of provisions and goods flowing across coastal waters. The effectiveness of these precautions was questionable, however, because one month later, the Governor of both these free enterprise zones, William Livingston, explained to army officials who complained that New Jersey had not provided its share of wheat and flour to the army, that "great quantities are carried into the Enemy's lines from the counties of Bergen and Monmouth" which the frustrated Governor found it "not in my power to prevent."[33]

The maverick entrepreneurial verve of enterprising operators had struck New York State as well. In August 1779, a first page newspaper essay deplored the "criminally infatuated" lot of traffickers, engrossers, and forestallers who enriched themselves "at the expense of their country." These "barefaced offenders . . . barbarously and cruelly protracting the war" could only be controlled, claimed the anonymous author, by reinvigorating the local committees, who would ferret out trade with the enemy as well as any internal trafficking. "Let us divest ourselves of the fatal principle of self-interest," intoned the essayist, "that has too long disgraced America."[34]

But the principle of self-interest had already taken sufficient hold that it could not be uprooted by the rousing rhetoric of civic virtue. No group seemed to have a corner on righteousness. Even the military, typically held up as the paragon of civic virtue, was not immune to the lure of money. In May 1780, a Colonel in the New Jersey militia, Sylvanus Seely, faced a court martial on charges of running an elaborate organization dedicated to illegal trade in Elizabethtown. According to the prosecution, he authorized goods from New York to be unloaded from flag ships, allowed individuals from those ships "to tarry all night on shore without any necessity," partook of this illegal booty himself, and gave permission for persons to go and come from the enemy on a regular basis. The court found him "not guilty," but Governor Livingston was so convinced of Seely's guilt that he published the list of charges in the *New Jersey Gazette*, proclaiming that he did not approve of or confirm the court's finding.[35]

Colonel Seely figured in another case featuring individuals thought to be unlikely participants in illegal trade. The women of the new nation—as harmless, soft, apolitical creatures—were allowed greater mobility in the military theater than men. When an American soldier at Elizabethtown seized a trunk destined for a Loyalist lady in Philadelphia, he passed it on to Colonel Seely, who recruited a woman to claim it as her own as it made its way south towards Philadelphia. This underhanded behavior sparked the suspicions of the woman being used as a cover for his mysterious trunk, and so she reported the soldiers involved to American authorities. Just as men sometimes dressed as women to spy on the other side, they also used women to facilitate illicit trade. Since women could move about more freely, so also could the goods they claimed.[36]

This fact did not escape venturesome women who conducted their own business affairs. A Connecticut man crossed the Sound three times on smuggling ships and each time, found the majority of passengers heading toward Long Island were females. The amount of flour and fresh provisions traveling this route was "immense," according to one informant in 1780. In the State of New York, a literal parade of Tory women crossed the lines at Philipsburgh, armed with passes granted by civil and military officers. A civil official on the scene related to Governor Clinton that in addition to the men issuing passes, the water guards on the river were very indulgent in getting women to and from the enemy. He urged that Clinton end this practice "for as long as everyone goes and comes when they please," warned the vigilant official, "an underhanded trade will be carried on, not only in bringing out goods but in carrying in provisions." Further upriver, General Heath reported to Governor Clinton that women and children coming out of New York typically brought "presents from people in New York for their friends in the Country," but being mixed with the effects of those coming out, it was impossible to detect them.[37]

A year later, in 1781, the same problem plagued county officials. Sheriff Isaac Nicoll at Goshen urged Clinton to stop the traffic of women in and out of town, as those who returned brought with them "larg Quantities" of goods with which they supply "their fammalyes and disaffected Neighbors," creating resentment among the "well affected Inhabitance [who] must go with a Patcht Shirt and a ragged Cote." Governor Clinton wrote Nicoll a very defensive reply, stating that he granted permission to certain individuals "for particular Reasons which I cannot communicate." Neither man mentioned the names of the offending females, but it is not unreasonable to suggest that the local sheriff, with his rough way of expressing himself, voiced the resentment of a poor man about the liberties enjoyed by wealthier, well-placed individuals who got mysterious passes from the state's Governor. Although committed to stamping out "the wicked practice of Traficking with the Enemy," Governor Clinton, whose state had fewer holes to plug than did Connecticut or New Jersey, was not successful in controlling this flow of goods, even in the fourth and fifth years of the war.[38]

New Jersey's Governor had his problems with women entrepreneurs as well. When one woman requested a pass to move to the city, the Governor refused on the pretext that her son was a notorious trader with the enemy. Livingston suspected that the woman wanted to move so she could serve as her son's on-site manager in New York. But even Livingston had his complaisant moments. He ultimately decided to approve the move provided that Mrs. Gautier sign an affidavit swearing that she had not been involved with her son's mischief nor would she help her son in future in any illicit commerce.[39]

The governors of those states surrounding the occupied city tried in vain to stop this illicit traffic. In 1783, a "considerable number of armed boats" still plied the waters between Egg Harbor, New Jersey, and New York to carry on "a trade with the disaffected inhabitants." That same year the people of New Haven, Connecticut, were so disgusted with "the artifices of smugglers" that a crowd of fed-up Whigs burned the ship of a perennial offender in the town square.[40]

The Governors were not alone in battling traffickers and smugglers. Their partners in state government, the legislatures, duly passed laws forbidding all trade with the enemy. The early laws were framed as embargoes on exports. New Jersey enumerated its list of embargoed items in June 1777, including wheat, flour, rye, Indian corn, rice, bread, beef, pork, bacon, livestock, and other provisions. In November 1777, the New York Council of Safety stopped the exportation of flour, meal, and grain, threatening offenders with the death sentence. Despite punitive laws in place, the establishment of flag boats, and the distribution of militia to inspect and seize, the trade continued. In 1778, a frustrated William Livingston could only shake his head as British flag boats landed at ungarrisoned places, ostensibly to shuttle people with passes back and forth, but also to conduct clandestine trade at night along a deserted shore. Livingston complained to Washington that the state's measures had some success in preventing people from carrying provisions to the enemy. But now, griped New Jersey's governor, "we shall have the mortification of seeing them fetching it from us." The ingenuity of inveterate businessmen managed to make the laws seem about as valuable as Continental currency.[41]

The Continental Congress periodically urged the states to exercise new energy with respect to illicit trade. In the summer of 1778, prompted by a resolution of Congress, William Livingston enjoined the civil and military officers of the state to exert themselves more vigorously, particularly officials in Bergen and Monmouth counties. But by February 1779, he had to temper the enthusiasm of his men. They had seen golden opportunities in enforcing the laws, forming bands to roam about the state, seizing goods with abandon. Such depredations had to stop, demanded Livingston, and all future posses were to be led by an officer. In Connecticut, refugees from Long Island received special dispensation to bring into the state furnishings and valuables from their former homes in the British-occupied sector. By the spring of 1779, this privilege was revoked as too many Long Islanders had used this pretext to carry on illegal trade. Try as they might, state authorities could not stop their citizens' money-making proclivities. In November 1780, the Congress once again urged states to curb this "criminal practice" of illegal trade by instituting the death penalty if they had not done so already.[42]

The states continued to revise their laws throughout the war, plugging holes and attempting to control improprieties in enforcement. In the fifth year of occupation, a New Yorker voiced his pessimism on the efficacy of such laws, noting that "trade with the enemy is carried on all along the Lines of this state to a degree that would astonish." Although acknowledging that there were still a few men left who tried to stop "this growing Evil," the pessimistic observer saw no effective means to stop it. "The State law notwithstanding," he concluded, "its severity does not appear hitherto to answer the Purpose."[43]

Undeterred by the busy doings of its constituency, the New York legislature passed a new, stricter law in April 1782. A bemused spectator in New

Jersey wrote a friend in New York State about his reservations as to the law's potential efficacy. "Your legislature seems to have been determined to outstrip every of their neghbors on the subject of illicit trade," he commented. Noting that his state legislature tried this tactic at an earlier period, the writer continued, "They now begin to think of slackening the cord at least in some instances, and well they may if they wish to preserve and cherish the small remains of reverence and Obedience to Law and Government." He further opined that "the People will risk anything to enjoy the cheapest market and if we may judge from their conduct, they conceive it no violation of the Rights of Conscience to transgress the penal statutes on this head." Whether civilians were right or wrong about this reasoning, the writer concluded, "This however is evident—that penal laws are more suitable to the nature of Monarchy than a Republic and it becomes the wisdom of the Latter not to institute any but such as are absolutely necessary for the Existence and Preservation of the State."[44]

Despite the writer's sour prognostication on the enforceability of any law on trade, his state passed its own new law in June 1782. By December, the New Jersey legislature had to add yet another iteration because "great Quantities of Provisions and Produce of this and the neighboring states, are through the Arts of the Disaffected, constantly conveyed to the Enemy."[45]

Although less exercised about the trade with enemy farmers, the British occasionally took a citizen to task for possibly combining trade with spying. The judges at the trial of Jesse Waln got a thorough lesson in the porosity of both lines when Waln was accused of "carrying on a correspondence with the enemy." The judges learned of the race of men and women called the London Traders, farmers (not considered as enemies) from New Jersey who were permitted into the English lines and returned with papers authorizing the transport of tea and other commodities signed by the Office of Police. The judges were also informed of the lively trade that occurred with the Jersey shore without the knowledge or consent of British authorities. In fact, one witness testified that anyone of any political persuasion could trade on the western side of Staten Island. Finally, the judicial panel learned that the very behavior that sparked suspicion about Mr. Waln's activities in the first place was a common occurrence. Flagmasters (captains of flag of truce vessels) often absented themselves for an hour or two at the enemy-controlled Elizabethtown, and often took the opportunity to trade. Waln was acquitted.[46]

While some citizens were in the "Business [of smuggling] great quan-

Elizabethtown, New Jersey Looking up Broad Street from the Stone Bridge, 1795. Elizabethtown was a popular meeting place for legal and clandestine meetings between residents living on both sides of the line. Nearby was Elizabethtown Point, where flag-of-truce vessels frequently docked. New Jersey Historical Society.

tities of Provisions" across the lines, others took a few necessities with them when they went into or out of the city. The intention was not to sell the items but to use them themselves or offer them as presents to friends and family. Rebecca Franks, a charming young woman of Tory proclivities, wanted to send a set of handkerchiefs to a friend in Maryland so that her friend would be up to date on the latest fashions. At an evening's entertainment, she asked British General Sir William Howe if she could send a packet to her friend, who was, Rebecca explained, the wife of a member of the Continental Congress. Sir William "very politely" assented to her request, telling her she could send anything she wanted to the delegate's wife. Howe acquiesced to Miss Franks's appeal at about the same time he vetoed a move to open up New York City trade to England. But to this charming lady, "very elegantly" dressed, with feathers in her hair and a twinkle in her eye, the gallant officer could not say no.[47]

Rebecca Franks accosted the British general at a public event, mischievously choosing her moment to make it impossible for the old man to deny such a charming lady's request. But for all her guile, at least Franks asked for permission. Rebecca Shoemaker, another refugee Philadelphian in New York sent a steady stream of items to her daughters in Philadelphia: gowns, dolls, books, bonnets, and buckles. There is no record that the Shoemaker family obtained anyone's permission on either side of the lines.[48]

The American authorities were less complaisant about the movement of goods for private use. When a New York City resident wanted to move back to New Jersey, he requested to bring over a stock of goods. Despite the services this man had performed for American prisoners of war, Governor Livingston refused his permission as it would "give the highest Umbrage to those among us who have borne the heat and burden of the day."[49]

As in the case of Mrs. Shoemaker behind British lines, there were those in American-held territory who went about procuring necessities with airy disregard for the law. Governor William Livingston's twenty-year-old son, Henry Brockholst, had the distinct pleasure of escorting two British aristocrats, Major and Lady Ackland, back to New York on their parole after the Battle of Saratoga. Through the intercession of Lady Harriet Ackland, "a most amiable character," Livingston was to receive "some articles" from the city which in his indigent state, he had "the utmost need of." Apprehensive that the British would detain him because of his notorious family name, young Livingston escorted the aristocrats only as far as the British lines, where he waited for the return of the sleigh that had transported the Acklands to New York. The sleigh returned with "several Articles"—very fine linen, cambrick cloth, and other items. When writing to his sister two weeks later from New York State, Henry asked that his sister keep the goods-laden sleigh "a profound secret between Mamma, Kitty, and yourself." He had apparently learned in the interim that "tis death in New Jersey to trade with the enemy. If this be true," he pleaded, "the Necessity of Secrecy is obvious." Although safely in New York, Henry obviously feared for his reputation in the state headed by his staunchly virtuous father. As a way of excuse, William Livingston's son informed his sister that the authorities in New York State did not deem this activity to be criminal.[50]

While Henry Brockholst Livingston writhed at the prospect of being unmasked, his kinsman, Robert R. Livingston, one of the highest-placed officials in the new American government, betrayed a more subtle discomfort about his correspondence with a Tory lawyer in New York City. Livingston sought Samuel Jones's legal advice in the matter of a will. Calming any scruples he might have felt in asking a favor of a notorious Tory,

Livingston wrote, "a communication so remote from politics as the one in question will meet with no interruption from the different sides of the lines on which we are placed." The passive construction "on which we are placed" implies that some greater force put them in their respective locations and not the choices each man had made. Livingston conveniently separated business and politics but still felt obliged to make this distinction, indicating that he was not totally at ease with the communication he had initiated. Other businessmen trading with New York shared this same dilemma.[51]

The wealthy and well-connected had more opportunities to benefit from these little favors than did the average citizen. They certainly had more access to people like Lady Harriet Ackland and Samuel Jones, and more money with which to trade. All the while supporting the American war effort, they may well have asked themselves how a few vest buttons and handkerchiefs could subvert the cause. An enormously wealthy general in the Continental army might well have reasoned this way as he kept a running account of purchases with a firm in New York. A bill dated January 6, 1778 (and deemed important enough to be retained in William Livingston's Papers) listed General Schuyler's purchases of Irish linen, superfine cloth, buckskin gloves, white-ribbed silk hose, and large gilt buttons. The bill also shows that Schuyler's balance was reduced through the friendly offices of Lady Harriet Ackland, who carried gold from the American general to the firm in New York.[52]

How did one rationalize one's position as a Patriot while trading with the enemy? For those businessmen considering themselves good Whigs, the answer varied. In 1775, Mingle Minthorne maintained that his business practices, frowned upon by the committee, betokened no inkling of his political leanings. He was simply acting like everyone else. In 1782, when Dirk Romeyn wrote the pessimistic note on the efficacy of new laws limiting trade, he pointed out that "the People will risk anything to enjoy the cheapest market." He further blasted penal laws in general as "more suitable to the Nature of Monarchy than a Republic." His conception of Liberty did not encompass government interference. Others, particularly those who lived out the war in dwellings other than their own, pointed to the sacrifices they had made. They found the legislative demands to be unreasonable. How could their little piece of velveteen or cask of madeira harm the war effort?[53]

Businessmen were no different from soldiers or family members who determined which proclamations and laws would apply to them. The Revolution presented average citizens with a number of compelling issues to weigh and place in some sort of order. With few ardent Revolutionaries or Royalists prepared continuously to sacrifice all to the war, each community must have encompassed a vast number of citizens who, at times, put their own self-interest above the larger cause.

5

Crossing Freedom's Line

EVERT BYVANCK WAITED until he could actually hear the Battle of New York before vacating his country house in August of 1776. He had taken the precaution of moving out of his city residence before the cannon thundered from across the East River. Now, on August 31, Byvanck realized that his person and possessions would not even be safe at his Corlear's Hook country estate. Consequently his slaves, Sam, Cato, and Prince, loaded up Byvanck's skiff with two chests of clothes, one box of earthenware, one box of periwigs, and a bundle of clothes for themselves. They sailed up the river to Harlem where the three slaves hauled the boatload of articles to a gentleman's house near the slip. Next morning, Byvanck dispatched Sam and Cato to help Byvanck's son move his household to the new family refuge at Horseneck, Connecticut. The elder Byvanck instructed his remaining slave, Prince, to load a cart with his master's small trunk, the master's son's books, and a treasured spy glass, after which master and slave proceeded to Horseneck.

Once they had arrived in Connecticut, Byvanck sent Cato with a bundle of clothes to his wife and child at Alexander Forbush's house in Hackensack, where Cato was to work for his victuals until Byvanck had need of him. With Cato gone, and Prince busy setting up the new household, Byvanck had to hire a Negro man named Jack to accompany Sam and his eldest son to Manhattan, where they were to retrieve chests of clothes, two feather beds, furniture, linens, guns, powderhorns, saddles, bridles, and Byvanck's sword. Sam had hardly returned from that excursion when he turned around again toward Manhattan, this time with the elder Byvanck, to gather up yet more of the contents of the country house.

By the time they left on this trip, the war had reached their once-tranquil country retreat. A heavy cannonade peppered the Byvanck estate with shot and ball. Byvanck climbed over the back fence and crept up to the house to find the overseer and his family taking shelter behind the building. With much prodding, the overseer ventured down to unlock the back gate so that Sam and the wagon could come up to the house. Whether crouching on top of the rig or leading the cart by the horse's reins, Sam made a clear target for the guns across the river. Yet the cannon's fire was imprecise, and so the slave and cart negotiated a cratered field with no incident. The following day, Sam drove Byvanck into the now-quiet city, where the slave ran errands while his master got a shave and had his wig dressed. Byvanck bought a quarter mutton and "lett Sam carry it to my House." But no sooner had the turnips and other greens flavored the meat than the final alarm warned that the King's troops were about to land in the neighborhood. Byvanck ordered Sam to harness the horse to the chair and off they went to Connecticut.[1]

In their complex, multi-stage retreat to safety, the Byvanck family made not a single move without its slaves. Every juncture of Mr. Byvanck's progress featured Sam, Prince, or Cato. For one solid month, from mid-August to mid-September, Sam lifted upholstered chairs, looking glasses, and periwig boxes onto carts, and then coaxed horses or oxen to move the tightly packed vehicles over the rubbled roads of Manhattan and the rutted lanes of rural Westchester County and southern Connecticut. In terms of energy expended, this month of toil may have been nothing out of the ordinary for Sam. As a slave, his daily routine revolved around the needs and wants of his master. In all of the various exoduses from the city between the spring of 1775 and the summer of 1776, thousands of enslaved people like Sam did the actual moving of people and goods to safe havens.

The enslaved population was mobile in other ways as well, often independent of the wishes of their masters. The war provided unique opportunities for freedom as British and Americans vied for the labor of African Americans, at the same time striking a blow to the other side by depriving it of black workers. Shortly after installing the Byvanck family in their new abode, one of the Byvanck slaves ran away to Long Island. Overcoming fear of the unknown, the new refugee placed his bet on the British as the more likely liberators of America's enslaved population. Thousands of African Americans did the same, creating another network of people on the move in the region of occupied New York. Like so many of their white counterparts, the blacks put their personal hopes above the dictates of political or military authorities. They were certainly savvy enough to realize that an ardent attachment to King or Congress was unlikely to be of benefit to them. So they maneuvered among the rival claims of both sides, ever alert for openings that the war's permeable boundaries might furnish for a better life.

And yet the experiences of those who fled to freedom are not the only African American story in Revolutionary New York. The newly freed joined masterless slaves, the already freed, and those still in bondage to Loyalist masters. Opportunities for men far outweighed those for women. The ease with which African Americans could cross the porous military lines gave great leverage to those in occupied New York as well as to those still enslaved in the American-controlled periphery of town. This complex story begins with the African American situation before the war and then charts the journey from apathy to hope as this black population on the move found a new voice in the midst of war.

Enslaved men like Cato, Sam, and Prince formed a striking presence in Revolutionary New York. Among the novelties of the colonies noted by newcomers was the presence of substantial numbers of African Americans on the islands of New York Bay. One Hessian soldier found a significant number of slaves present in the city when the British force marched into town, as well as some free blacks on Staten and Blackwell's islands. The use of slave labor was so widespread on Staten Island that nonpropertied white men, unable to find employment there, tended to make their living on the sea.

The Hessians took note of the African American community not only because it was an interesting novelty, but because it constituted a substantial part of the New York Bay population. According to the 1771 Census, blacks comprised 14 percent of the city's inhabitants. In the western counties of Long Island, almost a quarter of the population had African ancestry. On Staten Island, one in five faces was black. The African American population threshed the grain and herded stock on Long Island. Blacks swept the chimneys, drove the carriages, and dressed the hair of their masters in the great houses of New York. They worked the docks, cobbled shoes, and performed other artisanal trades in the public world of the city's business community.[2]

African Americans had been performing these jobs since the early days of Dutch rule in the island city. With the introduction of British rule in 1664, the laws governing black life became more restrictive. On two occasions, groups of the city's blacks attempted to use violence against the white regime. In both cases, in 1712 and 1741, the white community crushed the agitators and then passed more repressive laws to further curb the movement of the city's black population.[3]

When Parliament passed tax measures in the 1760s, thousands of Americans raised their voices in protest. Men who had taken for granted the presence of slave labor and expressed nary a quibble over its morality suddenly thundered about the great evil. Of course, these blistering condemnations which appeared in American newspapers had nothing to do with the slavery hitherto known and lived by Americans, but with a slavery to come—an imminent slavery that the English would foist on the Americans if not stopped. During the summer of the Stamp Act controversy, New Yorkers read and discussed a series of articles in the *New York Gazette or Weekly Post Boy* written by John Morin Scott under the alias "Freeman." "The English government cannot long act towards a Part of its Dominions upon principles diametrically opposite to its own," claimed Scott, "without losing itself in the Slavery it would impose upon the Colonies." Another animated essayist on the Stamp Act crisis envisioned slavery's diffusion over time. "Awake! Awake, my countrymen, and, by a regular and legal opposition defeat the designs of those who enslave us and our Posterity." The visionary writers of the protest movement could see far afield in some respects, but their scope did not encompass the slave advertisements just inches from their editorials in the city's press.[4]

In the ten years after the Stamp Act, blacks also witnessed their neighbors challenging the natural order of things. While the enslaved community realized that the rhetoric of freedom and slavery did not apply to them, they could take some heart in the occasional pronouncements of one small group in town, the Society of Friends, or Quakers. Even though a number of New York Quakers owned slaves, individuals in their community had testified against chattel slavery since early in the century. In 1718, an influential Friend from Flushing, William Burling, publicly proclaimed his concern in meeting about the enslavement of human beings. The sporadic nature of these pronouncements in an enclosed religious meeting of a small and normally quiet sect may not have been much of a beacon to the oppressed objects of these concerns. But blacks might have gained hope from happenings in Pennsylvania, where in 1755 the powerful Yearly Meeting of Friends condemned the slave trade and in 1758 placed offending members "under discipline." Three years later, the Pennsylvania Assembly slapped a prohibitive duty on each slave imported into the colony.[5]

It would take until the eve of the Revolution for New York Quakers to move on the slavery question. Spurred by the Philadelphia Meeting pronouncement, New York Friends moved at their 1774 Yearly Meeting to discipline those who bought or sold slaves or those who held slaves past the age of 18 (if a woman) and 21 (if a man). Such "disorderly persons" would be put "under dealings," that is, a committee of Friends would visit to discuss this issue with them. In May 1776, a committee charged to deal with slaveowners reported that "a considerable number" still owned slaves. It was not until late 1778 that the meeting first disowned slaveowners in the New York area.[6]

Such movement on the slavery issue was in the future for Prince, Cato, and Sam in the summer of 1776. While they may have been aware of promising glimmerings from the small meeting house on Green Street, the actions of an eccentric little sect did not affect the slaves of most staunch Protestants. New York's enslaved community found more hopeful signs originating from English sources.[7]

An event that no American slave could ignore occurred in Virginia in November 1775. By the fall of that year, the debate about Parliament's power over the colonies had erupted in full-scale military action. Minutemen had faced off against the redcoats in Massachusetts; Americans had invaded Canada; and in Virginia, the Royal Governor, John Murray, the Earl of Dunmore, had fled to a British warship in the face of a determined rebel force. Dunmore figured that this desperate situation called for desperate means. On board his floating haven on November 7, the Governor issued a proclamation which declared "all indented servants, Negroes, or others (appertaining to Rebels) free, that are able and willing to bear arms, they joining His Majesty's troops, as soon as may be, for the more speedily reducing the colony to a proper sense of their duty, to His Majesty's crown and dignity." While inducing nightmares of slave insurrection in the dreams of whites, Dunmore's Proclamation gave concrete hope in the here and now that any male slave working for a rebel master could reap the benefits of freedom—determining his own destiny, protecting his family, and passing a legacy of freedom to his descendants. News of Dunmore's gamble raced up the coast.[8]

The American army was not about to emulate the British. The words and actions of both sides made it obvious to the observant slave that his chances for a better life rested with the British. To a white man like Lutheran minister Henry Melchior Muhlenberg, the belief on the part of the black community that a British victory would mean universal manumission seemed preposterous. But to a black man sizing up the conduct of both sides, it is not at all surprising that he might decide to support the only party that had made a promising offer.[9]

Still, it was the war itself that provided the real opportunities for black men and women, particularly around New York. War upset the smooth-running combination of legal authority and neighborhood custom that upheld the institution of slavery. Chaos shook the mainstays of the social order to create new spaces and new options for oppressed people: the master's absence; additional opportunities for hiring oneself out given enlistment demands on poor white laborers; the value of a slave's muscle to both armies; the existence of other networks that operated between the British and American zones. The enslaved had more options than ever before, and they moved in variant ways to improve their lot. A distinguished historian of African Americans in the Revolution encapsulated the community's motivation in this way: "The Negro's role in the revolution can best be understood by realizing that his major loyalty was not to a place nor to a people, but to a principle"—namely freedom.[10]

Yet this did not mean that the enslaved community of the New York City region acted with but one response. Some opted to actively support one side or the other; others chose to see what openings each new day would bring. Some blacks in the countryside around town had families, a bearable routine, and a decent master. They weighed the risks of running away, along with the probability of getting their entire family across military lines, and decided to stay with "the devil they knew." Others chose to support the American cause, figuring that if they proved themselves in the Revolutionary War effort, they could make the words of the Declaration of Independence apply to them.[11]

A sizable number of blacks, however, took another risk. They ran away from their masters and set their eyes on the Promised Land of English guarantees. Thus, "what in peacetime was a rivulet [of runaways] became in wartime a flood." A statistical study of runaway ads in the mid-Atlantic Revolutionary-era newspapers shows an enormous jump in number during the revolutionary period, particularly in the war years.[12]

On December 23, 1776, a refugee from the Beekman family made a simple notation in a pocket diary: "Hanover and John went off." Hanover and John, both in their early twenties, had served the wealthy Beekman family in New York City and, like Evert Byvanck's slaves, had assisted in moving their master's household, this time to Essex County, New Jersey. Like the Byvanck example and thousands of runaways before them, the

Beekman slaves chose to risk capture in order to realize a better life. What propelled them to bolt is a mystery. Perhaps the enticing prospect of work for pay and freedom to go where they would had emboldened them to fly from what they knew toward the unknown.

Of course, Beekman did not take this outrage lying down. Even though he had moved out of the city, he enlisted the aid of a Tory printer in New York City, Hugh Gaine, to get his money's worth from his human investment. "You may well believe that this leaving me at this time, is very aggravating and ungrateful," wrote Beekman to Gaine. "The disappointment is the greater as they are both able and sober fellows and good [drivers?]." Determined never to have either man under his roof again, Beekman asked Gaine to have the men picked up and sold at either private sale or public vendue. The irritated slavemaster certainly acted as if there were no war and no new boundaries between him and his friends in New York. Whether Gaine felt inclined to perform such a favor or not, the British did not allow such transactions. Thus we find that Hanover and John were subsequently seen "strolling about the town." Beekman soon realized that a new order prevailed in New York City.[13]

Hugh Gaine was unlikely to gratify Mr. Beekman because the British army continued Lord Dunmore's offer when they moved to New York, at first through General Howe and then through General Clinton. The British issued no universal manumission decree. They encouraged the slaves of rebels to come in and work for the army while at the same time supporting the property rights of Loyalists in town. At first, the situation was murky enough to encourage such rebel slaveowners as William Beekman to think that they could somehow extricate their property from town or arrange to sell their runaway slaves on the block in New York. But then in 1779, in anticipation of the southern campaign, the British reiterated the status of refugee blacks through official pronouncements. On June 7, 1779, the Commandant of New York, David Jones, issued the following order to his troops: "All Negroes that fly from the Enemy's Country are Free— No person whatever can claim a Right to them—Whoever sells them shall be prosecuted with the utmost severity." Unlike Dunmore, Jones made no distinction between men and women. However, an official proclamation issued later that month by the British Commander-in-Chief of the army, Sir Henry Clinton, hinted that this arrangement was limited to male slaves. Setting the scene of his proclamation by noting the use of Negroes in the Continental army, Clinton promised that captured blacks in rebel uniform would be sold back into slavery, while those who took refuge with the

British army could not be sold. "I do promise to every Negroe who shall desert the rebel standard," wrote Clinton, "full Security to follow within these lines any Occupation that he shall think proper." The inclusion of the male pronoun in the last sentence betrays the intention of the British. But the proclamation was vague enough to offer hope to all members of the African American community. Within a year of the proclamation's issue, the British complained about the number of black women and children flocking to British posts. General Pattison instructed an officer at one New Jersey stronghold to prevent women and children from "passing the North River" because otherwise, they would become "a burden to the town."[14]

The enslaved people who took the British up on their offer used strategies both old and new to achieve their goal. They used time-honored methods like forging papers, passing themselves off as freemen, or, if light skinned, claiming they were white or painting their faces to enhance their light color. The war's chaos also helped. Jabey, a thirty-five-year-old six-foot-three-inch runaway, availed himself of the greater need for able-bodied seamen on British ships and civilian privateers by heading for the Hudson, there, conjectured his master, to sign up on a ship. The permeability created by Loyalist sympathizers in the American-occupied zone also aided aspiring freemen. One thirty-year-old man named Pomp, described as Guinea-born but a good English speaker, fled his master in Poughkeepsie and was thought to be across the river in Ulster City with "some disaffected people." His master was convinced that he was bound for the British lines. Boston King, originally from South Carolina but enslaved in New Brunswick, New Jersey, noticed that at the ferry on the Raritan River, people would wade across at low tide. After midnight on one Sunday morning, with the guard either asleep or in the tavern, he waded across and made his way to the shore opposite Staten Island, where he found a boat and reached the British lines safely.[15]

Evidence of the black community's new mobility exists as well in the letters of jilted masters who complain about the scarcity of labor in their communities. With Hanover and John in New York City, William Beekman complained to his brother that there was no "boy" to be had in rural New Jersey. Even local farmers forbade their sons to work for anyone else. A Beekman in Esopus, New York, grumbled that with the unannounced departure of his "once faithful [but] by now ungrateful villin" coachman (a white servant), he was "now obliged to do all the work" on his place since he could not "hire any Person here either black or white." Yet another Beekman refugee, this time Gerard Beekman in Philadelphia, developed a new appreciation for his runaway slave; although the man was a "Teeser and a Drunkard," he had been the only slave left in the Beekman household. "My Wench and my Little [York?] Sam is run to New York," complained the now servantless merchant. Gerard Beekman was hurt and inconvenienced, but worst of all, he was a master with no one left to master over. His fury was evident when he ended a letter to his brother with the request that his love be conveyed to his sisters and brothers and "all the wites in the house." A fortnight later, Beekman had settled down and found it in his heart to send his love to *all* in the house.[16]

New Yorkers took notice of the movement of blacks to British encampments throughout the war. The Revolutionary authorities regularly scooped up slaves whom they suspected of planning to defect to the other side, subjecting them to incarceration and interrogation. Their masters would then be required to post a bond "for their Good Behavior in future," thus guaranteeing added vigilance on the part of owners. New York authorities also regulated the types of servants allowed to accompany Loyalists sent to New York. Governor Clinton denied Loyalist William Smith the use of able-bodied slaves. "The slaves he might have sold if he had pleased," groused Clinton. But the Governor, a law clerk in Smith's office before the war, relented on Smith's "hardy Scotch hireling[s?]." Those he would exchange for Americans held by the British in New York City.[17]

In New Jersey, legislators constantly modified the act preventing movement from and to enemy lines. No sooner would the Assembly plug one hole than its constituents would find another. It took the fifth iteration of the movement laws to acknowledge that blacks posed a special problem, they finally being singled out for whippings, ear croppings, pillories, or service on board a vessel of war. Later in 1782, the State Assembly specified the exact punishment for slaves and minors—lashes on the back not exceeding thirty-nine in number.[18]

The American reaction to Clinton's proclamation was muted because the pronouncement did nothing to change the de facto situation behind British lines. Clinton simply made official once again what had transpired for years. The state assemblies, however, responded with long overdue laws forbidding the seizure, kidnapping, or sale of "Negro slaves belonging to Persons residing within Places under the Power of the Enemy, which have absconded from their owners and come into this State." Although claiming humanitarian motives, the New Jersey Assembly waited for the British offer to extend its own. But the motivation of state legislators mattered little to slaves of Loyalist masters in New York. Neighboring New Jersey had extended an offhanded invitation, couched in penalties for those who re-enslaved blacks fleeing from New York.[19]

In response to these unprecedented offers by the powerful, African Americans moved between the lines at a time when many other people traveled the same roads. Fleeing slaves joined smugglers, Quaker ministers, black servants, soldier wives, people with passes, and people without them. The porous nature of the lines provided some camouflage for those whose movement would result in a dramatically different future. The newly free crossed into a city brimming with strangers—Loyalists from various colonies, British soldiers, European merchants, Hessian mercenaries, and other African American refugees. In such a place, it was easier to melt into the crowd, particularly useful for those African Americans who fled Loyalist masters in the area around the occupied zone. The once-enslaved also found themselves in a city in crisis where less attention is typically paid to societal norms in the interest of employing all available hands.

This permeable city expanded the number of scenarios possible for African Americans. Most noticeable were the newly freed people under the British proclamation who joined the blacks already free before the war. The newcomers also walked the streets next to still-enslaved blacks under Loyalist masters. There were masterless slaves, too, who were charged with watching over their master's property in his absence. Although still technically enslaved, their schedule was now their own, and if their masters were deemed rebels, they now had the option of never returning to their former lives. Occupational categories expanded especially for those black men who now wielded a gun. This new array of African American roles merits a closer look, for the black experience in occupied New York was not limited to those who directly benefited from the Proclamation. The influx of newly freed people created opportunities for those still enslaved in both the British and American-occupied zones.

Whereas a significant number of blacks had to find a way into the city, others had never left it, whether by choice or by command of their masters. When William Smith fled the city in the 1775–76 exodus, he left a black man and woman at his townhouse. Many families, if they could spare them, left slaves in town to watch over their homes and forward any letters. Smith's slaves may have felt fortunate that they were the ones left behind, even after their master's house burned down in the 1776 fire. Similarly, William Beekman left three of his slaves in the city, hiring them out to a Loyalist friend. Beekman's sister, another refugee in New Jersey, owned a family of slaves who stayed with her Loyalist nephew, whether by command or choice is not clear. In all three cases, the enslaved experienced a loosening of control in their lives: the Smith slaves were now masterless; the Beekman group could qualify under the British Proclamation as William Beekman was a Whig; and so too could Cornelia Walton's slaves although her Loyalist nephew stood to inherit these people and might effectively block any move.[20]

Slaves were not the only blacks to remain in town at the British invasion. Freemen too wagered on the British. David King, a shoemaker, carried letters back and forth between the city and British warships in 1776. His service to the Royalist Governor, William Tryon, ended when crew members of the *Duchess of Gordon* deserted to the Americans, informing them that King and other blacks were playing a double game. With a price on his head, King fled to Rhode Island.[21]

John Jackson, another shoemaker in town, paid a high price for refusing to serve in the rebel militia. He ultimately lost his house and everything in it. Later on, while serving in the British navy, he lost his right leg as well. John Ashfield, a free black, worked for the British during the war. Afterward, Ashfield's father elected to stay in New York City, while his son went to England, there to wait table in a public house. While father and son may not have seen eye to eye on the political issues of the day, each gambled on the best option available to him at the end of the war.[22]

So many slaves and free blacks remained behind that a slavemaster from New York City remarked in 1776, "I believe the Chief of the Blacks are encouraged by some secret enemies to stay in the city as they were seen to muster in large companies." For the blacks who remained, the British could not arrive soon enough. They joined their white neighbors in presenting a scene of "universal joy" to the British invasion force. Such large numbers of liberated African Americans could now help the most vulnerable group in the occupied city—those enslaved people secured under the daily vigilance of solidly Loyalist masters.[23]

By arbitrarily freeing certain blacks and keeping others enslaved, the British heightened the tension in the occupied city. Blacks who had the misfortune of belonging to Loyalist masters watched as others were freed in a trice. We cannot fathom the heart of a well-dressed and refined female house servant who beheld the presence of rough field hands from New Jersey, suddenly freed. How did she feel when friends and neighbors who were enslaved before the occupation returned to town as new people, simply by dint of the political persuasion of their former masters?

Unlike her freed brethren, the female slave was especially subject to the vagaries of her condition. The buying and selling of slaves continued in occupied New York. She may well have seen her own future when a "Negro Wench with Two Children" was put on the block in 1777. As she passed by the coffee house in the fall of 1780, she might have seen the public auction of "a likely Negro Girl, about eight years old."[24] Female slaves comprised three-quarters of the sale ads in Rivington's newspaper (the few males who were sold were most often boys). One such sale involved a Loyalist master who decided to leave for England, divesting himself of all human property including a fifteen-year-old "wench."[25]

The fact that some blacks were freed and others were not made the vulnerability of the enslaved population all the more apparent. A few female slaves elected to avoid being sold by running away. The porosity of the city and the numbers of freed brethren helped them in their flight. Sarah, a mulatto woman, ran away after being accused of theft by her mistress, and was "known to be secreted in this city." The ad for two runaway wenches with a baby boy indicated that they were "lurking about this city," and promised trouble to those who harbored them. When a Virginia woman named Pamela ran away, her owner imagined that "some evil-disposed persons encourage her in this way." Whether those who harbored runaways comprised a network or were simply individuals who responded to specific cases, their presence in town was all too keenly felt by masters.[26]

Twice as many men as women ran away. Males simply had more opportunities. The army could absorb them and ships in the city's harbor could spirit them away. Luke, an eighteen-year-old hairdresser, had last been seen with an officer to whom he had hired himself out. The owner of Peter had seen the fourteen-year-old a number of times with an officer of one of the new corps. The owner believed that Peter had tricked the officer into believing he was a freeman. Masters of vessels were often warned not to hire runaways. Many young men were thought to have gone off "a-privateering"; some fled one ship to take advantage of better opportunities on another. One sage master bowed to the reality that once his slave was aboard ship, the possibility that he would get his man back was slim. So the master made an offer. He stipulated that the ship captain could keep the slave provided he paid the slave's wages to the master. Virtually all runaway male slaves were below the age of twenty-five. The rigorous life on a privateer might not have appealed to older men with families they were not prepared to desert.[27]

While some African Americans fled from British authorities and Loyalist masters, other enslaved people, once the property of American

Revolutionaries, risked their lives to get to New York City, there to be free under the protection of the British army. But freedom in New York City still entailed great dangers. If a slave managed to cross the Hudson River into the city, his troubles were far from over. Young black men were as vigilant as their white counterparts when the rumor spread that His Majesty's fleet was in search of "volunteers." Not only freemen but slaves of Loyalists could be swept up in an impressment action. A refugee could also face the nightmare of successfully crossing the lines only to be claimed as a slave by a white Loyalist in New York. Dinah Archey of Virginia said that she had come in five years earlier "agreeable to his Excellency General Hows Proclamation." A certain William Farray had since claimed her as his slave. Although Farray could produce no bill of sale, the police vacillated on making a decision on the case, forcing Dinah to appeal to General Carleton. Casting herself as a "Poor pensioner," Dinah suggested how the British General should proceed in this matter: if Farray had no legal paper, Dinah asserted, then he had no claim.[28]

As part of the civilian community of New York, African Americans had many of the same headaches their white brethren did with respect to the demands of the military. But if a black man's house were confiscated by the army, he had fewer options at his disposal and could expect no alternate accommodation to be provided by the military. Although John Jackson exhibited enough disaffection to be driven from his home by the Americans in 1776, he returned to British-occupied New York to find his property and goods in the possession of His Majesty's troops. Jackson's best alternative was to join the British navy.[29]

Another black New Yorker, Thomas Farmer, saw his house taken by the barrackmaster. Like Jackson, Farmer saw his best option as joining the military, becoming an officer's servant in the 64th regiment. Yet another freeman, Inchu Moore, rented a cellar kitchen in the city for eight pounds per year until a white man offered the landlord double that amount. Although Moore claimed that the landlord wanted to keep his original tenant, the determined white renter apparently had connections. Moore appealed to the Mayor's office, where an official told him "that it was a Pity that we Black folks that came from Virginia was not sent home to Our Masters." Moore found it "hard" that he got no satisfaction from the town officials and "very hard" to be "abused so by this Man and his journeyman." While Moore had to swallow such talk, he felt confident that he could lodge a complaint with no damning repercussions and that justice might prevail—a situation undreamed-of in his slavery days back home.

Undeterred by the initial rebuff, Moore continued up the line of power to present his case to the Commander-in-Chief.[30]

When the British invited African Americans to New York, they framed their invitation as a work contract. A black man could choose any occupation, but the range of possibilities was limited. Most found work on privateers or as teamsters. Approximately fifty blacks even managed to procure coveted carting licenses because of the scarcity of white laborers in town. Otherwise, refugee blacks occasionally found work as drivers when the army needed them. Ten blacks comprised one-tenth of the British Commissary Department in 1781. In 1779, General Clinton appointed a Commissary of Captures whose job was to convert captured moveable property to use for the King's army. An offshoot of this office was the Commissary of Captured Cattle, managed by three cattle rangers, each with a party of ten mounted blacks. While employing blacks in one area of the Commissary of Captures, the British enumerated "Negroes" along with cattle and rice in another area of this department, the Commissary of Captured Forage. Expediency, not justice or humanitarian motives, ruled the day with respect to black men.[31]

The war nevertheless created new spaces for African American males. The army and its vast labor pool periodically moved out of the city on campaign, leaving jobs vacant. The war also made possible individual instances of extraordinary opportunity. Samuel Burke, a black man from Charleston, South Carolina, managed to get to England before the war, where he entered the service of a Royal Governor, William Browne. En route to the Bahamas, Burke and his master were captured and imprisoned in Hartford, Connecticut. Once exchanged and in New York City, Burke "assisted in raising his [Governor Browne's] regiment" because Burke "could speak the Irish tongue." Samuel Burke's fortunes continued to rise when he married a free Dutch mulatto woman who had a fine house and garden. His domestic arrangements at Number 5 Dutch Street were interrupted when the barrackmaster expropriated the house for His Majesty's use, leaving Mrs. Burke "in a very distressing condition." The best the displaced New Yorkers could do was to obtain a certificate from Governor Browne indicating the value of the house. This provided little comfort to Mrs. Burke, who reckoned that her best option was to join her husband "in all his Marches and Routes" when he went south with the army.[32]

Samuel Burke, Thomas Farmer, and John Jackson decided that their best move was to join the military when their houses were occupied by the British army. The high officials whose signatures graced the British proc-

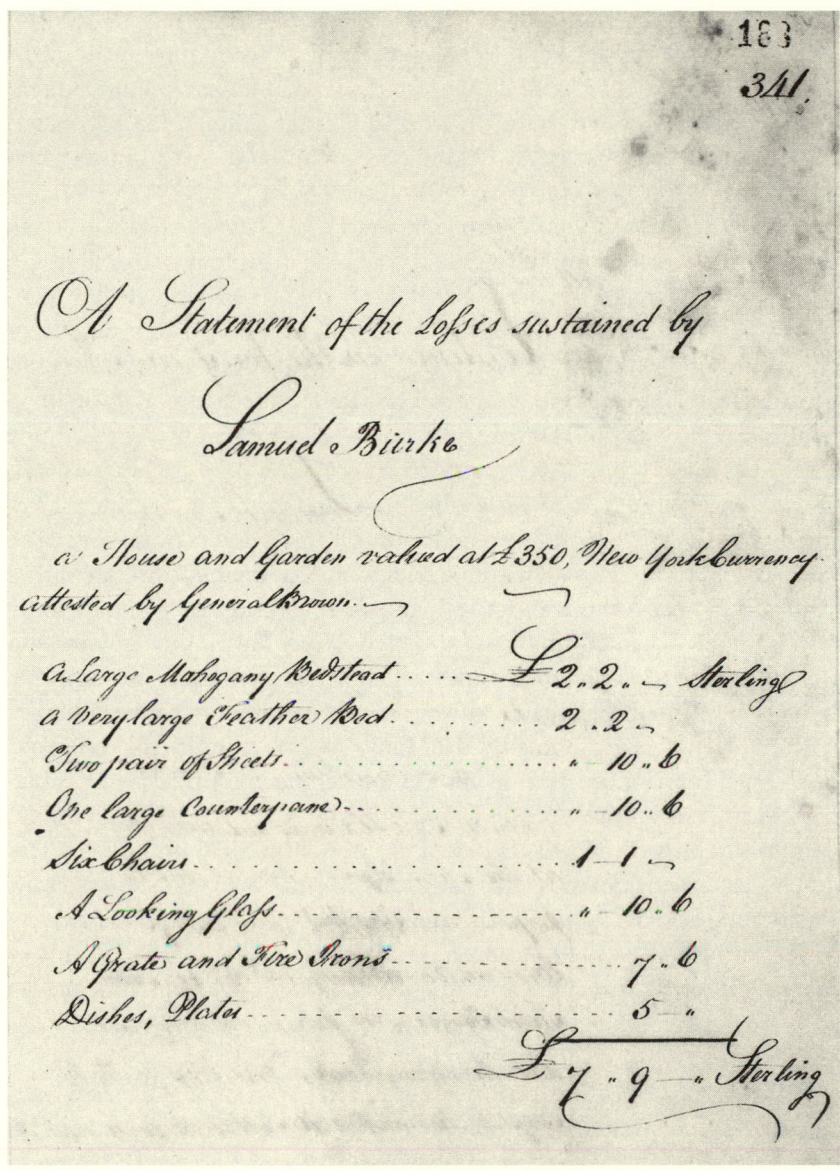

A Statement of the Losses sustained by

Samuel Burke

a House and Garden valued at £350, New York Currency attested by General Brown.

A Large Mahogany Bedstead	£2.2..	Sterling
a Very large Feather Bed	2.2	
Two pair of Sheets	".10..6	
One large Counterpane	".10..6	
Six Chairs	1.1	
A Looking Glass	".10..6	
A Grate and Fire Irons	7..6	
Dishes, Plates	5."	
	£7."9."	Sterling

Statement of losses sustained by Samuel Burke. A black man who married a Dutch mulatto woman with a house in New York, Samuel Burke served as a recruiter in New York City and was later wounded in the British service. In England after the war, Burke applied for compensation for his losses. The British allowed him twenty pounds sterling for his losses but rejected the bulk of his claim "for want of satisfactory proof of loss." Public Record Office.

lamations wanted blacks primarily as laborers for the British war effort. As an orderly book put it, Negroes' "employment will save the troops much Toyl and Fatigue." Blacks could wield a shovel and pickaxe, drain a ditch, and perform menial duties for British and Hessian officers. Blacks' contributions to the war effort gained a kind of recognition on occasion, as when a fortification in town was called "The Negro Fort."[33]

Every black man who crossed the lines provided yet another service to the British, namely military intelligence. After five days of hiding in a barn, Joe, the servant of a militia captain, fled Morristown with his wife, Dinah; later he disclosed troop movements and the very low morale of American soldiers. Another black refugee, named Mermaid Loo, crossed the lines with information about militia drafts raised around Fishkill to confront the Tories and Indians just north of Albany. Three of Loyalist David Ogden's Negro slaves managed to cross the lines to Long Island, where they informed their master that his estate, including the three slaves themselves, were to be attainted and sold. The messengers must have been taken aback when their master directed his anger at them for fleeing, rather than at the rebel authorities for the imminent confiscation of his worldly goods. Ogden claimed that once the New Jersey authorities understood that he had crossed the military lines to get medical treatment, his property would be restored. He chastised his servants for lessening his credibility with the New Jersey authorities. In March of 1779, the British command kept the entire city on alert because of a black's testimony about a rebel-led insurrection whose aim was to burn down the town (a Hessian soldier complained that he and his fellows were not allowed to undress for several nights). Occasionally, blacks gathered information in a systematic way, functioning as spies for the British. Benjamin Whitecuff circulated in New Jersey for two years before capture by the Americans. Whether as informants, guides, or spies, African Americans brought valuable information to powerful men, thereby enhancing their own sense of importance.[34]

When the British enticed African Americans to their side, they envisioned vast labor battalions in the service of the army. But the exigencies of war increasingly made them think of black men as soldiers. When expedient, the British used armed freemen to complement their fighting force. With the advent of the southern campaign, the British turned even more to the black soldier.

With the main army directed southward, some New York Loyalists volunteered to shoulder military duties which included harassing the enemy around New York. These units felt no compunction about including blacks in their numbers.[35] The Loyalist regiments were a different breed from their European counterparts. They had a long history with their enemies that had in recent years concluded with the Loyalists' flight from their communities and the confiscation of their worldly goods. Many were eager to seek revenge, to inflict damage for damage's sake, and to confiscate goods with abandon as partial compensation for their own losses. Officially constituted military organizations like the Associated Loyalists would also provide an object lesson to the laconic British about how the war should be waged—with conviction and unremitting drive.

The exploits of the Associated Loyalists were faithfully chronicled in the Tory newspapers of the city, although the racial composition of these bands was not mentioned. One such unit at Bergen Point, headed by Major Thomas Ward, was dedicated to "annoying" the Jersey coast. One quarter of Ward's four-hundred-man force was black, and from the complaints lodged against them, it is obvious they were armed. A Loyalist sympathizer living near Orangetown claimed that a "party of negroes" raided his farm and carried off horses from the property. Suspecting that the raiders came from Ward's company on Bergen Neck, the victim's nephew trekked down to the post only to see his uncle's horses hauling wood about the neighborhood. The uncle then enlisted the help of a prominent merchant in town, William Bayard, which necessitated some quick explaining on the part of Major Ward. Ward claimed that he bought the horses from the blacks under the impression that they were rebel property. As Ward had only made a down payment on the horses, the committee charged to arbitrate the case recommended that Ward hold back any monies due the blacks until the money value of the horses had been collected. The arbitrators' report included no testimony of, or defense by, the accused.[36]

When not raiding rebel territory, Ward's company cut wood in the neighborhood of its post, which raised more cries from loyal landholders in the region. In 1782, the civilians procured the help of William Van Schaack, a prominent lawyer refugee in town. The complainants charged that Ward's men continued to cut more than the allotted amount of wood, giving little compensation to the owners. The main offenders, they claimed, were "the Negroes" of Ward's group. So thorough were Ward's men that of the 3,825 potential cords on Justice Freeland's land, they left standing trees for only one hundred cords of wood. Johannes Van Buskirk estimated that on his seventy-two-acre farm, only 45 of 1,800 cords of wood remained. Other landholders were wiped out.[37]

Refugee military units alienated Loyalists and Rebels alike on their missions to round up prisoners, cattle, and cords of wood for the city. After the British defeat at Yorktown, the refugees' activities elicited less support from the community they served. In the waning days of 1781 and into 1782, many Loyalists saw, if they had not already, that a day of reckoning might well come at the hands of the rebels. The Associated Loyalists viewed these concerns as overanxious fretting, continuing to believe that they could still prevail if only they could pound the rebels harder. Perhaps in an attempt to distance themselves from the Associated Loyalists, the city's newspapers began to highlight the group's African American members. In February 1782, American forces raided the Bergen post. It was reported that the advanced sentry for the Loyalist refugees was "a Negro Man" who suffered a bayonetting by the rebels. In June, a band of refugees, "forty whites and forty blacks," raided the town of Forked River, destroying the saltworks there. Despite the British order to cease offensive war, the racially mixed Loyalist bands persisted in carrying the war to their enemies, exacting a last measure of retribution before they abandoned the stage to their adversaries. The Forked River raid even elicited disgust on the part of the Loyalist newspapers. "Thus are they conciliating the affections of the Americans," William Lewis noted with irony in *The New York Mercury*.[38]

By the time the Loyalist press had acknowledged the African American presence in Ward's company, the period of blacks' active service was coming to an end. Not three weeks after the Forked River raid, a group of twelve to fifteen blacks from Ward's unit ambushed and killed a white slavemaster who had gone to New York to sell the wife of one of Ward's African American soldiers. Armed black men acting in maverick fashion were not to be tolerated. After the fearsome report of their neighbor's murder, the people of the Bergen vicinity heard the cheering news that refugee blacks would henceforth be disarmed.[39]

The American Revolution provided the first real opportunity for the African American population to radically alter its fate. Under slavery's yoke, one's range of choices was limited. A slave could slow the pace of work, feign illness, or even run away, though runaways typically headed for an uncertain future in a new neighborhood, where if caught they would be returned to their master's fury. Never before the Revolution had runaways a place of asylum secured by one of the most powerful armies on earth. The war also claimed many masters around New York, whose absence from the household emboldened servants to set their own work schedule or even flee. And African Americans joined a steady stream of people on the move who crossed the lines for a variety of reasons. To an eighteenth-century African American, who normally had to swallow humiliation on a daily basis and could not protect his family, life in the occupied zone must have seemed a great release, despite continued hard work and a double standard with respect to fairness.

The porous nature of the boundary separating the two sides in the New York theater of war allowed a degree of leverage never before experienced by African Americans. In the occupied city, the new freemen made employment decisions, petitioned government, and aided still-enslaved individuals to escape the hold of their masters. For those still in bondage on the American side, permeable boundaries meant that black men and women could easily and successfully run away, thus promoting more accommodating government officials and masters. For one such obliging mistress, a city refugee living in the Hudson Valley, a move to the town of Esopus was out of the question because her "wench," Sarah, had refused to go. Mrs. Bancker's husband acquiesced to this state of affairs although the Banckers' son, Abraham, could not fathom why their decision should be "held in competition with the stubborn will of a slave."[40] Another New York City refugee noted a distinct change in her slaves' demeanor once her husband died. They had become "very saucy," and when an "ill-natured Person" told them their master had freed them, they demanded to "go to the office" and look at the will. One of the "wenches" struck Mrs. Beekman as so intransigent that her mistress gave the woman to her daughter and son-in-law, as "she wanted a Master."[41] Yet another husbandless woman in the Hudson Valley pleaded for the return of her mate, imprisoned by American authorities for disaffection, because her "servants have got so bad as they will do nothing but what they please." The woman's brother, an officer in the American army, entreated Governor Clinton to allow his sister's husband "to make his own House his Prison" because "the Negroes have got to be ungovernable and of consequence but very little labour Done and no care taken." Without black labor, Colonel Woodhull saw his sister's family "a-going to Destruction Head Long in a most Rappid manner." The freeholders of Flatbush also fretted about the attitudes of the town's black inhabitants when they petitioned the British to authorize no more taverns because they had enough "parties in the town" and because they needed no more watering holes for "our Negroes already sufficiently loose and licentious."[42]

While some masters were supremely vexed about servants they could not control, others strove to accommodate their slaves who could cross the lines or disappear on a privateer. One sale ad featured a twenty-four-year-old black sailmaker who wanted to continue in town laboring at his sails rather than go to sea. The advertisement was most forthcoming in admitting that the craftsman could simply walk his master's investment onto a boat and into the wide horizon beyond, never to return. Another advertisement announced the sale of a young Negro woman with four children. "They are not sold for any fault," claimed the seller, but because the woman had a husband in town and the mistress did not want to part them. While entirely possible that the owner acted out of humanitarian motivation, her liberality may have been influenced by her slave's enhanced chances for successful flight.[43]

The odds of successfully escaping bondage were heightened in a wartime city that already had a large number of freed blacks. Masters suspected that persons in town abetted the independent behavior of their enslaved servants. The most common suspects were masters of ships, as the sea had traditionally offered employment to black men. But the owners also suspected the black residents of the town, whether family members, sweethearts, or friends. In January 1782, an ad appeared featuring "a small black girl named Sue or Mary stolen by her mother, named Pender, a Virginia wench." In October, fourteen-year-old London ran away and was believed to be living with his mother in or about town. In November 1783, a husband plucked his wife out of her master's house. These family reconstitutions occurred after the battle of Yorktown, when talk of the British abandoning the city was rife. A master's decision to leave would mean that a mother would never see her child again, impelling her to insure her child's continued residence in town.[44]

Family networks were not the only ones operating in the city to spirit away enslaved people. When twenty-two-year-old Mattis ran away, his master believed he had no intention of fleeing but was "seduced and is still secreted by someone." When sixteen-year-old Jack left his owner, the latter offered one guinea for the slave's return, and five guineas for "discovering such person or persons who may have employed, harboured, concealed, or entertained such negro boy." When twenty-six-year-old Venus walked out of her master's house, the newspaper advertisement offered a three-guinea reward for information about the persons who put an ad about Venus in another city newspaper the previous day. Venus's former owner suspected that these people were "the persons who decoyed the wench away, and if they are not black in color, they are black in actions," he declared. Directing all his ire and frustration at Venus's collaborators, her owner concluded, "they may be ashamed of their name, for they dare not sign it to the advertisement." The advertisement in question, written in black dialect, exposed Venus's master as a cheat who stole the money with which she planned to buy her freedom.[45]

Evidence of greater leverage on the part of blacks was not limited to the point of sale or the networks aiding runaways. Slaves could inform on masters who violated the laws. When an escaped American sailor made his way from a British prison ship to Long Island, he found a sympathetic woman to feed and clothe him. Letting his guard down, he moved freely about the property only to be warned by his protector to be more careful. "For God's sake, don't let that black woman of mine see you," she exclaimed, referring to the slave woman washing on the stoop of the house, "for she is as big a devil as any of the King's folks and she will bring me out." The possibility of incarceration in the Provost put the soldier's hostess in mind of the lot of her husband, who had died in prison three weeks earlier after languishing there for two years. The tables were turned for the woman washing clothes on the stoop; with a mistress closely associated with an enemy of his Majesty's government, the enslaved woman had new power over her mistress—a scenario scarcely to be imagined before the war.[46]

Another scenario made possible by the war involved Jack, an enslaved New Jersey man, who had fled to the British. By December 1779, he had had enough of the occupied town and returned to New Jersey, but not to his master's farm. He instead made tracks to his wife's master in another county. There, according to his temporary master, Jack performed "trifling" tasks for almost a year and then asked that he be allowed to stay until his wife gave birth to their child. Jack had leverage because he could easily cross the Hudson in the event that his owner denied his request.[47]

The latitude experienced by African Americans can even be seen in situations that on first glance appear dire. Enough "idle" black men were seen in the streets of New York to induce the British authorities to summon "all male Negroes not employed in any of the public departments or are not the property of inhabitants." Ordered to assemble in front of a prison, such men were told that they would be expelled from town if they did not get to work. There is no evidence that the authorities carried through on their threats, although two years later, they had to summon "Negroe Vagabounds and Straglers" to the commons where once again they threatened those with no verifiable employ. Every slave who crossed the lines represented labor power that the Americans could not deploy. Sending labor power back to the rebels was certainly not British strategy. African Americans knew this and so continued to vex the authorities by controlling their free time.[48]

African American men strolled the streets and also at times spoke up with little reserve. The father of an American prisoner in New York complained that his son was marched through the city streets followed by "Negro Boys" who "grossly insulted" him. One can only guess at the elation felt by these young blacks, who could now belittle men who resembled their masters. A Loyalist officer's court martial revolved around the "impudent" behavior of an African American servant who refused a white man's order to leave the room, then argued openly with the officer whom the black man called "that Damned Fellow with wings on his coat." An enslaved man in New Jersey so incensed his master that he found himself in jail awaiting the auction block "for no fault," said the newspaper ad, "but a fancy tongue."[49]

A "fancy tongue" could take many forms: defiance, sarcasm, rage, or sullenness. Milford Smith of Philadelphia demonstrated yet another variation of "fancy tongue," or threatening speech, when he used the unbowed, intelligent, rational speech of a self-assured man. Milford had labored as a slave in Philadelphia for Mrs. Margaret Childe, a widow in financial difficulties. When the British entered Philadelphia, Milford had been hired out to an American resident of the city, Robert S. Jones. By the end of the British occupation, Milford decided to join the exodus to New York City, signaling his new life with the addition of a surname, a marker typically denied black slaves. Milford the slave now became Milford Smith, a man who could control his own identity. Milford Smith had not been in New York for two months when a friend, probably Anthony Benezet, the prominent Philadelphia Quaker, crossed the lines and informed Smith that Mrs. Childe was anything but quiet about his departure. Indeed, she had tried to enlist the support of the New York State Assembly as a "distressed widow" who had promised Milford his freedom once she died, but now was so angry at his action that she wanted him sold or arrested. In her deposition, Mrs. Childe singled out the baneful meddling of Anthony Benezet, who "makes it his business to help all Negroes in obtaining their freedom." Benezet apparently had drawn up the legal document that left the slave free after her decease, which was sealed and put with her will. In a fit of anger, she destroyed the addendum on hearing that Milford had run off with the assistance of a certificate that Benezet had made, replete with Mrs. Childe's forged signature. At the end of her appeal, the jilted mistress was forced to acknowledge Milford's new surname. "[He] calls himself Milford Smith," she noted.

As for the newly surnamed Smith, now of New York, he was quite anxious about his status behind British lines because his mistress was not one of the rebel supporters who fled Philadelphia at the British advance. She stayed behind as a loyal, law-abiding civilian under the occupation. The British never encouraged the slaves of Loyalists to abscond, which forced Smith to make his side of the story the official one. He wrote to Mr. Jones, the man for whom he worked before his flight, and asked that Jones take the certificate from Benezet's hand and have it recorded in the proper office. It is the tone of Milford Smith's letter that is most striking. "Hon'd Sir," wrote Smith to Jones, "I beg leave to return you my sincere thanks for your kindness to me when I was in the family and I am heartily sorry it was not in my power to wait upon you before leaving the city with the King's army." Here is a most genteel communication whose formality is indicative of equal writing to equal. That Smith could not "wait upon," that is, pay a social call on Jones' family before his departure, sounds odd coming from a fleeing slave. There is no hint of sycophancy, inferiority, or subservience in this letter, which may have irritated Mr. Jones, for instead of aiding Smith, he turned the letter and certificate over to Mrs. Childe.[50]

The appearance of surnames in the African American community of Revolutionary New York was a harbinger of future developments. While still-enslaved blacks were denied the dignity of a surname, those who crossed the lines appeared in newspapers and military records with family names, even when they committed infractions. When four men from the "Virginia Company of Blacks employed as laborers in the service of the Royal Artillery" deserted, the advertisement proclaiming their disappearance and probable resort to privateers listed their full names — Toliver Pearce, Benjamin Sawyer, Ralph Henry, and David Cooper. In other efforts to retrieve their property by providing all possible information, masters were forced to acknowledge the runaways' surnames. "Tony" sometimes called himself "Anthony Frost"; "Caesar" also went by the name "Julius Caesar"; "Jem" went among his companions by the name "James Jackson." The men of the black community (in contrast to the women) transformed diminutives and added the dignity of a surname, thereby erasing a marked distinction between the free and the unfree.[51]

African Americans signaled their new status in other ways as well. A 1782 letter to Rivington's *Royal Gazette* lamented that, with every passing day, blacks were increasingly "aping the dress and manners of their masters and mistresses" to the extent that one could not tell from behind whether a woman in a silk gown "fashionably festooned" was white or black. The letter writer further lamented that in addition to black-sponsored dances, assemblies, and concerts, the African American community had started its own Charade Clubs, a piece of frivolity previously enjoyed only by whites.[52] A Hessian chaplain attending the horse races on Long Island in 1778 remarked that "even the lovely female Negroes were given time off by their mistresses, and appeared in such finery that, when seeing them from the rear, we immediately prepared to pay our respects." Catching himself from such a mistake at the last minute, the Hessian was amused "to see a pitch-black person wearing a white summer dress with a white velvet sun hat and black velvet gloves."[53]

The ability to choose, engendered by the British proclamation and New York's permeable boundaries, charged many African Americans with a new confidence. Milford Smith's genteel letter, Dinah Archey's petition to Sir Guy Carleton, and Inchu Moore's complaint to Sir Henry Clinton all bespeak an assurance that black freemen before them rarely exhibited. Freemen before the war had learned that the best policy was to lie low in the barely tolerant white society that surrounded them. While occupied New York was little more tolerant, the likes of Smith, Archey, and Moore were among those in the community who dared to test the limits of their new-found freedom. No case better illustrates this new confidence (and the bounds within which it operated) than the testimony of Murphy Steel, a soldier in the Black Pioneers. He wrote to the military commander of New York City not as a petitioner or a complainant, but as a mouthpiece of God. While sitting in the barracks on the East River, Steel heard a disembodied voice that called him by name and instructed him to "go and tell Sir Henry Clinton to send word to General Washington that he must surrender himself" lest the wrath of God fall upon the rebels. And who would be the instruments of the wrath of God? The Voice ordained that if Washington did not heed Clinton's request, then Clinton should threaten to "raise all the Blacks in America to fight against him." The Voice instructed Clinton to inform King George of his command.[54]

The Voice was persistent in its attempt to rally Steel into action. After several more episodes, the Voice greeted the black soldier on one of the main streets of New York City. Steel in effect pleaded with the Voice to leave him alone, admitting that he was afraid to do the Voice's bidding "as he did not see the person that Spoke." Steel's interlocutor then revealed that he was the Lord. Murphy Steel could not then resist the command of God to inform Clinton and Cornwallis that "the Lord would be on their Side."

A black man presumed to tell Sir Henry Clinton what to do. Sir Henry elected to keep this testimony to himself, perhaps surprised and amused or perhaps moved by it. But the only way Steel could have presumed to instruct a British Major General was to couch his instruction as a religious imperative. Steel, one of a long line of oppressed people to use religion to cross new boundaries and to give public utterance to thoughts and aspirations, made clear to General Clinton that God impelled him to act.

While we can watch Murphy Steel build his case in his letter to Sir Henry Clinton, we cannot as readily ascertain his motivation. In the summer of 1781, he may have felt frustrated that he lingered in New York while the real military action was being played out in the southern campaign. Perhaps Steel was angling for a transfer to General Cornwallis, whom he mentioned at the end of the letter. On the other hand, Steel may have been a man of deep religious conviction who marveled at the wondrous changes ordained by God in his own life. If God could deliver him from his master, put a gun in his hand, and allow him a freedom of movement he had never experienced before the war, Steel may well have thought that he and his black colleagues could bring Washington down and "put an end to this rebellion." His wartime experiences certainly emboldened him to write an exhortatory letter to a major general, suggesting that he and his brothers could take care of a situation that the British army could not.

Black voices continued to probe, push, and challenge throughout the British occupation of New York. In the last months of the war, a small contingent of African Americans who had not already fled to the British warships expressed their anger at being "delivered in so unwarrantable a manner." They objected to the arbitrary assignment of their persons to the departing ships, "insisting on their rights under the proclamation," noted a Hessian observer, even if that meant making personal deals with the rebels so as to stay in America.[55]

Unlike their fellows under American rule, African Americans in the British zone insisted on their rights as early as 1783. For them, a British proclamation rang out more loudly than the Declaration of Independence. For all Britain's inconsistency and less-than-humanitarian motives, the British army was the first major institution to liberate significant numbers of the enslaved in American history. While the Americans talked a fair game and struggled with the reality of slavery in their society, the British literally paid blacksmiths to remove iron shackles from slaves' feet.[56]

The relationship between the British and the enslaved population created the most unusual network in the New York theater of war. Unlike the others, the African American relationship with the British was not one between equals, but rather one in which the most powerful found common cause with the most vulnerable. Family members knew one another before the war; so too did many of the businesspeople who profited from illegal trade. But the African Americans had no previous connection with the British army, no history of affectionate or lucrative exchange to mitigate the disturbances of war and its aftermath. The British proclamations were devised with the balance of power in mind. Once the British army departed (accompanied by thousands of blacks), the remaining African Americans were left to shift for themselves. Their powerful partners were gone. Hence, the black community strove to downplay its wartime alliance with the British, stressing instead its contribution to the American cause. But the significant movement across military lines during the war was so dramatic that the memory died hard in the white community, particularly since continuing controversy about compensation for departing slaves lived on through the turn of the century. Unlike its neighbors who passed gradual abolition legislation earlier, New York did not put a gradual emancipation law on its books until 1799.[57]

No matter what the callous motivation or inconsistency of the British, an enslaved African American could cross the lines to a better life between 1776 and 1783. Like others during the war, New York's blacks put their own priorities before adherence to either cause. Even for the minority who remained in familiar surroundings rather than face the unknown in 1783, the experiences of the war years could not be extinguished. The black community learned that liberation need not come only in isolated instances of flight; that those who held power could be moved to hasten the day of deliverance. African Americans also learned more about preserving their families in circumstances that dwarfed the already fierce challenges of everyday life in slavery. Their ingenuity in spiriting their brethren out of the master's grasp would serve future generations when the children and grandchildren of the Revolutionary cohort crossed new lines to freedom. The black participants in the New York theater of war carried their stories with them into the new era of American independence, thereby creating new networks of hope in the African American community.

6

The Late Unhappy Commotions

THE COMMUNITIES OF Loyalist New York City and the Patriot periphery collapsed into one another in the closing years of the war. After the American victory at Yorktown, Loyalist Americans tried a number of strategies to salvage what they could from a fast-deteriorating situation. The private and public faces of the Loyalist community did not at first send a unified message. While many individuals sought to solidify connections with the other side, the Loyalist press initially tried to breathe new life into the war effort. But when the news of the Peace Treaty reached the city, the stringent voice of the public print fell into step with private strategies by appealing to the "reasonable" Whigs for fairness, sobriety, and discernment.

After the American reinvestment of the city, the returning victorious forces did not speak with one voice on the continued presence in town of Loyalists. One part of the Whig community saw danger in making room for former enemies. Another part of the community believed that stability and reconciliation were crucial to establishing a permanent American society. Thus did New Yorkers turn their attention to reestablishing their city at the close of the war, and into the early days of the new municipal administration.

In all of the movement in and out of New York City during the war, none was greeted with more acclaim and fanfare than the arrival on September 25, 1781, of George III's son, Prince William Henry. The sixteen-year-old Prince Royal was paraded around town, feted by the city's leading soldiers and citizens, and lauded by a flurry of poems printed in the Loyalist press. "The Satisfaction felt by every Loyalist was very visible in seeing one of the royal family in America," wrote one observer. Such joy on the part of the King's supporters probably mingled with relief, for the prince's arrival signaled Britain's commitment to continue the war.[1]

And as far as the Loyalists could tell, the war was going well for His Majesty's forces. The southern army had captured the south's two major cities, Savannah and Charleston, and was moving up the coast into Virginia. The city's newspapers had not made people fully aware of the damage inflicted by rebel forces in North Carolina. By the Prince's arrival, New Yorkers knew, however, that an important engagement was imminent. In October, a call for volunteers had gone out in support of Cornwallis's forces in Virginia. Elsewhere, the signs augured well for the British side. America's most effective fighting General had defected; the American army was plagued by mutinies; the money issued by the Continental Congress, playfully referred to as "King Cong" by the Loyalist press, was not worth the paper on which it was printed. Reports of civilian dissatisfaction and unrest filtered back to the city. So Prince William Henry's arrival provided a pretext to huzzah about a series of hopeful signs.

[handwritten margin note: Brits assumed they were doing well in war]

But the glow of celebration lasted little more than a month. One of the Loyalist luminaries actively involved in toasting the Prince Royal, William Smith, received a handbill from New Jersey on October 24 that must have made his stomach drop. The southern army under Lord Cornwallis had surrendered to the combined French-American force five days earlier after a long siege at Yorktown, Virginia. The town was "greatly agitated" at the news. By month's end, New Yorkers had read about the Yorktown surrender terms which placed Loyalist refugees in Virginia in the hands of rebel civil authorities. The Loyalists were "vexed and despondent on the Fate of the refugees left there to the mercy of the Usurpers," declared one city resident.[2]

Few heartening developments counterbalanced the Yorktown fiasco in the ensuing months. Although in May 1782, news reached New York City of the British fleet's victory over the French fleet that had turned the tide at Yorktown, the city's inhabitants continued in a state of high nervousness. The spring fleet from Europe had already brought word that a prominent English General, Henry Conway, had publicly moved for American independence. On August 2 the new military Commander-in-Chief, Sir Guy Carleton, informed his Loyalist colleague, William Smith, that King George had agreed to the independence of the colonies, contingent on the security of Loyalist life and property. Smith lost no time in spreading the news, reporting the next day that the town was "thrown into the most painful Anxiety by the report."[3]

Another Loyalist, Hudson Valley landlord Beverly Robinson, reported his reaction to Sir Henry Clinton, then back in England. What did the recently arrived packet bring from England, wrote Robinson, but the news that "the independence of America [was] given up by the King without any condition whatever, the Loyalists of America to depend on the mercy of their enemies for the restoration of their possessions, which we are well assured they will never grant." Robinson wondered what would become of himself and his family as he had conspicuously supported the British cause "and had too good an estate ever to expect forgiveness." As he saw it, his best alternative was to repair to England "with the hopes that the government of Great Britain will not suffer us to starve but allow us a small pittance."[4]

Robinson was not alone in his decision to leave town. Throughout late 1781 and into 1782, large-print newspaper ads began to appear that conveyed the idea with elemental simplicity. "I intend to leave this Province soon," William Torrance declared in a November 1781 announcement. "I intend to leave for Britain in the first fleet," declared Robert Pringle in January of 1782. Pringle and others undoubtedly wanted to wrap up their affairs in town as soon as possible.[5]

While some city residents found no reason to stay, others banked on their unoffending, quiet lives under British occupation to spare them from any American backlash, thereby allowing them to remain in their native country. The support of friends and family members outside town was now more crucial than ever. Even those city residents who had maintained a steady correspondence with Whig family members throughout the war felt the need to explain their decision to remain behind British lines. One such individual was Abraham Bancker, a young man of complicated political leanings who stayed on the British side of the lines during the war. When Abraham initiated a correspondence in 1779 with his Whiggish cousin living in New Jersey, also named Abraham, his letters were brief, owing to the "necessity of the times." However abbreviated his first forays into hazardous correspondence beyond the military lines, he managed to communicate to his cousin his heartfelt affection for his relations on the other side of Newark Bay. By mid-1780, Abe felt comfortable enough to pen full, flowery, showy letters to his fortunate cousin. Perhaps Abraham's mood had lightened because of his removal to Manhattan where he procured a position with a city merchant. Still, he remained weary of "the Public Discord," assuring his influential kinsman that "we sicken at the Loss of the Company we esteem." However weary and disconsolate he felt about the separation from his kinsmen, Abraham did not choose to join them on the American side of the lines. He opted instead for a business career in New York City.

Despite the constant flow of affectionate correspondence, Abraham nonetheless felt compelled to explain his choice to his correspondent. By May of 1782, it looked to everyone as if the Americans would prevail. Abraham had undoubtedly read the American newspapers which characterized those who remained in town as traitors who had lived in the lap of luxury long enough. Abraham made sure that his cousin of high Whig credentials understood his motivations and his sufferings during the war. "Few individuals have greater Cause to abominate the War than myself," he wrote in a May 1782 letter. "In the commencement of the revolution, I was proceeding thro' a Course of Study, with great Pleasure, and under Singular Advantages," mused Bancker. "Ambition rendered the Paths of Literature delightful, and the Progress I made, still brightened the Prospect I had in view, which was not merely to render myself conspicuous, but to become an useful Member of Society." His studies were cut short by the conflict, or as he put it, "this calamitous war intervened [to] cut me off from the Avenues to Science and blasted all my Expectations." He called the first four years of the war on Staten Island "a confinement" when he seldom went abroad and became "absorbed in a deep melancholy which much impaired my Constitution." Only when he realized that this disposition might prove fatal did Abraham venture into the city to find employment. He assured his cousin that his position as a clerk in one of the city's merchant houses was not lucrative but served "to amuse my Mind and instruct me in that useful branch of commerce." Only to save his life, claimed Bancker, did he choose to become a part of the British economy in the occupied city. But lest his cousin surmise that he enjoyed himself in town, Abraham gave full vent to his melancholy at seeing his cousin's city house occupied by someone else. His "Breast laboring under Anxious Concern," Abraham confessed that "many a Sigh escapes me when I cast my Eyes towards the well-known Mansion."[6]

There may have been no need for young Abraham Bancker to justify his choices during the seven years of war. He had sustained a friendly correspondence with his influential Whig cousin for over three years. In his cousin's eyes, Abraham's heart was in the right place. Still, he felt the need to explain himself. His nervousness in that regard is understandable. While family members knew who he was, having had a positive prewar relationship that disposed them to be understanding, the other refugee New Yorkers with no comparable personal acquaintance might not be as sympathetic to a man who had chosen to remain behind British lines for the duration of the war. The average New Yorker might look at Abraham Bancker of Staten Island and see a young man who could easily have stolen across the military lines to American-controlled territory. He never cited any kind of family emergency in his father's household. To a Whig who did not know him, Abe was at worst a Tory, at best an unpatriotic neutral who lived a relatively comfortable life at home surrounded by his immediate family—a far cry from the wartime experiences of thousands of dispossessed New Yorkers who were now on the verge of taking their city back. As an informed man who read "the prints" throughout the war, Abraham Bancker had to be aware that a possible misinterpretation of his motives and actions could lead to stern retribution by those who could only assess his actions at face value. He consequently made sure that his influential relatives understood his choices and his sufferings during the war.

William Walton had more reason to be nervous than did Abraham Bancker. Walton's wealth and standing in New York City made his loyalism all the more apparent and consequently all the more egregious to the American authorities. To live a quiet, unobtrusive life was not in his nature. William Walton signed the loyalty oaths to the King, became a high official in the civilian police department, and headed a battalion of Loyalist city militia. He lived in one of the town's great mansions and socialized with the city's military and civilian leaders during the war. Seeing the handwriting on the wall in 1783, Walton reached out to his aunt's Whiggish family in New Jersey whom he had hitherto ignored, in the hope that with their support he could stay in New York when the Americans returned. His strategy paid off. Although enjoying no loving relationship with his Aunt Cornelia, a Beekman by birth, William Walton managed through his aunt's assistance to thrive in the new American republic.

The Walton story featured no unalloyed family love, but family ties did nonetheless prevail over political differences. When Cornelia Walton left her mansion house in 1776, she depended more than ever on the annuities due her from her Loyalist nephew in New York, who acted as the executor of her husband's will. Her hopes of money from that quarter were dashed, however, when she received no communication from her nephew and no reply to her own letters to him.

Finally in April 1782, Cornelia tried to get the attention of young William by writing to the British General, James Robertson, asking him to intervene with her delinquent kinsman. Cornelia wrote to her nephew that she saw herself as "easy and silent" about the money "and by no means as pressing as probably you would have been had the case been reversed." Having no luck with the British authorities, Cornelia called upon a sympathetic city resident to visit the mansion house and inquire about her money.

Finally, with the prospect of censure from Robertson and the inconvenience of neighbors knocking at his door, William responded to his aunt in a letter bursting with outraged resentment. He enumerated the reasons he could not send any money in the past but he nonetheless included a note for three hundred pounds. At the news that she had written to Robertson, her nephew haughtily assured his aunt that the British General "has never mentioned the receipt of it to us nor do we suppose he will."[7]

Whether from total engrossment in his own affairs or outright disinclination to acknowledge an elderly aunt, William Walton turned a deaf ear to Cornelia's entreaties until it became clear that the English intended to make peace with the new American government. The condescension so evident in William's 1782 letter had evolved into total obsequiousness a year later, as evidenced in William's April 24, 1783, letter to his aunt. William had heard from a Beekman cousin that Cornelia intended to move back into her own house, the house in which William was then residing, as soon as the British left town. On hearing this news, William reversed his haughty tone and hastened to explain all his actions to his "Dear Aunt," his "dear Madam" and "Friend." The upheaval of the war prevented him from sending his aunt's annuity payments, and the penury of his own family was such that he was forced to accept the position of justice of the peace (a euphemism for a high official in the civil police). Having explained away two of the knottier problems of his collaboration with the British, William invoked the Walton family name in an effort to elicit his aunt's support. "It is my duty now," wrote the newly solicitous nephew, "to call on you in the Name and by the Love you had for your late respected and worthy Husband, to beg you will be the Friend and Assistant of his and your nephews." He urged his aunt not to "join with our enemies in endeavoring to crush a Family you have so long been happily connected with." In conclusion, this "affectionate nephew" attempted to soften Cornelia's heart by reminding her of his children, who would suffer too if she abandoned him.[8]

Cornelia Walton reciprocated the wish for family reunion in as affecting a way as did her nephew. She longed for "that former family friendship" and wished that "mutual good offices" be restored. But however much she showered her nervous nephew with protestations of family solidarity and affection, she did not lose sight of the fact that her nephew had ignored her during the war and owed her money. She first suggested that William stir himself with respect to the rent money owed her from city residents and military personnel during the war. Then she demanded that he pay the annuities promised in her husband's will to the slaves who stayed in the city

John Wollaston, *Mrs. William Walton (Cornelia Beekman)*, ca. 1780. Cornelia Walton spent the occupation in New Jersey, attempting in vain to procure money from her Loyalist nephew in New York City. With the American reinvestment of the city in 1783, Mrs. Walton made her errant relative squirm. Her nephew's descendants had the last word, however, when they wrote her out of the family history in an 1832 newspaper article. Accession number 1902.4, negative number 6072. © Collection of the New-York Historical Society.

during the war. Next, she moved to acquire her "dear nephew's" attainted property in Monmouth County, New Jersey. The Treasurer of that county still held the proceeds of the land sale, which Cornelia suggested that she claim in partial payment of the debt outstanding to her. While continuing to assure her nephew of her love and devotion, Cornelia next informed him that Governor Clinton wanted to rent her mansion house when the British vacated. As William had not paid a farthing in rent over the last eight years, she thought it "inconsistant with reason that you should have it any longer."[9]

As a refugee in the countryside, Cornelia Walton had been disconnected from the one source of power available to her—her money. But the upheaval of the Revolution created new options. She took advantage of property confiscations to retrieve some of the money that her nephew owed her. She had it in her power to renounce him totally, and indeed, she had the satisfaction of seeing him writhe. After seven years of accumulated helplessness, Cornelia may have enjoyed the scene. Possessing real power over her errant nephew and heir for the first time in her life, she decided to punish and support him at the same time. Her strategy may have sprung from the fact that the financial well-being of Mrs. Walton and her nephew was intertwined. Most of Mrs. Walton's wealth consisted of real estate holdings and the all-important account books of her husband's estate. William Walton could have emptied her home of all its furnishings, sold her city property to gullible buyers, and departed for England with the records of all outstanding bonds and debts owed to her estate. This may well explain the carrot-and-stick approach she used in her letters, opening and closing each one with protestations of affection while dishing out the bad news to her less-than-filial relation.

Despite rumors to the contrary, the high-profile Loyalist, William Walton, resisted the pressures to leave town with the British. His trust in his relatives was not misplaced. His Aunt Cornelia's influential Whig family spread its influence over him, enabling him to remain in New York City. He felt comfortable enough to apply for a Loyalist pension in 1785, ever professing himself a British subject.[10]

While it is obvious that William Walton waited until the last moment to effect a reconciliation with his aunt, the motives of other refugees were not as transparent. Samuel Shoemaker, a former mayor of Philadelphia, had headed the civilian police wing of the British occupation there, and chose the prudent course of following the British out of town in the summer of 1778. He took up residence in New York as a valued Loyalist official.

Shoemaker was as resourceful as his family members in arranging to correspond with kin in his native city. He used to jot his illegal communications in the margins of newspapers that were more likely to escape the censors en route to Philadelphia.

In the March 31, 1781, edition of Rivington's *Royal Gazette*, Samuel Shoemaker noted on the bottom of page four that he had managed to effect the release of a Pennsylvania soldier incarcerated in New York. This was the first mention of such service. It would be another nine months before Shoemaker would again note his efforts on behalf of Pennsylvania soldiers. From December 1781 onward, Shoemaker sent steady reports home on his progress in finding, succoring, and freeing Pennsylvania mothers' sons from British jails.

His efforts swung into high gear on December 22, just two months after Yorktown, when like Walton and others he might have figured that the odds of British victory had precipitously declined. In an effort to ingratiate himself with Whiggish authorities back home, he may well have worked more assiduously for American soldier prisoners once he realized that the Americans would prevail. Each liberated prisoner might be an insurance policy for his family, his property, and ultimately himself. On the other hand, he may have acted on purely humanitarian motives, and, like other participants of the war, chose personal connections over political ideology. His activity on behalf of the prisoners before the decisive battle in Virginia may have been hampered by British disinclination to release prisoners until the Americans snagged thousands of British prisoners at Yorktown. No matter what Shoemaker's motivation, he relayed news of prisoners' health or burial place back to Philadelphia, inquired as to the whereabouts of imprisoned soldiers, conveyed money to them, and managed through his influence with the British to secure several sailors' release. All his activity centered on the most vulnerable prisoners in New York, those on the city's old hulks in the harbor. After a particularly busy week when he had passed forty dollars to soldier Tobias Norman, made inquiries into the health of two acquaintances' sons, and sorrowfully reported that John Eckhart from Reading was feared dead, Shoemaker wrote in the February 23 edition of the *Royal Gazette*, "I cannot easily describe the trouble [and] difficulties that have attended my endeavors."[11]

In the waning days of the war, Samuel Shoemaker had no idea whether this reservoir of accumulated favors would work to his advantage. Abraham Bancker and William Walton wondered as well if their efforts at family reconciliation would pay dividends. Certainly these men and all the Ameri-

WEDNESDAY, NOVEMBER 27, 1782.

THE
ROYAL GAZETTE.

New-York, Published by JAMES RIVINGTON,   Printer to the King's Most Excellent Majesty.

HIGH WATER at NEW-YORK, this WEEK.	
Sat. 48 m. after 11	Wed. 13 m. after 3
Sun. 44 m. after 12	Thu. 1 m. after 4
Mond. 33 m. after 1	Fri. 46 m. after 4
Tuesd. 22 m. after 2	

Sugar House Paper, To be sold, enquire of the Printer.

Swords, Cutteaux, and Pistols of various kinds.

☞ The most beautiful CANES in great Variety for Gentlemen and Ladies.

Samuel & Robert Elam

HAVE IMPORTED, In the BRIG ABBY, From LIVERPOOL, AND BY THE EDWARD and ROSAMOND, From LONDON, Which they are now opening At their STORE, No. 111, Queen-Street,

A Large and general Assortment of Yorkshire superfine and coarse CLOTHS,—twilled and plain Coatings, Duffils, low priced forgathies, Rattinets, Shalloons, Durants, Callimancoes, and other stuff goods; check'd bread Buttons, best scarf twill, sewing Silk, &c. &c.

They have also for Sale, Lancashire Sail-Cloth, No. 1 to 6. Durham Mustard, of the first Quality, in tin canisters of 25 to 30 pounds each. A few quarter-casks of old Sherry Wine. And a variety of other desirable Articles in the Haberdashery and Linen Drapery line, which they will sell low for Cash.

For LIVERPOOL,

Will sail in 10 days if no convoy offers.

The BRIGANTINE ABBY, WILLIAM TAYLOR, Master.

A strong double decked vessel, burthen 140 tons, will be ready to take in goods in three or four days. For freight or passage apply to said Master on board the vessel at Moore's Wharf, near Beekman's Slip, or to

WILLIAM KENYON, Who has just imported in the said vessel, Mould Candles, Poland Starch, a few Crates Earthen Ware, consisting chiefly of Cups and Saucers, and a box of Men's fine fashionable Hats.

November 15th, 1782.

For LONDON,

The Ship ROSAMOND J. GEAVES, Master.

Has excellent accommodations for Passengers, and will sail with the first Convoy. For Freight or Passage, apply to JOHN MILLER, at No. 14, Water-Street, or to Captain Geaves, on board, at Wells's Wharf.

John Miller,

Has for Sale, No. 14, Water-Street, CHEESE in hampers, Hams in hogsheads, draft Porter in casks, Queen's Ware in crates, Window Glass in boxes, Brown Soap in firms, Mess Beef and Pork in tierces, Callicoes, Chintzes, Muslins, Lawns, Cambricks, Shalloons, Linens, Teas, Flannels, Coatings, Groswords in half, whole and quarter barrels, also Old Madeira in Pipes. New-York, Oct. 1, 1782.

TO BE SOLD,

At FORT KNYPHAUSEN,

A NEW built convenient HOUSE, one story high, with two front parlours, and a back parlour, a kitchen and shop adjoining the front; likewise a good garden, well inclosed, in the rear of the house, and a stable,—the property of Christian Stracker. For particulars, enquire of his late partner, Henry T. Marchand, No. 15, Maiden-Lane.

N. B. The above House is fit for a Tavern or Store-keeper.

Just arrived in the ship Nancy, Captain Clark, from Cork, after a passage of 40 days, A parcel of choice New MAY BUTTER, Of the first Quality, Mess pork, London porter in bbls. and bottles, cheese and soap, To be sold by Eddy, Sykes, and Co. No. 152, Water Street.

RICHARD HALL,

No. 4, Beekman's Slip,

HAS received by the late vessels from Halifax, and pickled and, cod sounds, pickled mackarel and herrings by the barrel, salmon, in quantity. Also now Cork Butter per the firkin, by the best vessel from Cork. An also a general assortment of liquors, wines, groceries, &c. Indian corn and oats by the bushel.

TO BE SOLD,

At Public Auction, By Taylor and Bayard, On Monday the 2d of December next, At Twelve o'Clock at the Coffee-House,

THAT excellent well built house No. 59, Maiden Lane, the property of Judge Bayard, at which time the conditions will be made known, and an indisputable title given to the purchaser; also to be let and lawmade in possession given, an elegant House, with a good Garden, Coach House and Stables, at Bloomingdale. Enquire of Taylor and Bayard.

AT Frederick Cockles Store,

No. 167, Water-Street, Corner of Burling-Slip,

MAY be had, Brasiery by the cask, as imported from England, in the like fort. Also, stockings, Gloves, and Shoes, by the dozen; Flannels by the piece.

N. B. For the conveniency of those who do not wish to purchase Brasiery by the cask, he has at the above Store, on the most reasonable terms,

Wine bottles by the box	Pewter Dishes,
Mustard do.	Do. plates,
Copper tea do.	Basons,
Brass chasing dishes.	Light theatres,
Do. weights.	Tinkards,
Do. Candlesticks.	Ten pots,
Do. warming pans.	Salts,
Do. do. cullars and locks,	Quart and pint mugs,
Do. skewer and pepper	Porringers,
boxes.	Table and tea spoons,
Night and lock horn cocks	Also, plated buckles and jewellery. [✳ 3 t.

RUN AWAY,

From the Subscriber, On Sunday last, the 17th Instant.

A Likely young Grison NEGRO fellow, named NERO: He had on when he went away, an ordinary suit, a blue frieze Shooting jacket, lined with green baize, had four thick pockets and blue buttons, brown cloth tower-ers, and an old stopped hat; he also carried with him a new suit of grey clothing, hat waistcoat and coat lined with green baize, with plain white metal buttons, and a pair of boots. Whoever will secure the said Negro and deliver him to the subscriber, at Newtown, Long-Island, or to Mr. Robert Dunbar, No. 17, Maiden-Lane, New-York, shall receive FIVE GUINEAS Reward.

Newtown, Nov. 20, 1782.   WM. OAKDEN.

GENUINE PORT WINE,

In Pipes, Hhhds. and Quarter Casks, Just landed from on board the Brigantine Knyphausen from Oporto, and to be sold by Samuel Donaldson, at No. 20, in Smith Street, next door to the corner from Wall Street.

For LONDON,

To sail with the first convoy, The Ship VENGEANCE, JOHN BARRON, Master.

For freight or passage, apply to the Captain on board at Murison's Wharf,—Two thirds of her Cargo already engaged.—There are good accommodations for a few Passengers in this well appointed and excellent ship. For particulars enquire of JAMES RIVINGTON.

FOR LONDON,

To sail with the first Convoy, The Ship NEW-YORK, CHARLES GRANT, Master. Burthen 400 tons, with valuable accommodations for passengers. For freight or passage apply to Pollock and Urquhart, Dock-Street, or to the Captain on board, at the Ordnance-Wharf, Counties-Dock. c. t. f.

This Day is published, Price 4s.

And to be had of the Printer,

RIVINGTON's NEW-YORK Pocket Almanack

For the Year 1783.

Being the Third after BISSEXTILE, or LEAP YEAR.

CONTAINING, Besides the usual Calculations,

1st, A Drawing the Weight and Value of Coins; a list of Post Roads through the Continent, Tables of each Water at New-York, and Places adjacent, &c.

Also, BIRTH Days of the Royal Family of Great Britain; Years of the other principal Sovereigns of Europe; and Tables shewing the Value of Guineas from 1 to 100, in Dublin, Sterling Money, and New-York Currency, &c.

WILKES, & Co.

No. 59, Smith-Street, Have still remaining on Hand a few CHESTS of Excellent Claret, Which they will sell for Cash only at Three Pounds Currency a Dozen.

N. B. The prime and the charges. The Partnership of WILKES and Co. being dissolved is the only motive for disposing of their Wine so cheap.

For SALE, by the PIECE,

At the MANUFACTORY STORE, No. 50, Water-Street, between the Fly-Market and Burling-Slip, cheap as usual,

A Large and fresh importation of the following GOODS: Twilled Sashes, Superfine, Second Broad Cloths, London Brown, blue, scarlet, Drabs of the newest colours; those twill'd for ever. Coats (water proof) Super and Second white Cloth, &c. A few very fine Carpets, a large quantity of Men's fine Shoes, with many other articles too tedious to mention.

A few Pieces BUFF CLOTH, Sold by   S. HOPKINS.

JUST imported in the Brig Abby, Captain Taylor, from Liverpool, and to be sold by Benjamin Birkett, No. 45, Hanover-square, a complete assortment of Gamblets, Tammies, Durants, Shalloons, Rattinets, Callimancoes, and Moreens.

SAMUEL DONALDSON

At No. 20, in Smith-Street, next Door to the Corner from Wall-Street, has for Sale,

OLD Port Wine, in Pipes, Hogsheads, and Quarter Casks, warranted genuine. Barcelona and Teneriffe do. in Bottles. Madeira, Sherry, Teneriffe and Fayal ditto, in whole and half Pipes. Old Cunber Brandy, in Butts and 20 Gallon Casks. Clest in Hogsheads. Muscovade and Powdered Sugars in Hogsheads, Barrels and Boxes. Bohea and Hyson Tea, in Chests. Mould and ship Candles, and Red and Turpentine Soap, in Boxes.

ALSO A small parcel of well chosen DRY GOODS, at a low advance for ready money, or on a short credit.

For LONDON,

To sail with the first Convoy, The Ship EDWARD, Capt. COUPAR, For freight or passage apply with Samuel Franklin, or the said master on board, at Brownjohn's Wharf.

---

cans behind British lines had cause to feel nervous about the change in command at New York.

Six months after the devastating news of the peace conference in Paris and the King's permission to his negotiators to grant independence if necessary, the civilian population of occupied New York learned of the formal cessation of offensive war in February 1783, followed the next month by the publication of the preliminary articles of the peace treaty. The Loyalists read the fifth article with a particularly heavy heart as it provided no guarantee of Loyalist property, merely a promise on the part of Congress to "recommend" to the states that they return Loyalist property. No one on either side seriously believed that this vague recommendation would restore property to anyone. The community that plighted its future to Britain felt abandoned and betrayed by the mother country.[12]

[handwritten marginal note: Restoration of Brit's property]

When the Loyalist community turned to the American side for some hopeful signs, they found little comfort. The rebel press gave full vent to angry voices calling for retribution against the people who occupied their homes for the past seven years. A broadside from Poughkeepsie made quite plain who had reason to fear the wrath of an injured people. Titled "To All Adherents to the British Government and Followers of the British Army commonly called Tories who are at present within the City and County of New-York," the publication erased all hope of any Loyalist evading retribution. "Your feelings must be callous indeed," warned the aptly named author, Brutus, "if you do not with exquisite anguish anticipate the horrours which infallibly will seize you when the *final* evacuation takes place." Brutus promised blood or banishment to *all* Tories who dared to stay, regardless of their motivation. The "safety of the state," noted Brutus, "forbids the experiment of making distinctions." The broadside also an-

Samuel Shoemaker letter in Rivington's *Royal Gazette*, November 27, 1782. A prominent Loyalist who fled Philadelphia after the British occupation, Shoemaker communicated with his family back home be secreting his letters in newspapers. He wrote on only one side of the page (see bottom left) because the newspaper was folded lengthwise down the middle. His text reads: "family in good health. Novem 27.82. / Papers M&N to 21 / No. 14 & 15 etc: etc: inst' recd. / I have obtained permission for J. Fisher to come to this city & shall send it down to E. Town with this packet—I expect Geo. Brown & the other prisoners whom the Admiral ordered to be sent out at my request, will go today or tomorrow by way of Dob's ——— / The picture in the magaz intended for Sr.ly C———N is not in the least like him." The Library Company of Philadelphia.

ticipated Loyalist appeals to the American government or to influential friends, labeling these tactics as delusional and hopeless. A free people, explained Brutus, would quash any bribery or flattery or special "contracts." Adopting the character of the soldier who slew an arrogant Caesar, the broadside's author concluded, "we have fought for the country, and therefore we have an undoubted right in common with our fellow citizens to say, who shall possess it."[13]

The identity of Brutus was probably William Malcom, a politician who eventually sat in the New York Assembly. Complaints reached Governor George Clinton that such inflammatory talk pushed "at least 100 families" to leave New York, people who "might have proved greater ornaments to society than even Mr. Malcolm appeared." Alexander Hamilton wrote as well about the efficacy of these pamphlets. In August 1783, he was one of the multitude to enter British-occupied New York because, he said, his wife insisted that he go. While there, he noted the exodus of many good people who had hitherto intended to stay. Hamilton equated each of those departures with so much wealth and industry departing the country. "Our state will feel for twenty years at least the effects of the popular phrenzy," he wrote in disgust.[14]

Equally demonstrative and emphatic was another New York publication from the summer of 1783 that fingered eight specifically named Loyalists. The point of the pamphlet was to assure these prominent men that there was no place to turn in their efforts to remain in America. Connections, position, or money was to no avail. The pamphlet's author, Cives, addressed the following warning to William Smith, a prominent Loyalist politician: "If you mean to rely on your numerous and wealthy connexions in the country, as the wall of your preservation, you may be assured of having but a very slender support." To Charles Inglis, the leading Episcopal minister in town, Cives warned that even Inglis's "sacerdotal character" could not protect him, "even at the horns of the altar." Frederick Philipse, advised Cives, should not put too much faith in the treaty's fifth article with respect to retaining his enormous domain of Philipsburg. "For you may be rest assured," proclaimed Cives, "that the worthy inhabitants of Philipsburg who have at all times disputed that ground inch by inch, with the enemy, and *purchased* it with the price of their best blood, will never become your vassals again. They will not," continued the pamphlet, "submit to become tenants *at will*, to you or your son, nor to any other *enormous landholder on such base terms.*" Driving his point home, the writer concluded that tenants "have not, as formerly, been contending who should be their master, a Phillipse or a Vanhorne, a Livingston or a Delancy—No, they have been fighting for freedom and will enjoy it." To any wealthy Loyalist merchant, like Hugh and Alexander Wallace, who thought he could buy his way back into the American community, Cives directed this salvo: "You may rely that the virtuous Citizens, when collected, and who have undergone an infinite variety of hardships, for nearly eight years, will not permit you nor such as you, to insult their honest patriotic sufferings by a parade of your traitorous gotten wealth." Cives exhibited marked concern that the Tory community would escape justice by resorting to family and friends, religious ties, or the monetary influence of the business community. For the Loyalist in search of hopeful signs in the summer of 1783, there were few comforting voices of moderation in the American Whig press.[15]

The Loyalist press greeted the ongoing series of defeats in 1782 and 1783 with artful flexibility. After news of the English concession on independence in August 1782, but before the preliminary articles of the treaty in March 1783, the Loyalists directed their propaganda toward the British, demonstrating anger and resolution that independence would not become a reality. They asked that the King give them a chance to win the war; they predicted that other British colonies in the Western hemisphere would fall, one after another, to an independent America.[16]

This bellicose talk largely stopped when news of the provisional treaty, with its infamous fifth clause, shocked the Loyalist community into the realization that England was cutting the colonies adrift, leaving its American subjects to their own devices. Loyalist writers then turned their full attention to the American scene where angry demands for retribution against those behind British lines were flying fast and thick; they started to respond to the likes of Brutus and Cives, but their target audience was not the radical reformers but the "sober minds" of moderate Whigs.

The dialogue piece was the weapon of choice for Loyalist publicists. In one such piece, a country justice and a committeeman met on the road one day. The committeeman was elated that "all those vermin called Tories" would soon vacate the thirteen states. The country justice, a Whig himself and clearly the voice of reason in this story, patiently explained to his riled neighbor that a distinction should be made between criminals like robbers, horse thieves, and murderers, and upright types "who acted from principle only and in all respects agreeable to the rules of war and honour." The country justice went on to point out that indiscriminately banishing all Tories would mean millions lost to the American states. He chastised local committees for spreading "anarchy and confusion," and at the same time, exposed the money-grubbing motives of those who pressed for total Loyalist expulsion. He labeled the present political structure as a monster of nature because it was a body with many heads. This barrage of reasoned argument made an impression on the now-sobered committeeman who vowed in future to treat the good Loyalists "with more gentleness and mildness." The enlightened committeeman had learned his lesson well. "Why should I quarrel with them for not thinking as I have done," reasoned the converted moderate, "any more than for not looking just as I do, and wearing the same coloured cloth as I do; the God of nature has not permitted us to think alike, no more than to look alike, and shall we hate the handy work of our Creator?" The country justice smiled with approval.[17]

The same themes were played out in various dialogues whether between a committeeman and a country justice, a moderate Loyalist and his firebrand Whig nephew, or a woman within the British lines and a man outside them. In each case, the authors tried to vilify the radical element as motivated more "by the private emoluments arising from their offices, than by any desire to contribute to the public weal." In isolating the radicals, the Loyalists tried to make common cause with that portion of the Whig community that hungered for peace and a return to blessed routine.[18]

The newspapers that had periodically reported with relish the demise of the peripatetic Benjamin Franklin now featured favorable histories about the great man. A similar makeover of George Washington appeared in the Loyalist press. Once "the murderer of André," Washington had become the embodiment of virtue. Now if a report hailed from a neighboring Whig community, it was no longer labeled as from "the rebel press." As one returning Whig saw it, "Even the greatest Tories talk now as Whiggish as myself to my amazement—they all cry on—'Now Doctor, you will soon lie in your own city—the rascals will soon be gone.'"[19] One such flexible character, Cadwallader Colden, Jr., a civilian official under the British, wrote to New York Governor George Clinton that although they had differed on the political front, they were each men of pure heart. "There are other sentiments more essential to society," claimed Colden, than mere political differences, namely their "long and intimate acquaintance." Having established this verity, Colden felt free to inform the Governor of New York of his apprehension that "numbers of Useful honest men" were being driven out of America "throo fear of a Mob or Rable." Colden claimed that these honest and honorable victims would "be better and more faithful subjects to the States than thousands you now have among you."[20]

As the Loyalists worked to create common ground with those Whigs of similar temperament, education, and wealth, the radical Whigs played right into their hands by proudly distinguishing themselves from luke-warm allies. There were meetings for "Real Whigs," complaints against "white-washed whigs," and "buttermilk whigs." This name calling inten-sified after the evacuation, when the radicals witnessed the inevitable: the rapprochement of citizens who had more in common on the social and cultural plane than they had differences in the political arena.[21]

But in the spring and summer of 1783, this rapprochement was far from inevitable in people's minds. Henry Addison, a refugee from Mary-land, wrote about the confusion reigning in the city. At one moment, it seemed that the rebels would be moderate; at the next, they talked nothing but confiscation and banishment. "Yet after all," a weary Addison wrote, "I know not which way to set my face." William Smith also recorded the wildly varying temperatures of the exiled Manhattanites. On April 19, 1783, he wrote, "There appears to be a general desire to construe the Peace as perfectly completed, so anxious are the people for a return to the Employ-ments of a state of tranquility." The next day, Smith recorded, "The confi-dence of those who come in fills the Loyalists with inexpressible Anxiety." From confidence to fear and back again, the Loyalists tried to read the hearts of their victorious neighbors.[22]

Smith's mention of "those who come in" referred to the increasing stream of exiled New Yorkers who entered the city after the Preliminary Articles became common knowledge. The Commandant of New York, Sir Guy Carleton, set up a commission to oversee the transfer of property, in-viting out-of-towners to lodge claims at this new office. When the weather broke in the spring, exiled New Yorkers by the hundreds staged their own invasion of the city. In early April, the British tried to regulate the flow with an order that, as usual, few people heeded. The eager curiosity of people who had been separated from their homes for seven years clearly over-whelmed the trivial technicality of a passport. The volume moving back and forth concerned American officials. From New Jersey, Elias Boudinot noticed that the worst offenders were of the better sort. "I heartily wish," he wrote in April 1783, "that General Carleton would send all the Gentry who are flocking into the City, to the Provost [prison] as they have no business to put themselves in the Power of the Enemy." From Philadelphia came word that "great numbers in this town are forming plans to go into New York on speculation." From New York, John Morin Scott wrote to Gover-nor Clinton that the "unwarrantable Liberty" of crossing enemy lines had to stop. Although a "friendly Intercourse with the disaffected there" could produce "an Assimilation that may eventually prove beneficial to the Liberties of this State," Morin Scott thought it improper for New York's citizens to make so free with the enemy when no definitive peace treaty had as yet arrived.[23]

On the American side, the prohibition on movement into the city was still in force. William Smith noted the efficacy of government attempts to control the movement of the population. "The people have flocked hither from the country since the proclaiming of the Cessation of Arms," he wrote, "without any regard to the authority assumed on the other side of the lines. There are now upwards of 2,000 in town." Up the Hudson, Margaret Livingston noted that a ban on movement to the city did not prevent people from crowding into sloops, "fighting for their passage," a movement Mrs. Livingston characterized as "quite the rage." Mrs. Shoemaker noted the "perpetual motion" in town. "We see strange faces every hour almost in this place," she wrote in May 1783, "and it is incredible what numbers come up and go down every day from Elizabethtown [New Jersey]." A Hessian soldier ventured into town to buy clothing in anticipation of his departure and found that prices had shot up because the "country people since the peace was known came in crowds," thus fulfilling Rhinelander's predictions of pentup demand. The Maryland refugee, Henry Addison, wrote in the same month, "Our streets here are crowded with rebel officers (I ask their pardon, they are no longer so) in their uniforms which you may suppose is not a little mortifying to us" and all the more so because "they do not always behave with propriety." Addison reported that his son in the Loyalist Provincial corps had to bear insults from American soldiers while drinking at a tavern.[24]

Tensions in town rose as large numbers of Whig refugees met Loyalist refugees for the first time in several years. The returning Americans demanded seven years' back rent, payments for missing furniture, money for repairs on their property, and payment of longstanding debts. Abraham Bancker, a New York resident through the war, wrote to his Whig cousin that he should come to town to secure his father's property. "You may enter without obstruction," claimed Bancker, "provided you'll observe a little Regulations which have been established by Sir Guy Carleton for preventing that Scene of Confusion which would necessarily arise among People of different Sentiments and fired with bitter resentment towards each other." One of the Whig refugees of the Beekman family, in town to inspect his family's property, wrote about soldier Loyalists who were wildly resentful that certain civilian Loyalists had acquired immense fortunes. He predicted that "there will be a dreadful Squabble among 'em before they go off."[25]

In the midst of this tense atmosphere, friendly reunions also occurred. On the streets of New York, Philip Van Rensselaer ran into an old friend in the person of a British captain for whom Van Rensselaer acquired a pass to Albany so his old chum could visit with friends before he sailed. William Livingston, the ever-vigilant Governor of New Jersey, sent a state legislator into New York in June on an errand to buy some port wine. The Governor asked his Loyalist brother, John Livingston, to check the quality of the wine before Livingston's emissary purchased it. He explained to his sibling that his "republican pride" prevented him from going to New York himself to see his "friends . . . at the expense of being beholden to the English for such a permission." Livingston then articulated what so many people felt with respect to relatives and friends behind British lines. He made a distinction between *his* loved ones and the rest of the population that chose to live under the British during the war. "I would give you an invitation to come here," wrote Livingston to his brother, "but our people still continue so enraged against the Loyalists, that although you do not come under that description of those against whom their resentment is levelled, yet they do not always clearly distinguish."[26]

Indeed, why should the citizens of New Jersey distinguish John Livingston from the rest of the loyalist community? Unlike their Governor, they did not have a half-century relationship with him and so had no opportunity to build a store of trust and affection. Yet many of William Livingston's constituents had relatives behind the lines whom they too distanced in their minds from the despised Loyalist collaborators.

This phenomenon might explain why some Loyalists were more optimistic in the last months of occupation than were others. One citizen might see the glass half empty: "The town now swarms with Americans whose insolence is scarce to be borne. Many of the Yorkers are [meanly?] cringing and currying favor."[27]

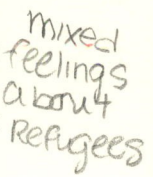

mixed feelings about Refugees

Another resident saw the glass half full: "Our old inhabitants are beginning to come in and mix with us again; and I think matters will terminate here much better than many people were led to believe. Those that have come to town seem well pleased and wish for a speedy reconciliation with their old friends."[28]

If Loyalist refugees hailed from outside the New York region, the likelihood that they would receive an encouraging visit from family and friends would be slim. In the absence of such comfort, the only reading a Virginian or a New Englander could glean from the American side was the vengeful rhetoric of a wounded people. Henry Addison was one such refugee. In July, he reported that "all here is gloom and suspense and consequently irresolution which way to turn ourselves." He read the resolves against the Loyalists' return "which would shock the humanity of a savage," and concluded that "there can be no Peace here for half a century to come."[29]

Henry Addison was not alone in his belief that rancor and strife would continue after the British evacuation. Thousands prepared to leave the city for England, Canada, or the Bahamas. These people had to consolidate their belongings, collect debts, sell off what they could not take with them. Every day, incoming Whigs could attend auctions for items as varied as Chippendale sidechairs, horses, and books. Mrs. Shoemaker bought up some landscape paintings on the cheap and offered to buy her son, William, some of Joseph Galloway's old law books. Given that the evacuation was imminent, New York was definitely a buyer's market. Americans looking for a more advantageously situated store, home upgrade, or investment rental property could purchase Loyalist estates for as low as one-twentieth of their value. One enterprising New Yorker who had just purchased a store noted that he need not have shopped as sellers came to him offering their houses and lots. His only apprehension was whether he would lose money later on if the property were attainted.[30]

Departing Loyalists also had to make decisions about their human property. Sale ads began to appear in newspapers specifying that a slave was sold "through no fault of his/her own" but rather because the owner was bound for Europe. In the last year of occupation, the number of male slaves sold through Rivington's *Royal Gazette* exceeded the total number of all the previous years of British rule. With respect to women, the last year of occupation accounted for 30 percent of the ads for female slaves from 1777 to 1783. The possibility of being sold sparked considerable anxiety for those who had faithfully served masters. Slaves who had anticipated working the rest of their lives for a certain family suddenly found themselves subject to the auction block. This anxiety translated into a greater number of blacks fleeing New York City. Half of the male and female runaways during the occupation occurred in 1782 and 1783. Whether canceling their day on the block or avoiding a voyage that would distance them from all that was familiar, the enslaved community chose the age-old risk of running away.[31]

The mental anguish for those who were shunted about was vibrantly

[handwritten margin note: Thousands of Loyalists leave America]

[handwritten margin note: British slavery at war's end]

captured by the Hessian noblewoman Baroness Van Riedesal, whose "faith-ful negroes" were claimed at the last minute by a man who had turned from rebel to Loyalist. Arriving at the dock with a legal paper ordering the re-turn of his slaves, he demanded that the Hessians turn them over to him. One of the three slaves fainted. When she came to, "she threw herself at my feet," related her mistress, "and embraced them with clasped hands so strongly, that they were obliged to tear her away by force." The departing couple offered to buy the slaves, but the owner named too high a price. The young slave who had fainted, named Phillis, now frantic with despair, ran from passenger to passenger, entreating them to take her on board. "None of these persons were confident in the matter," recollected the Baroness. Later, she "repented" that she did not pay off the slave's old master, not because the woman's screams haunted her dreams, but because "the female domestics in Canada were too simple and too clumsy."[32]

The still-enslaved population was not the only portion of the Afri-can American community to experience high drama in the war's waning days. The city's free black population had to decide on its next move, a sub-ject of intense interest to their former masters in the periphery. John and Hanover "went off" on December 23, 1776, as noted in a Beekman family diary. Abraham and William Beekman received reports about their former slaves from their contact in the city who, in March 1783, spotted them in the streets. He labeled them "ungrateful chaps," but added, "I think they are sorry for what's past as they speak always very submissively to me." Two weeks later, John and Hanover let their former masters know that they wanted to see and talk to the Beekmans in town, probably to read their faces in an effort to gauge their responses. Hanover apparently liked what he saw because by July he was back with the Beekmans, while John still had not decided where to go. After a search for John's residence, an acquain-tance of the family's city contact found him and another family slave, Mary. The Beekmans received the comforting news that neither was in danger of going away. But still, John needed assurances. He asked that Hanover come to town to talk with him before he made any definitive answer.[33]

Cornelia Walton had a vested interest in a family of slaves who had served her before the war and then stayed in New York City to work for Cornelia's Loyalist nephews. The terms of Mrs. Walton's husband's will stipulated that each of Mando Ashton's daughters was to receive fourteen pounds per annum until the death of Mrs. Walton, when they would be freed. Not wishing to wait for that eventuality, Mando informed her mis-tress in August that she and her children intended to leave for Jamaica.

Mando Ashton's decision sparked an unpleasant exchange of letters between Cornelia Walton and her Loyalist nephew, William, about the annuity payments due Mando's children. As the executor of his uncle's will, William Walton had been living in New York City during the war with full control over his aunt's estate. Mando claimed one figure while William claimed a much lower one. When questioned about the money by Mrs. Walton, Mando and her daughter, Ann, could not recollect exactly what they had received in the last seven years, a memory loss that exasperated Cornelia Walton. By September, the greatly agitated Cornelia expressed her desire "to gett rid of that unprofitable and troublesome family" at a time when she began "to entertain some doubt of their going off." Whether her daughters decided to leave or no, Amanda Ashton stayed, whether out of affection for the old lady or a belief that Cornelia Walton's days were numbered. The "mulatto wench" received sixty pounds when her mistress finally died in 1786.[34]

Evert Byvanck, the master of Sam, Cato, and Prince, also busied himself with retrieving lost human property. He knew that any effort to reclaim the man who ran away in 1777 would be fruitless. But Byvanck owned another slave behind British lines who was there, according to Byvanck, against his will. This man, Tom, had been captured by a party of Loyalist refugees in Connecticut who had sold him to a gentleman behind the lines. The Loyalist raiders considered the black man as booty. Tom, as a slave of a rebel master, was not entitled to the benefits of Clinton's 1779 proclamation, freeing those who fled rebel masters, because he did not come in of his own free will.[35]

While Byvanck resorted to British authorities, other slavemasters tried to spirit out their human property by deceit and force. Jacob Duyree of Poughkeepsie had left his slave, Frank, in New York City to look after the Duyree townhouse in 1776. During the British occupation, Frank Griffin married a free black woman. By the war's end, Griffin put out feelers to his master that he might return to Duyree (under what conditions is unclear). The elated master promised that he would hire Frank's wife for wages and give the couple the option of staying in New York City or living in the country. The British would give Duyree a permit to remove Frank Griffin only if Griffin himself came to the Office of Police to request the permit. Not sure about his final decision, Griffin told Mayor Mathews of New York City that he wanted permits to leave and return. Griffin departed with his old master and then came back to town having decided that he wanted no further relationship with Duyree. The frustrated master had had enough of coddling a slave and toadying up to British authorities. Enlisting a cart driver and a sailor, Duyree put a rope around Griffin's neck and made off in a sloop. Luckily for Griffin, another black man saw the abduction and ran to a city inspector. This witness, another black man, and the city inspector jumped into a boat and went off in hot pursuit. They overtook Duyree, delaying him long enough for a boat with eight Hessian soldiers to arrive. Duyree and his accomplices faced a court martial at which the chief defendant argued that "Frank" had put himself back into slavery by returning upriver with his master. Not so, proclaimed the British judge. Duyree was forced to pay a fifty-guinea fine to go toward the relief "of the Poor and sick Negroes" to be expelled from the King's lines.[36]

Many a freed black man like Frank Griffin reached no accommodation with their masters. It has been estimated that three thousand blacks joined the British evacuating New York. The British commandant's office printed special forms certifying that the bearer "being a free negro, has the commandant's Permission to pass from this Garrison to whatever place he/she may think proper." One Whig newcomer to New York City in 1783 noted that no Negro was forced to go anywhere, although he observed that blacks from Virginia formed a conspicuous group in their unanimous intention to depart on British ships. This wish to be gone from American dominions probably reflected the more stringent conditions of enslavement in the South as well as the inability of distant masters to cajole and make promises to their former slaves.[37]

The subject of departing blacks caused consternation and outrage on the American side. "They are extremely out of temper about their negroes," a Loyalist wrote in 1783, "and accuse Sir Guy Carleton of a Breach of Treaty on that Head." The two commanding Generals, George Washington and Guy Carleton, had discussed the matter face to face at a meeting in May at Orangetown. According to a Loyalist witness, Washington opened the meeting with three points, "delivering himself without animation, with great slowness and a low tone of voice." The first item on Washington's agenda was the "preservation of property and especially the Negroes." Carleton responded that the British had been keeping a registry of departing blacks so that owners could be paid. "Here Washington affected to be startled—'Already embarked!' says he." Washington had a point. The Provisional articles stipulated that the British would leave the United States "without causing any destruction or carrying away any negroes." Countering that one could read a document in many ways, Carleton observed "that no interpretation could be put upon the articles inconsistent with prior engagements binding the National Honor which," insisted the officer-gentleman, "must be kept with all Colours." According to the Loyalist witness, this rejoinder about honor effectively silenced the American Commander-in-Chief. Washington moved onto the next item.[38]

Carleton kept the British promise to the blacks freed by British proclamations. Three of Washington's representatives suffered the humiliation of helplessly watching as thousands of blacks registered to leave American shores. The issue of slave departures and compensation would cause rancor between the United States and Britain for years to come.[39]

In the last year of the war, the business community readied itself to resume normal operations. In February 1783, Frederick Rhinelander wrote to one of his British contacts that with the prospect of peace, the English should get ready to send "a very large and general assortment of Earthenware." Rhinelander anticipated a general boom due to pentup demand. The Loyalist merchant demonstrated no sense of impending doom in his correspondence, only unbounded optimism about market opportunity.[40]

The English merchants, too, jumped on the peace wave to send greetings to their old American friends. James Beekman received at least four letters from merchant houses in London and Bristol in the summer of 1783 in which the British lauded the removal of every obstacle to their lucrative exchange and reminded the Americans that they, too, suffered during the war in paying interest on their American friends' debt for seven years. Anxious to collect these debts, some English houses lost no time in sending representatives to American shores in order to collect. This struck American sensibilities as undue haste. But except for a few misunderstandings and startup complications, the trans atlantic business community lost no time in reestablishing the unimpeded flow of goods and credit between Britain and America. "The most distinguishing feature of the present times," claimed a New York newspaper in September 1783, "is an ardent spirit of commerce."[41]

While some in the business community joyfully anticipated the return of fat times, others faced the dismal prospect of selling off what they could before departing American shores. Alexander Hamilton, a man weaned on commerce in the Caribbean, mentioned the plight of these unfortunates on his visit to British-occupied New York City in August 1783. Hamilton, a former Continental army officer and aide to Washington, deplored the effect of "violent papers sent into the city." People were leaving, the very people whom Hamilton wanted to stay: "Many merchants of second class, characters of no political consequence, each of whom may carry away

8 or 10,000 guineas have I am told lately applied for shipping to convey them away."[42]

Indeed, the exodus had started before Hamilton's visit to New York as thousands of Loyalist Americans poured onto British ships when the ice broke in the spring of 1783. By May, General Carleton reported to Washington that 6,000 had already been evacuated. In June, 3,000 more shipped out; and in August, 8,000 Americans including many men from the provincial regiments stood on the decks of their ships and watched New York disappear from view. In November, the remainder sailed out with Sir Guy Carleton and the last soldiers.[43]

Why did these people leave? Some were simply too notorious to stay. Abraham Van Buskirk, a prosperous Bergen County doctor, formed a Loyalist regiment early in the war. He burned too many barns and Presbyterian churches in his old neighborhood and was one of Arnold's high-ranking officers in the brutal raids on the Connecticut coast. William Smith, the well-known New York politician who could not stomach American independence, collaborated on a high level while a refugee in New York City. He considered himself a voice of moderation in the councils of the powerful and held himself aloof from the more bitter element of the refugee community whom he labeled as "the Loyalists." But in the eyes of the returning Americans, there was no difference between Smith and the most treacherous Loyalist. Once a high-level Whig politician, Smith turned coat and was ever at the side of former Governor William Tryon and the British military commander, Sir Guy Carleton. Still, Smith thought he had a chance to stay, and requested asylum in Connecticut. Although assured by some supporters that he might settle in New Haven, the Connecticut legislature rejected his request.[44]

There were less infamous Tories in the Whig account books, some of whom chose to leave town just the same. Martin Lawler was a truckman from Philadelphia; Francis Staple was a cartman in New York; Mary Airy was a widow who sold provisions in the city. The poorer emigrants were probably lured by British promises of land in Nova Scotia and simultaneously frightened by the Whiggish promises of retribution. For those emigrants who came from some distance, there were no family or friends from the other side to mitigate the effects of the angry Whig attacks on traitors.[45]

Some of these emigrants felt they could stay with minimum repercussions but decided to forgo the opportunity. Their experience with the new Republican groups in power had precipitated their initial flight to New

York. They consequently had no hope that the New Order would bring justice, stability, and prosperity to American life. A London newspaper reported that some of the departing New Yorkers "have not been proscribed" yet they left because, reported the newspaper, "they see the storm gathering and that the difficulties of the inhabitants of this western world are not yet over."[46] The *Pennsylvania Packet* wrote of similarly motivated people: "Many of them pretend that it is not fear of treatment after the departure of the army that urges them to leave the country so much as a conviction that the new republics must sink in a short time under their immense national debts and the exorbitant taxes with which they will be loaded."[47]

Both Stephen Skinner and David Colden, Loyalists who eventually left America after the evacuation, shared these gloomy prospects for the fledgling Republic. Skinner wrote in June 1783 that "tottering committees" aping the "giddy multitude" ruled as dictators and will sow "anarchy and confusion . . . for some years to come." "The power," he wrote to a friend in London, "is in the hands of the lowest sort of people, and they will not easily part with it." He saw no light on the horizon "till the reasonable and thinking part of the community step forth, men of character and moderation." David Colden painted a similar picture in a September 1783 letter to his niece. He complained of committees, hell-bent on the destruction of all Loyalists. "We are told that these committees have allarmed the people in power," he wrote, "who wish to suppress them, but know not how." "The people have been taught a dangerous truth," concluded Colden, "that all power is derived from them."[48] Both Skinner and Colden acknowledged the presence of more moderate heads on the scene who at that moment could not control the Revolutionary verve of the lower sort.

So, in their decision to go or stay, Loyalists were helped along by the depressing prospects of finding happiness in America, and by the glowing picture of Nova Scotia described in the city's newspapers. According to the Canada promoters, their prospective abode to the north possessed good soil, excellent water, spacious harbors, and a climate so good "that Fevers and Agues" were unknown. The government was "mild," collecting very few taxes "raised solely for the Benefit of the Island," claimed those who had already arrived. Once better communication was established between Canada and New York, the newspapers worked double-time to counter the less than rosy information about St. John and Nova Scotia that trickled back to town. True, claimed the *Royal Gazette*, the place looked like a vast wilderness, but the essentials were there to build a flourishing society, and as for the weather, it was warmer at St. John than it had been in New York the past summer.[49]

Alongside the promising descriptions of Nova Scotia, the Loyalist press faithfully printed statements from New York localities and beyond that Loyalists were not welcome back. Readers of Rivington's and Gaine's newspapers also read corroborating accounts of Loyalists who tried to return to Whig-controlled areas only to find themselves attacked by angry locals. In early June 1783, the level of violence against the Loyalists in New York State was so elevated that Sir Guy Carleton informed American officials that the evacuation would be delayed to accommodate the additional Loyalists who chose to depart. One such American official in New York City, Gouverneur Morris, then went about town assuring Loyalists that they had "nothing to fear as to life or estate." Here again, the aristocratic old guard leader was not in step with the lower-level political neophytes of the local committees, which led to mixed signals to the city refugees.[50]

Sir Guy Carleton oversaw a logistical nightmare as he arranged for the departure of 20,000 soldiers and at least 30,000 civilians. The vortex of this movement of 50,000 people centered on the minuscule area of Manhattan island's tip, where confusion reigned. Carts were piled high with household goods and furniture. A mother kidnapped her daughter to keep her from going off with her Loyalist husband to Canada. One ambitious emigrant even tried to move a two-story house onto one of the departing ships. "There is no end to auctions and vendues," proclaimed a Pennsylvania newspaper, "everything is selling off." Taverns hosted last-minute meetings of departing citizens as well as last-minute deals between Whigs and Tories. Ever-vigilant businessmen hurried to make the last shilling on this bonanza of the unfortunate. A Connecticut trader, for example, thought he could unload a cargo of trenchers called Hinghamware but found no buyers in New York. The enterprising businessman donned a British uniform and entered the shop of John Peters, a prosperous merchant in town during the war. He claimed the army needed trenchers for the voyage. Peters immediately bolted for the Connecticut ship to snap up all the trenchers he could buy so as to resell them to the British. And, of course, he was stuck with a cargo of trenchers that nobody wanted. "The story was long remembered," recollected one of his neighbors years later, and Peters was regularly asked if he wanted any more Hinghamware. Swindlers also used the confusion at war's end to prey on victims and then flee to the other side of the lines. Other, less sophisticated criminals preyed on neighbors and found themselves taking the place of departing military prisoners in the city's jail. A crime wave swept the city in late summer and continued through the end of the occupation.[51]

Loyalist's ultimate decisions

The average Loyalist New Yorker found himself in late 1783 making life-transforming decisions under immense pressure in a crime-ridden atmosphere. He watched as ebullient Whigs shook the hands of fellow travelers in the streets. He witnessed the return of the cursed Presbyterian congregation that lost no time in repairing its meeting house. He saw British generals talking with arch rebels like Gouverneur Morris and Egbert Benson. Feeling thoroughly betrayed, the average Loyalist swallowed abuse and humiliation in the last months of British tenure.[52] To keep street brawls to a minimum, the British posted sentries on every corner of the city. New York was a thoroughly uneasy place.

This chaotic scene fostered palpable tension in town. The subject of general conversation on the street, according to one resident, was the worried or ecstatic inquiries as to when the British would finally vacate. "The Loyalists have faces as long as my arm," wrote one witness. In late August, this city resident advised a Whig to stay in New Jersey because the tension of imminent departure had exacerbated tensions. "It would be more dangerous for a good Whig to go now to town than two years ago as they are upon the eve of departing," he wrote to his friend. For William Smith, the Loyalist flight was painful "not only to the wiser sort who see the evils of it on general policy, but to private debtors, executors, and Administrators etc. etc. [who] go away to the confusion of all that have settlements to be made with them."[53]

For those who made the decision to go, their last hours in New York were on board British transports. Sarah Frost, bound for Canada, received what she thought was a last-minute visit from her father, only to find that her ship lingered another two weeks to collect a full complement of passengers. "There is great confusion in the cabin," she wrote on June 9, "We cope with it pretty well through the day but as it grows toward night, one child cries in one place and one in another while we are getting them in bed. I think sometimes I shall be crazy." Meanwhile, on a ship bound for England, William Smith experienced a calmer scene as he wrote to his wife who stayed behind. "It is very inconvenient to write in a cabin, where five pens are scribbling around the table, and persons of business at every chair."[54]

Both Mrs. Frost and Mr. Smith had an admirable perch in the harbor from which to watch the fireworks in town. As the beaten Loyalists boarded British warships, the remainder of the elated Whig community streamed into the city. "New Yorkers [were] shaking hands with one another as joyfully as if they were arrived from the Dead," wrote a city resident to a friend about to return. A committee of army officers and civilians met at Cape's Tavern to plan festivities for the auspicious day. Aside from appointing a committee to meet the next night at another tavern, the men did nothing but underscore that any person who chose to live behind British lines was not welcome to participate in this exercise. The very first order of business, in fact, was the request that anyone "whatever his political character may be," who had remained in the city during the late contest, should leave the room forthwith. The victors wanted no characters of questionable credentials to sully their day of triumph.[55]

On the morning of November 25, American troops marched from Harlem in upper Manhattan to Bowery Lane, on the outskirts of the city. On their march toward town, the troops might have smiled at the additional six stars in a field of thirteen stripes recently painted onto the sign of the Seven Stars' Tavern. At 1 P.M., the British evacuated their Bowery posts and marched for the city docks. Once American troops under General Henry Knox secured the city, the parade commenced. The military commander, General George Washington, and the chief executive of civilian government, George Clinton, rode side by side, neither man taking primacy of place. The support organizations of the two men could not ride side by side, and so the civilian branch came first. Clinton's chief advisors were followed by Washington's officers, eight abreast. Bringing up the rear were citizens on horseback, followed by the Speaker of the Assembly and citizens on foot. Noticeably missing in the parade accounts were representatives of the rank and file of the army. A contingent of privates and noncommissioned officers might have formed a part of the body of Westchester Light Horse escorting Clinton and Washington, or they might have mixed in the crowd as proud citizens, but the low-ranked were not highlighted as featured players in the newspaper or personal accounts.[56] Later that day at Fraunces's tavern, the after-dinner toasts memorialized the army's contribution—the fallen heroes, the "military children," the "vindicators of the rights of mankind." The thirteenth sip of Madeira went down with the wish that "the remembrance of this Day be a lesson to Princes." Less than a week later, another dinner featuring the same participants ended with a round of toasts in which the theme of soldier sacrifice was replaced by wishes for "uninterrupted commerce" and the success of those in trade who had been good Whigs. It took little time for Americans to turn from the past towards the future.[57]

Christian Inger, *Washington's Triumphal Entry into New York, Nov. 25th, 1783*, 1860. This chromolithograph shows that the whole community, young and old, rich and poor, Native Americans and African Americans, turned out for the American reentry after seven years of British occupation. Understandably absent are those people who did not rejoice to see the Americans return. The Library Company of Philadelphia.

The city was jammed with those who wanted to see the spectacle, celebrate the victory, and perhaps gain some perspective on the ordeal they had just experienced. City residents invited friends from out of town to share their homes and watch from their windows. Thousands sported a laurel in their hats and the official union cockades of black and white "ribbands." John Pintard, the Americans' point man in New York for prisoners of war, hired a cartman's large horse for the parade, though it proved skittish around crowds and gunfire. Pintard still managed to follow his friend, James Beekman, Jr., to the cavalcade's conclusion in Queen Street. Benjamin Tallmadge, one of the men so smitten with John André, could not summon up the words to describe the joy of meeting friends from whom he had long been separated "by the cruel rigors of war." Abraham

Delanoy, who lived behind British lines for the duration of the war, called the Americans' entry into the city "the most beautiful sight I ever saw."[58]

Delanoy's eyes were further charmed by a fireworks display one week later, featuring a Chinese fountain, a balloon of serpents, the Moon and Seven Stars, horsemen fighting, an illuminated pyramid, and seven bee-hives interspersed with rockets and tourbillions. The houses on the city's major thoroughfares were packed and "the Street itself was scarcely capable of containing another Spectator." The "prodigeous concourse" roared their wonderment and approval, the sound of which (and the illuminations that inspired it) wafted out into the harbor and onto the Loyalist ships waiting for a good wind.[59]

According to newspaper accounts, the participants of this gala week were one in their joy and gratitude, yet there were citizens on land who were as heartbroken as their former neighbors now en route to Canada. Benjamin Tallmadge acknowledged the presence of a few Tories whose dour countenances could not dampen the ebullient mood of those who had reason to celebrate. There were probably other erstwhile disaffected who stayed home or joined the party with happy faces in the hope that their participation would begin the process of their reintegration into the newly constituted New York society. Washington certainly hoped that New York would act with moderation and prudence toward all its citizens. During the Evacuation Week festivities, he received a letter from arch-Loyalist Andrew Elliot on board a ship in the harbor, asking Washington to look after his daughter, Mrs. Eleanor Jauncey. Washington complied with Elliot's request, waiting on the lady and promising to render her any service. With his chivalric duty done, Washington reported back to Elliot. "I am confident Sir," wrote the Commander-in-Chief, "it must give you great satisfaction to be informed that the most perfect regularity and good Order prevail in this city, and that every description of People find themselves under the protection of the Laws of the State." But if the General paid a social call on a Tory lady and comforted a notorious Loyalist leader, other victorious Americans did not share Washington's generous mood.[60]

Once the festivities had ended, the freshly returned refugees looked around and saw more than a few Loyalists who continued to walk the streets of New York City. For some members of the Whig community, this was too much to bear. Just as the Evacuation Day organizers expelled any person who had lived with the British during the war, an element of the returning Whigs called for the total expulsion of all those, no matter what their motivation, who had chosen to live behind enemy lines. And this contingent of returning New Yorkers was powerful enough to dominate the city's newspapers in the first months of American rule.

The enraged New York Whigs first tried threats. They addressed themselves expressly to the Tory community, promising violence if the Tories did not make haste to leave. In the December 13, 1783, edition of *The Independent New York Gazette*, they left a calling card with "Messieurs TORIES," reminding them that the calm after the storm could be succeeded by "a bitter and *neck-breaking* hurricane" if they did not decamp. A month later, they noted the presence of businessmen who lost not a day's profit whether under British rule or American rule. All "good whigs," they claimed, found this fact to be "very obnoxious."[61]

One such objectionable character, William Walton (Cornelia Walton's errant nephew), had made himself doubly obnoxious to all good Whigs by his high-profile collaboration with the British and his very public profile in the post-Revolutionary city. In the spring of 1784, a piece appeared in the newspaper addressed to "William Walton Esq: Late Magistrate of Police." Angered by Walton's baldfaced shamelessness in staying behind and "wriggling" himself into a public office, the author, "A Republican," warned him not to put too much faith in the handful of Whigs who supported his presence in town. The Republican assured Walton that the former Loyalist's connections would one day "no longer stem the tide of popular indignation" and would indeed join in "the sacrifice" of Walton with as much relish as they now snapped up the estates of attainted individuals. The author represented himself as "the voice of the people, which, though at present may . . . only be heard in *whispers*, will if not attended to, sound in your astonished ears in all the majesty of thunder." Walton budged not an inch.[62]

Other city residents, nervous from all this talk about expulsion, busied themselves procuring testimonies from former American prisoners or government officials noting their services to the cause while behind the lines. Three widows in town had former prisoners sign a formal statement testifying to their ministrations to prisoners during the war. Hugh Gaine and James Rivington, both Tory publishers of the city's Loyalist newspapers, had managed during the war to pass enough information to the Americans to enable them to stay in town. By February 1784, Hugh Gaine advertized his business in the Whig papers. By 1786, he was "a respectable freeholder" in New York. Rivington had a harder time of it. He was the target of threats and was once kicked in the streets by a man who claimed that Rivington was responsible for his incarceration. The radicals also laid at his shop door the baneful influence of the market economy on the virtuous nation. Rivington was a purveyor of useless expensive fripperies, they claimed, and was himself "a greater curiosity than . . . all the Bijouterie in his shop." Although forced to give up their newspapers, both men lived on in the Whig city, conducting business there until their deaths. Another Loyalist resident, Dr. Richard Bayley, found himself accused of cruelty to American prisoners in his care during the war. Bayley published statements of prisoners and American officials testifying to his good work with the wounded. With such evidence on the record, Dr. Bayley and his ten-year-old daughter, Elizabeth (who would later become the first native-born American saint canonized in the Catholic Church), never felt obliged to leave the city.[63]

The radicals' early tack was to call for the expulsion of all Tories, which meant all those who chose to live behind British lines. The Tories were "the authors of war"; they kindled it and without them there would have been no war, claimed the victorious propagandists of early 1784. Their departure would not spark an economic crisis, claimed the radicals. In fact, their money could subvert the Revolution by insuring their control of "public affairs." The Loyalists' continued presence in town could mean only mischief and violence and would discourage any recruits in future crises. With no consequences for actions, they reasoned, why would anyone sacrifice?[64]

[handwritten marginal note: Tories Remain in town]

While the radicals thundered, another part of the newly returned American community criticized their arguments while finding reasons to become reacquainted with their erstwhile enemies. Their voices did not find space in the newspapers of early 1784 but rather in private letters. Robert R. Livingston predicted disaster because these mouthy advocates of change insisted on retaining their place at center stage. "We have many people who wish to govern this city," he wrote to his conservative friend, Robert Morris, "and who have acquired influence in turbulent times which they are unwilling to lose in more tranquil seasons." By January 1784, Livingston feared that the Loyalists were becoming too impudent thus giving "a handle to the warm Whigs to attack them." Still, he believed that with a little training and cross-breeding, the Loyalists would be rendered "useful animals in a few generations." Alexander Hamilton agreed with his friend, Gouverneur Morris, that New York was a scene of "strange doings." An exasperated Hamilton wrote, "if some folks were paid to counteract the prosperity of the state, they could not take more effectual measures than they do."[65]

Ironically, it is the protest of these new men on the public scene which provides the best evidence of the quiet process of reconciliation taking place in New York. In the week after the evacuation, they railed against the formation of a dancing assembly. Such high-toned activity attracted the better sort of gay disposition, whether Whigs or Tories. Tingling with resentment, the poorer Whigs attempted to unveil this invidious combination for the public. "We are astonished . . . that a coalition is now forming in this city, between certain Whigs and some of the most atrocious and obnoxious Tories for the purpose of promoting a dancing assembly," cried the radicals. "Can it be possible that any men who call themselves Whigs, can be so lost to every degree of sensibility or so inconsiderate as to engage in a measure so cruel in its nature, and which is pregnant with such dangerous consequences?" they asked. Threatening anarchy, confusion, and more blood, the outraged essayist concluded, "Do they imagine we are so pigeon-livered as to look tamely on, while we behold these miscreants, insulting our feelings and wantonly dancing on the graves of our brave officers and fellow citizens, who have fallen victims to the machinations of these new friends of theirs." The essayist recognized the disheartening gap between poorer Whigs and wealthier Tories. He knew what that gap meant in terms of power and influence, especially since the radicals' natural allies, the wealthy Whigs, were engaged in the intricacies of the minuet with former Tories.[66]

With no war to complicate matters, like-minded, similarly educated, finely clothed people sought out their own kind with a vengeance. Such prompt reconciliation, hardly surprising given the degree of civility during the war, rubbed salt into the wounds of those who thought a New World would result from the Revolutionary crusade. The critics of the dancing assembly added to their list of insidious influences the sociable Whigs who did not discriminate at the tea table. "One of the People" wrote to *The New York Journal* that "some characters . . . adopt the language and sentiments of the British ministry." Another essayist, who styled himself "Discriminator," claimed that "these vindictive reptiles" [the Loyalists] and their "hireling tools" would try in vain to effect a permanent reconciliation.[67] Three months later, in March 1784, a "True Friend" to the happiness and prosperity of the state leveled his fire not at the Tory vipers, but at the men who supported them. He labeled these weak Whigs as "infatuated . . . or blinded by self interest." He warned his former Whig allies that the people would never become so "pusillanimous" as to "suffer paricides and miscreants, the adherents and blood-hounds of British tyranny to partake or share in the government of this state."[68]

On the same day that this radical voice threatened another revolution if Loyalists came to claim power in the new order, the *New York Packet* announced the new Directors of the Bank of New York. Three Loyalist names numbered among the management of this new and powerful institution, under the leadership of Alexander McDougall, one of the most radical leaders of 1776.[69]

McDougall's association with former Loyalists brought up another troubling issue for the radicals — the possibility that the new men in the power structure were not as committed to substantive change as were the radical forces in post-evacuation New York. As each month went by with no legislative action on "the bloodhounds of Toryism," the radicals began to question the motives of the Patriot government itself. "I hope I may never have to add the impolicy or ingratitude of government, among the dangers which the Whig spirit has to oppose," proclaimed a vigilant Whig. The radicals saw conspiracies everywhere, and in the process of fighting these dangers were painting themselves into a corner.[70]

The government now under suspicion by an element of the radical community saw an influx of new men who would never have had the opportunity to play power politics before the war. This block of political novices sat with the old seasoned families of New York State politics — Livingston, Morris, Van Cortlandt.[71] Although a new constellation of men ruled the state, this did not mean that radical changes flowed from the legislative chambers in New York City. The legislature trod with moderate step when it came to the city's Loyalist population. Lewis Morris, an old-style Senator, wrote in February 1784 that an Alien Bill had come up for debate and after some limited discussion was dismissed. Responding to the hue and cry about Loyalist auctioneers continuing their businesses, the legislature passed a law in February 1784 regulating public auctions. Although requiring licenses to be procured through the Mayor, a city recorder, or a judge, the law made no point of singling out the former political persuasion of the auctioneer. With respect to forfeited-land sales, the legislature released more lands already vested in the state for sale. New Yorkers had the satisfaction of seeing major real estate, formerly owned by prominent Loyalist families, sold to new owners.[72]

In conformance with the Treaty of Paris, these sales included only those estates that had been attainted before November 30, 1782. While releasing lands for sale, the legislature buried in articles 33 and 34 of the May 1784 act provisions to allow certain prominent Loyalists to buy back their city real estate. The sons of John Watts, Sr., a very wealthy Loyalist resident of London, were permitted to regain their father's city residence and outlying farm. Neither of Watts's sons was a Whig during the war; both chose to live under British rule for seven years. Yet these men could buy back their patrimony for a price assessed by appraisers partially chosen by the Watts brothers themselves. Robert wrote to his father in July that the family once again possessed Rose Hill, the country estate, as well as the town lot. "It seems hard to pay for our own," Robert wrote, but he was very pleased with the terms of the sale. The New York State authorities gave no reason in the law for such forbearance, but it could relate to Robert Watts's family connections; he was married to a Continental army General's daughter.[73]

In the busy month of May 1784, the New York State legislature also passed a law for the sole purpose of helping a former Loyalist resolve his family's debt problems. As Elizabeth Bend was infirm and incapable of transacting business, she assigned her estate to her kinsman, Grove Bend, who in turn discharged all the estate to its creditors. Grove Bend, a New York city merchant, had lived in New York under British rule. His signature even graced an Address of Loyalty to the Howe Brothers, yet he benefited from the help of the New York State legislature to lead his family out of a thicket of debt.[74]

While the legislature aided selected former residents of occupied New York, it also passed a law in May 1784 that clipped the wings of others who had opted to live in British New York. In "An Act to Preserve the Freedom and Independence of this State, and for other Purposes therein Mentioned," the New York Assembly denied voting privileges and any prospect of holding public office to those who served in a pro-British military unit or privateer as well as to any person who resided behind enemy lines after July 9, 1776. In the same law, the legislature welcomed twenty-seven attainted men back into the community. Despite this leniency, many in the community took great pleasure in this act, noting that the Tories finally got what they had always wanted—taxation without representation. Six months after this punitive anti-Tory law, only one year after Evacuation Day, the New York legislature mandated that any case against indicted persons that had not already resulted in conviction should be dropped. The new constellation of men in the assembly did not even approach the radicals' vision of a Loyalist-free state.[75]

No expulsion, no seven-year banishment, no proscription against Tory businesses: the legislature had taken a moderate line with respect to old enemies, and even began to chip away at the restrictions and punishments that wartime conditions had imposed. The men in power now sent a strong message to the community that stability, continuity, and prosperity were its priorities. Digging up incidents from "the late unhappy commotions" served no one.[76]

Such postwar legislation did not reflect maverick behavior on the part of politicians, who in all likelihood represented the views of their constituencies. As a statewide body, the legislature included representatives from areas that had suffered less in the war than had New York City or the frontier. Even in delegations from the most war-ravaged part of the state, however, there were moderate voices whose opinions prevailed in the law. Most people who lived through the war were exhausted, and many of them craved ordinary, conventional, everyday happiness in a peaceful and prosperous land. Richard Varick, a soldier in the Continental army for seven years, looked forward to "the happy return of the American Golden Age when every man may set under his own Vine and Fig tree enjoying the Fruits of his Labor where and when no one will distract his repose." Like Varick, many New York–area residents had maintained connections on the other side of the lines during the war, which no doubt contributed to the victory of moderate voices. Housewives, businessmen, and soldiers had traversed the lines on missions of mercy, profitable deal-making, and paroles of honor, in each case forging a link with people on the other side.[77]

Networks continued to play an important role in the American city of New York. Family and friends kept departed refugees updated on the situation in town, sometimes aiding them in buying back attainted lands or counseling them on their next move. Rebecca Shoemaker wrote to her husband in England about the political landscape of the liberated city in January 1784. "The violent party have carried the day here [New York]," she wrote, "and the motion made in council by the Attorney General for admitting every person to vote at the election without discriminating characters, was overruled." She then surmised that New York "at present must be a very disagreeable place to many." Back in Philadelphia, Mrs. Shoemaker wrote that Whigs and Tories alike were welcome at the French Ambassador's house. "The general temper of the people," she wrote, "must be considerably changed with regard to the Loyalists for here are many who walk daily and publickly about the streets without meeting with any kind of incivility or insult. That could not have been done some months ago," she added.[78]

The scene in New York did not take much more time to coalesce on the Philadelphia model, as described by Mrs. Shoemaker. American Whigs in New York furnished documentary support for many Loyalist claims, including men as illustrious as James Duane, the Mayor of New York, and as lowly as John Paulding, one of André's captors. Duane's signature graced certificates that testified to losses by very prominent Loyalists like the Coldens, Whites, and the Franklins.[79] Family members advised their kin when it might be safe to return. Cadwallader Colden, Jr.'s wife and children were "well received" when they returned to their Orange County estate. Mr. Colden, however, was advised to lie low until the evacuation took place when, according to his brother, David, the Banishment Act would be repealed. Colden's son intended to leave for Nova Scotia when he was suddenly taken ill. Father and son never did leave New York, living peaceably in the new Republic while each received aid from the British government for their wartime losses and services.[80]

On the eve of the British departure, Christopher Miller advised his brother, Thomas, to stay out of town until moderate men could wrest control from the radical element. "Committees must have their swing," he wrote, "and while that power reigns, I don't wish to see any old friend here that has taken a warm part with the British." Christopher was confident that once order was restored, the government would operate on "a liberal manly plan." Like the Coldens, the Millers were certain that the radical element would burn itself out, to be replaced by men of solidly conservative mettle.[81]

While planning his brother's next move, Christopher Miller also aided his sibling in purchasing back Thomas's land investments in Vermont. Contacts in America often helped exiled relatives in this way. Robert Watts not only busied himself retrieving family lands, but he acted as agent for other prominent exiles as well. Elizabeth Galloway, the depressed teenager who fled from Philadelphia to New York in 1778 and later departed for England with her father, started the process of retrieving her family's lands in the last months of the war. The large, loopy handwriting in her postwar letters contrasts dramatically with the neat, minuscule writing of the illegal letters she had smuggled to her mother from New York during the war. By the autumn of 1785, she expressed delight to her agents in Philadelphia about the cooperation of the courts in retrieving certain lands.[82]

Land was not the only form of wealth to flow along family networks. William Crucher of Oyster Bay drew up a will in 1784, leaving part of his money to his daughter, Sarah Valentine. Mrs. Valentine, a widow, saw her property seized by Revolutionary authorities for her loyalty. At the time of her father's death, she was in Nova Scotia. Mr. Crucher left it to his executors to figure out a way to get the bequest to his exiled daughter. To skirt around any potentially sticky legal problems, Crucher gave permission to give the money to Sarah's children if there was no other way to proceed.[83]

While Elizabeth Galloway and Sarah Valentine left the United States even though they were not forced to go, other Loyalists who had more to worry about than either of these women braved the consequences of staying. Evert Bancker, Jr., signed every Loyalist address to British authorities while a resident in occupied New York. His reputation was such that the Loyalist Mayor, David Mathews, appointed him "to pass any of the Guards and examine the boundaries of any Lands [of a rebel] which may happen to be near any of the Works." Mathews placed such trust in Bancker because the latter "had always in the most explicit manner testified his Loyalty." In July 1784, the Whig Mayor of New York, James Duane, appointed the same Evert Bancker, Jr., to a surveyor's post, "being fully persuaded of the integrity and ability of Evert Bancker." Satisfied with a simple oath of abjuration and allegiance, New York's Mayor made formal what was in fact going on in Bancker's business after the evacuation. As evidenced by his survey book, Bancker did not miss a beat in the surveying jobs he performed when power switched hands. His wartime activities cost him nary a farthing, whether because of important family contacts on the Whig side or a change of opinion in his own mind concerning politics.[84]

Frederick Rhinelander signed the same Loyalist addresses as did Evert Bancker, Jr. Rhinelander, a wealthy merchant, made all the moves typical of a departing Tory in the last days of occupation. He had a massive clearance sale, widely advertising special deals on crockery and picture frames. Perhaps anticipating that as a well-known investor in privateers, his stock would be confiscated, Rhinelander hastily converted his wealth into liquid assets to tide him over in whatever storm would follow. After the American return to the city, he found it necessary to lead a quiet life in New Jersey for a while, during which time New York City's government ordered him to remove an old hulk from the city docks. The Common Council knew the vessel was an old privateer but took no further action to punish its owner.[85]

The decision to stay paid off for both Evert Bancker, Jr., and Frederick Rhinelander. Both lay low long enough for the strident voices of the radical element to subside. They had not long to wait. By the spring of 1784, the Sons of Liberty themselves called for making distinctions between those residents of the occupied city who remained by "necessity, accident, or force" and those who were motivated by "a rooted enmity to the principles of freedom."[86] This is a far cry from their former demand for blanket expulsion. This new exercise in plumbing a person's heart to find the truth

left ample room for maneuver. Businessmen could now plead "necessity."
"Accident" could cover a variety of situations.

By spring 1784, fire and brimstone rhetoric largely disappeared from
the press. In May, former Tory Gerard Walton wrote to an exiled confrere
that the political situation in town had taken on "a more pleasing Aspect
then at any time since the change of Masters." Walton exalted in the defeat
of a "Discriminating Law" long pending in the legislature that had been
thrown out. In its stead, Walton reported that the assembly voted to let
return those who had petitioned the legislature to do so. (On this list were
two brothers of Walton's correspondent.) On top of all these promising
developments, Walton related the sweetest of all, "that Sears, Malcolm etc.
etc. who were in the Assembly and were for dealing Damnation through
this city are certainly cast out and a more moderate set elected in his Room."
Indeed, the entire radical New York City delegation in the State Assembly
was voted out, and the likes of Aaron Burr, John Lawrence, and Peter V. B.
Livingston elected in their stead. This shift in power comforted any nervous Tories in New York City, emboldening them to come out in the open
and breathe the free air of the new Republic. It is no wonder that in July
1784, Evert Bancker, Jr., applied for a surveyor post. The Tories realized
within six months of the evacuation that aside from a few financial penalties, the victors of the Revolution would live and let live.[87]

Given the sustained hardship with which the Whig refugee population
lived for over seven years, it is surprising that a return to business as usual
was so swift and relatively painless. Exhaustion no doubt accounted for
some of this complaisance. Many Americans directed what energies they
had to the wider horizons of opportunity provided by the British with-
drawal from American affairs. Unregulated trade to the east and an enormous land mass to the west fired the imaginations of robust entrepreneurs
and hopeful army veterans. With other activities taking first priority, many
American citizens were not prepared to make a major issue of the Loyalist
presence in their midst. They may have felt resentful toward the erstwhile
Tories, but they had other things to do.[88]

The nature of the war itself provides another explanation for the rapid
resolution of the conflict. In an effort to win over the substantial undecided
population in America—especially that of the Lower Hudson Valley—the
British chose to fight a contained war. They held the most violent Loyalist regiments in check while foreswearing an all-out war of terrorism and
destruction.[89]

But if the British pursued a more or less moderate tack with respect to military operations, they committed many blunders in their conduct toward the civilian population on the occupied islands of New York City. They made little sustained effort to cultivate the Loyalists under their control, arbitrarily seizing civilian goods and housing while pushing civilians around with impunity. So arrogant and arbitrary did British behavior seem to some citizens that many disenchanted Loyalists became Whigs. One thoroughly disgusted Loyalist wrote as early as March 1782 that if Washington attacked New York, fully half the people there "would receive him with open arms." Thus, when the American army reclaimed the city, many of its inhabitants were royally sick of His Majesty's troops and ready to join the American Republican experiment.[90]

Moreover, thousands of Loyalists left with the fleet, substantially reducing the number of problems with which Whigs had to deal on their return. The departure of approximately 30,000 Loyalists must have salved the wounds of many a bitter Whig exile, serving as expiation for the hardships borne by the exiled Patriots.[91]

The labors of Alexander Hamilton in the legislature certainly helped to defuse the awkward situation in post-evacuation New York. Hamilton saw nothing to be gained, and much to be lost, in expelling the Loyalists who remained. Why strengthen Canada? he argued. Thus, Hamilton ceaselessly maneuvered to dismantle the punitive legislation against Tories.[92]

Yet Hamilton's machinations in the legislature would have been to no avail had not a large segment of the public already been prepared for reconciliation. The moderates' program passed the legislature because the people of New York were primed for such a rapprochement by their wartime experiences. They had never entirely burned their bridges to the other side. They juggled a complex set of allegiances, of which the political was but one, and not always the most important. As a member of a family, a part of a trading network, or a civilian resentful of the arbitrary impressments of both armies, New Yorkers had lived out the war on many different levels, constantly shuffling priorities to survive in an active military theater. Once the smoke of battle cleared, and the war became characterized by such euphemisms as "the late unpleasantness," New Yorkers were free to recall all of the reasons they had liked one another before the guns had sounded.

When ministers of the city's various congregations preached once again from their pulpits, their message was one of rejoicing, not of retribution. The Presbyterian cleric, Dr. John Rodgers, led the way with a sermon based on Psalms 126:1,2—Yahweh brings Zion's captives home. John H. Livingston, from the North Dutch congregation, chose the verse from

Jeremiah chronicling God's great feat in bringing his chosen people back to the city. Not surprisingly, an Episcopalian cleric, Benjamin Moore, read a passage from Zechariah, stressing thanksgiving and reconciliation. Yahweh once sowed discord everywhere, Moore proclaimed, and now he would spread peace.[93]

However civil the resolution of the war, New Yorkers did not permanently put away their resentments. Politicians periodically launched the "Tory" epithet against opponents until the Revolutionary generation died out. Squabbling neighbors years after the war might resort to the old Revolutionary labels. Certain high-profile Tories could not come home after the war. Judge Thomas Jones pined away in England for his Long Island farm for the rest of his life, requesting his American relatives to send him dried clams and hominy from home. William Smith, Jr., returned to American shores as the Chief Justice of Canada, never to see New York again.[94]

Others returned from exile and lived long years in the new Republic. Hannah Lawrence Schieffelin, the Quaker poet who eloped with a British soldier, returned to New York City with her husband, who joined her brother in a business venture. Hannah continued to write, penning a memorial poem on the occasion of Washington's death which she had printed as a pamphlet. Her fellow member of the Sentimental Society, William Rawle, returned to Philadelphia even before the war's end, becoming a prominent lawyer there. Rebecca Shoemaker left New York City for her home before Evacuation Day and welcomed her high-profile Tory husband back in 1786. The Hessian soldier and diarist John Von Krafft returned to New York to join the girl he had secretly wed in the last days of the war. He changed his name to de Krafft and took up government service in Washington, D.C. And Henry Addison, the Maryland Loyalist who predicted tumults for years to come between American Whigs and Tories, never left the United States, returning from New York City to Maryland to live out peacefully the remaining years of his life. The number of Tory exiles who came back has never been determined, but the quiet return of those who chose to come home raised no tumults after the first months following the British evacuation.

This peaceful denouement is captured in George Clinton's phrase "Generous Enemies." Any number of private and public acts throughout the war muted the conflict's severity. In the military sphere, generous enemies were more in evidence when Americans confronted Europeans than when Americans faced one another. On the civilian side, they peopled the upper ranks of society more often than the lower. To be sure, acts of civility were often eyed with suspicion by more intransigent individuals. Washington and his Board of Officers felt this hostility during the André trial. So also did William Livingston when he refused to accord favors to wealthy friends and family because of a possible negative public reaction. Yet those who regarded episodes of amicable relations with suspicion did not at last carry the day. At the end, the radicals could not rouse a war-weary population to confront what they saw as a potential enemy within. New Yorkers got on with their lives, choosing friends and associates based on their own self-interest, a practice that many had never abandoned during the conflict. In effecting a quick and conciliatory resolution to the "late troubles," New Yorkers were aided by this simple fact: in 1783, they did not have to begin building bridges to one another; those bridges had never been destroyed during the war.

Notes

Introduction

1. War Office, 71–149, Public Records Office (hereafter PRO), London. One of the men was spared punishment because a British colonel testified on his behalf. This raiding across the Long Island Sound was a two-way affair. In March 1777, a Connecticut resident wrote that Tories from Long Island were constantly coming over to plunder and kidnap prominent persons. See James Cogswell, Jr., to Reverend Cogswell, March 17, 1777, in Misc. Mss., J. Cogswell, Jr., New-York Historical Society (hereafter NYHS). For an account of the Loyalist raid in Connecticut, see Joy Day Buel and Richard Buel, Jr., *The Way of Duty: A Woman and Her Family in Revolutionary America* (New York, 1984). Edward Countryman has labeled Cow Bay as an area of Long Island suspected of harboring many Patriot hearts. See *A People in Revolution: The American Revolution and Political Society in New York, 1760–1790* (New York, 1981).

2. There has not been a study of New York City during the Revolutionary War in over fifty years. Oscar Barck (1931) and Thomas Jefferson Wertenbacker (1948) focused on Manhattan, noting no permeable boundaries between the sides with the exception of some activity in the business community. See Oscar T. Barck, *New York City During the War for Independence* (New York, 1931); Thomas Jefferson Wertenbacker, *Father Knickerbocker Rebels: New York During the Revolution* (New York, 1948). More recent scholars chose to deal with other issues in the areas surrounding the city. See Adrian C. Leiby, *The Revolutionary War in the Hackensack Valley: The Jersey Dutch and the Neutral Ground* (New Brunswick, N.J., 1962); Joseph S. Tiedemann, "Response to Revolution: Queens County, New York, During the Era of the American Revolution," Ph.D. dissertation, City University of New York, 1976; Donald Wallace White, *A Village at War: Chatham, New Jersey and the American Revolution* (Rutherford, N.J., 1979); Philip Ranlet, *The New York Loyalists* (Knoxville, Tenn., 1986); Sung Bok Kim, "The Limits of Politicization in the American Revolution: The Experience of Westchester County, New York," *Journal of American History*, 80 (December 1993): 868–89. For a study of the city as a battlefield in 1776, see Bruce Bliven, Jr., *Battle for Manhattan* (New York, 1955); for a study of the prewar scene, see Carl L. Becker, *The History of Political Parties in the Province of New York, 1760–1776* (Madison, Wisc., 1968); Patricia U. Bonomi, *A Factious People: Politics and Society in Colonial New York* (New York, 1971); Joseph S. Tiedemann, *Reluctant Revolutionaries: New York City and the Road to Independence, 1763–1776* (Ithaca, N.Y., 1997).

3. Gregory Evans Dowd, *A Spirited Resistance: The North American Indian Struggle for Unity, 1745–1815* (Baltimore, 1992); John S. Pancake, *The Destructive*

War: The British Campaign in the Carolinas (University, Ala., 1985). Even in South Carolina, there is evidence of friendly communication in Charleston. See George Smith McCowen, Jr., *The British Occupation of Charleston, 1780–1782* (Columbia, S.C., 1972).

Chapter 1. The Seat of War

1. Thomas Anburey, *Travels Through the Interior Parts of America* (New York, 1969), 531–35 and 540–42; William L. Stone, ed. *Letters of Brunswick and Hessian Officers During the American Revolution* (New York, 1970), 18, 196–99; William E. Dornemann, trans., "A Diary Kept by Captain Waldeck," *Journal of the Johannes Schwalm Association*, 2, 3, (1983): 47. The Pharos was a lighthouse. James Murray to Elizabeth Smyth, August 31, 1776, in Eric Robson, ed., *Letters from America, 1773 to 1780 Being the Letters of a Scots Officer, Sir James Murray to His Home During the War of American Independence* (New York, 1950), 34.

2. Valentine C. Hubbs, ed., *Hessian Journals: Unpublished Documents of the American Revolution* (Columbia, S.C., 1981), 59.

3. Loftus Cliffe to Batholemew Cliffe, September 21, 1776, Loftus Cliffe Papers, Clements Library. For rapturous descriptions of the country estates just outside of town, see Anburey, *Travels*, 531–35; Stone, *Letters*, 201–2; anonymous journal in Hubbs, ed. *Hessian Journals*, 59.

4. Anburey, *Travels*, 532.

5. For a detailed discussion of these committees, see Carl Lotus Becker, *The History of Political Parties in the Province of New York, 1760–1776* (Madison, Wis., 1968), 115–94. For an explanation of New York City's riotous behavior in the 1760s to its more sedate protest in the 1770s, see Joseph S. Tiedemann, *Reluctant Revolutionaries: New York City and the Road to Independence, 1763–1776* (Ithaca, N.Y., 1997). For a discussion of the political scene in New York through 1770, see Patricia U. Bonomi, *A Factious People: Politics and Society in Colonial New York* (New York, 1971). See also Mary Lou Lustig, *Privilege and Perogative: New York's Provincial Elite, 1710–1776* (Madison, N.J., 1995).

6. Gouverneur Morris to Mr. Penn, June 20, 1774, in Peter Force, ed., *American Archives . . . A Documentary History of the English Colonies in North America* (Washington, D.C., 1837–53), fourth series, 1:343. For more on conservative leaders in a revolutionary situation, see Ronald Hoffman, *A Spirit of Dissension: Economics, Politics, and the Revolution in Maryland* (Baltimore, 1973).

7. Christopher Smith to John Alsop, October 19, 1775, Alsop Misc. mss. NYHS; Peter Keteltas to John Alsop, May 23, 27, 1775, Alsop Misc. mss., NYHS.

8. Robert Ray to Philip Van Rensselaer, May 6, 1775, Historic Cherry Hill Papers: Philip Van Rensselaer Papers, New York State Library.

9. Christopher Smith to John Alsop, October 19, 1775, Alsop Misc. mss., NYHS.

10. *New York Mercury and General Advertiser*, August 7, 1775.

11. *New York Mercury*, May 8, 1775. Washington ordered an end to all com-

munication with the ministerial fleet in April 1776. See *New York Mercury*, April 15, 1776.

12. Edward Floyd De Lancey, ed., *History of New York During the Revolutionary War and of the Leading Events in the other Colonies during that Period by Thomas Jones* (New York, 1879), 57.

13. For text of Prohibitory Act, see English Historical Documents IX: American Colonial Documents to 1776, #167, microfilm, DLAR.

14. Samuel Jones to Jacob Moses, March 2, 1776, Samuel Jones Misc. Mss., NYHS; *New York Mercury*, February 12, 1776; Robert Ray to Philip Van Rensselaer, February 14, 1776, Historic Cherry Hill Papers, New York State Library; Mercantile Library Association, *From New York City During the American Revolution: A Collection of the Original Papers from the Manuscripts in the Possession of the Mercantile Library Association of New York City* (New York, 1861), 86; William H. W. Sabine, ed., *Historical Memoirs of William Smith* (New York, 1971), 263; Garish Harsin to William Radclift, February 13, 1776, in Mercantile Library Association, *From New York City During the American Revolution*, 87.

15. "Extract of a letter from New York," *Morning Chronicle and London Advertiser*, June 7, 1776, in Margaret W. Willard, ed., *Letters on the American Revolution, 1774–1776*. (Port Washington, N.Y., 1925).

16. Edward Bangs, ed., *Journal of Lieutenant Isaac Bangs, April 1 to July 29, 1776* (Cambridge, Mass., 1890), 41.

17. Bangs, *Journal*, 23–60.

18. Provincial Congress of New York Proclamation, March 14, 1776, New York Misc. Mss., Box 12, #7, NYHS.

19. Bangs, *Journal*, 59.

20. William Tudor to John Adams, July 7, 1776, in Robert J. Taylor, ed., *Papers of John Adams* (Cambridge, Mass., 1979), 367.

21. Untitled interrogation dated June 24, 1776, New York Misc. Mss., Box 12, NYHS.

22. Solomon Drowne to Solomon Drowne, Sr., June 17, 1776, in Mercantile Library Association, *New York City During the American Revolution*, 99; Bangs, *Journal*, 43–44.

23. *Diary of Samuel Richards: Captain of Connecticut Line, War of the Revolution* (Philadelphia, 1909), 45.

24. Sir George Collier to unknown recipient, July 1776, Revolutionary Documents in the National Maritime Museum (Greenwich, Conn.), reel 1.

25. Peter Fithian to Betsy Fithian, July 29, 1776, in Frank D. Andrews, ed., *Philip Vickers Fithian of Greenwich NJ, Chaplain in the Revolution, 1776; Letters to His Wife, Elizabeth Beatty Fithian* (Vineland, N.J., 1932); *The New York Packet*, August 1, 1776; Solomon Drowne to Solomon Drowne, Sr., August 9, 1776, in Mercantile Library Association, *From New York City During the American Revolution*.

26. Dennis Ryan, ed., *A Salute to Courage: The American Revolution as Seen Through the Wartime Writings of Officers in the Continental Army and Navy* (New York, 1979), 33; Ezra Bronson to Samuel De la Plaine, March 7, 1785, Samuel De La Plaine Papers, NYHS; Samuel Burling, Loyalist Claims, A013/11/405, David

Library of the American Revolution (hereafter DLAR); *New York Mercury*, June 24, 1776.

27. Mary Airey, Loyalist Claims, AO12/24/78; Rachel Ogden, Loyalist Claims, AO13/16/270–274; *The New York Packet*, July 18, 1776.

28. William Livingston to unknown recipient, April 20, 1776, William Livingston Letterbook A, Massachusetts Historical Society, reel 5; "Case of William Butler Esq., Late Assistant Deputy Commissary General at New York," in Mercantile Library Association, *From New York City During the American Revolution*, 149; Bangs, *Journal*, 55; Robert G. Albion and Leonidas Dodson, eds., *Philip Vickers Fithian: Journal 1775–1776 Written on the Virginia-Pennsylvania Frontier and in the Army Around New York* (Princeton, N.J., 1934), August 18, 1776, and July 17, 1776; De Lancey, ed., *History of New York During the Revolutionary War*, 84; Wertenbaker highlighted this change as well when he wrote, "Seldom in history has a city been so completely transformed in so short a period, for the change was not merely one of military power but of civilian population as well." Thomas Jefferson Wertenbaker, *Father Knickerbocker Rebels: New York City During the Revolution* (New York, 1948), 97.

29. Ambrose Serle estimated that 15,000 men poured onto Long Island's beaches at the start of the battle. See Edward H. Tatum, Jr., *The American Journal of Ambrose Serle, Secretary to Lord Howe 1776–1778* (San Marino, Calif., 1940), 72. Albion and Dodson, eds., *Fithian-Journal*, August 18, 1776, and September 13, 1776. The Americans faced the largest expeditionary force Great Britain had ever assembled: 32,000 soldiers, ten ships of the line, 170 transports, and other vessels. See Bruce Bliven, Jr., *Battle for Manhattan* (New York, 1955); Oscar T. Barck, *New York City During the War for Independence* (New York, 1931), 74. Another source claimed that only 3,000 civilians remained. See Wertenbacker, *Father Knickerbocker Rebels*, 98. Yet another witness claimed that nineteen-twentieths of the population left town. See "Case of William Butler, Esq., Late Assistant Deputy Commissary General at New York," in Mercantile Library Association, *From New York City During the American Revolution*, 149.

30. For a vivid description of the battle from the cellars protecting the city residents, see E. G. Shewkirk [Schaukirk] to Nathaniel Seidel, December 2, 1776, *Pennsylvania Magazine of History and Biography* (hereafter *PMHB*) 13 (1889): 376–80; For the woman at the top of Fort George, see Tatum, ed., *American Journal*, 104.

31. The cause of the fire remains a mystery. Washington was ordered by Congress not to fire on the town. But there was no hue and cry from the Americans that the British now had 500 less buildings in which to take shelter. For more on the fire, see Wertenbaker, *Father Knickerbocker Rebels*, 99–101; Philip Ranlet, *The New York Loyalists* (Knoxville, Tenn., 1986), 74–76.

32. Abraham Brasher to John Fell, September 29, 1780, Pintard Papers, Box 8, folder 15, NYHS.

33. For more on the British soldiers, see Sylvia Frey, *The British Soldier in America: A Social History of Military Life in the Revolutionary Period* (Austin, Tex., 1981), 64–93.

34. Isaac Browne to Headquarters, March 27, 1777, Society for the Propaga-

tion of the Gospel (hereafter SPG) Letterbooks, Series B, v. 24, Doc. 56, DLAR; John André to Henry Clinton, [1779], Henry Clinton Papers, v. 82, #23, Clements Library; General Howe's Orders, January 10, 1777, in Stephen Kemble, "Journal," *NYHS Collections* (1883), 435; James Pattison to Lt. Walters, December 31, 1779, and James Pattison to Col. de Bishausen, May 28, 1780 in James Pattison, "Official letters of General Pattison," in *NYHS Collections* (1875), 332, 398.

35. For naming of "Holy Ground," see Frey, *The British Soldier in America*, 61; Peebles's Diary, December 31, 1776, microfilm, DLAR.; Howard Peckham, *Memoirs of the Life of John Adlum in the Revolutionary War* (Chicago, 1968), 78; John S. Littell, ed., *Memoirs of His Own Time with Reminiscences of the Men and Events of the Revolution by Alexander Graydon* (Philadelphia, 1846), 222; Israel Keith to John P. Palmer, December 1, 1776, Israel Keith Papers, New York State Library.

36. Peebles's Diary, September 30, 1776, December 24, 1776; General Grey's Orderly Book, February 23 to May 20, 1778, microfilm Rutgers University Library, New Brunswick, N.J.; Sylvia Frey states that the most common victims of rape in the occupied city were girls under the age of ten. See Frey, *The British Soldier in America*, 79; Peebles's Diary, December 24, 1776, DLAR; John Von Krafft, "Journal of Lt. John Charles Philip Von Krafft, 1776–1784," in *NYHS Collections* (1882), 71.

37. Peebles's, Diary, April 10, 1777; November 5, 1780; February 25, 1781; March 22, 1781, DLAR.

38. Rebecca Shoemaker to Anna Rawle, June 21, 1780, Am.13745, Historical Society of Pennsylvania (hereafter HSP); Rebecca Shoemaker Diary, #17848, New York State Library.

39. Rivington's *Royal Gazette*, October 25, November 8, 29, 1777.

40. General Pattison to the Board of Ordnance, November 7, 1779, in Pattison, "Official Letters," 133; Rivington's *Royal Gazette*, March 7, 1778.

41. For an example of a depressed and lonely teen whose father eventually takes her to Europe, see Elizabeth Galloway to Grace Galloway, January 4, 1779, Dreer Collection, HSP. For an example of a Boston refugee who commits suicide because he despairs of ever returning home and can envision only future poverty, see William Rawle to his sisters, May 3, 1779, Rawle Papers, 3, Letters of William Rawle, Sr., 1779–1834, HSP.

42. See "To William Livingston" by A Member of the Sentimental Society, September 12, 1778. See "The Sentimental Maid" by Lavinia, in Rivington's *Royal Gazette*, May 2, 1778. Lavinia was the nom de plume of Beulah Murray. The exact authorship of both pieces is still questionable.

43. For an example of this correspondence, see Beulah Murray to Anna Clifford, undated, Clifford-Pemberton Papers, 6, HSP. Anna Rawle wrote to her mother in June 1783 that she had just drawn a portrait of her sister, Margaret, in order to show Beulah Murray the type of hairstyle in Philadelphia. Beulah had just sent a doll sporting a New York style to Ann. Anna Rawle to Rebecca Shoemaker, June 1783, Am.13745, HSP.

44. William to Peggy Rawle, March 21, 1779, Rawle Papers, HSP.

45. William Rawle to Rebecca Shoemaker, March 21, 1779, Rawle Papers, HSP.

46. Leonard Cutting to Reverend Morrice, undated, SPG Letterbooks, Series B, 2, Doc. #153, DLAR.

47. Peebles's Diary, July 5, 1780, DLAR; Rivington's *Royal Gazette*, November 22, 1777.

48. "Orders and Regulations of the Superintendant General of the Police of the City of New York," December 7, 1778, in "Official Records compiled by General Pattison's Staff," microfilm, DLAR.

49. Pattison, "Official Letters," 235, 404; De Lancey, ed., *History*, 2, 66–67.

50. Pattison to Captain Waugh, December 13, 1779; Pattison to Major Cousseau, March 10, 1780; Pattison to Col. Clarke, November 9, 1778, in "Official Lettesr."

51. Sabine, ed., *Historical Memoirs*, v. 3, June 24, 1780; December 26, 1779; October 5, 1779; De Lancey, ed., *History*, v. 1, 163, 54, 171.

52. While historians have examined the ill will brought about by evictions, requisitions, and bullying behavior, there has been little work done on the cultural flashpoints between the British army and the Loyalists in New York. For more on the former type of tension, see Joseph S. Tiedemann, "Patriots by Default: Queens County, New York, and the British Army, 1776–1783," *William and Mary Quarterly*, 43 (1986): 35–63.

53. *New York Gazette and Weekly Mercury*, April 12, 1773; Rivington's *Royal Gazette*, October 28, 1778; *Journals of Congress*, October 12, 16, 1778. The Continental Congress could well have heard about the theatrical productions staged by the American soldiers at Valley Forge. The motion was voted down because it was felt it was an issue for the states to decide. The Congress strongly suggested that the states should enact this prohibition. George Clinton, the Governor of New York, passed along Congress's recommendation to the New York State legislature, recommending that body's "particular attention." See Hugh Hastings, ed., *Public Papers of George Clinton* (Albany, 1902), v. 4, 184.

54. Rivington's *Royal Gazette*, February 25, 1779. For more on theater in the American Revolution, see Kenneth Silverman, *A Cultural History of the American Revolution* (New York, 1976) and Jared Brown, *The Theater in America during the Revolution* (New York, 1995).

55. Rivington's *Royal Gazette*, April 21, 1779; *New York Gazette and Weekly Mercury*, January 20, 1777; Tatum, Jr., ed., *The American Journal of Ambrose Serle*, 176; Ewald Gustav Schaukirk, *Occupation of New York City by the British* (New York, 1969), 4, 12.

56. For more on the difference in religious practices between English soldiers and Americans, see Fred Anderson, *A People's Army: Massachusetts Soldiers and Society in the Seven Years' War* (New York, 1984), 196–223. For testimony on leaders, see Schaukirk, *Occupation*, 22; Sabine, ed., *Historical Memoirs*, v. 3, 70.

57. Schaukirk, *Occupation*, 10; Sabine, ed., *Historical Memoirs*, August 11, 1779.

58. Sabine, ed., *Historical Memoirs*, June 3, 1780.

59. Rivington's *Royal Gazette*, August 16, 1780.

60. Hannah Lawrence, "The Mall," Schieffelin Papers, New York Public Library.

61. George Washington to President of Congress, January 5, 1780, in Fitz-patrick, ed., *Writings of George Washington* (Washington, D.C., 1936), v. 17, 357.

62. George Washington to Gouverneur Morris, October 4, 1778, in John C. Fitzpatrick, ed., *Writings of George Washington* (Washington, D.C., 1936), v. 13, 21.

63. Evert Byvanck to John Byvanck and Garret Abeel, January 26, 1778, Henry Bogart Papers, New York State Library; Sabine, ed., *Historical Memoirs*, July 26, 1777, January 18, 1777.

64. Sabine, ed., *Historical Memoirs*, October 14, 1776, November 16, 1776; *Minutes of the Commissioners for Detecting and Defeating Conspiracies in the State of New York: Albany County Sessions, 1778–1781* (Albany, 1909). For complaints about the leniency of this committee, see Robert Byrd, Jr., to George Clinton, April 27, 1777, in Hastings, ed., *Public Papers of George Clinton*, v. 3, 745–46; George Clinton to Albany Conspiracy Commissioners, September 20, 1778, ibid., v. 4, 58.

65. Mr. Livingston to Richard Varick, July 28, 1776, Richard Varick Papers, NYHS; "Reminiscences of John Pintard," Pintard Papers, Box 3, NYHS; Abraham Brasher to Elias Boudinot, August 27, 1781, Pintard Papers, Box 8, folder 15, NYHS.

66. Susannah French Livingston to William Livingston, February 7, 1777, in Carl E. Prince et al., eds., *The Papers of William Livingston* (Trenton, 1979), v. 1, 218; Anna Zabriskie to Richard Varick, May 25, 1777, Richard Varick Papers, NYHS.

67. John Shy, "The Loyalist Problem in the Lower Hudson Valley: The British Perspective," in Robert East and Jacob Judd, eds., *The Loyalist Americans: A Focus on Greater New York* (Tarrytown, N.Y., 1975), 3–13. See also Paul H. Smith, "New Jersey Loyalists and the British 'Provincial' Corps in the War for Independence," *New Jersey History*, 87, 2, (Summer 1969): 76. For a study that challenges the notion that New York contained an inordinately high Loyalist population, see Ranlet, *The New York Loyalists*.

68. Hugh Hughes to George Clinton, November 13, 1777, in Hastings, ed., *Public Papers of George Clinton*, v. 2, 516.

69. Henri L. Bourdin, Ralph Gabriel, and Stanley T. Williams, eds., *Sketches of Eighteenth Century America* (New York, 1972); Crèvecoeur to Roger Morris, February 17, 1779, in British Headquarters Papers, #1756, DLAR. For rumors about this shadowy French character who suddenly appeared in New York City in late 1778 with papers hidden in a false bottom of his trunk, see Sabine, ed., *Historical Memoirs*, v. 2, 74, 126, 133, 146.

70. Adrian C. Leiby, *The Revolutionary War in the Hackensack Valley: The Jersey Dutch and the Neutral Ground* (New Brunswick, N.J., 1962), 40–41; Tiedemann, "Response to Revolution: Queens County New York during the era of the American Revolution," Ph.D. dissertation, City University of New York, 1976, 35; Boudin et al., eds., *Sketches*, 254–331.

71. Bourdin et al., eds., *Sketches*, 296.

72. Ibid., 291.

73. Sabine, ed., *Historical Memoirs*, May 10, 30, 1778.

74. Robert Boyd, Jr., to George Clinton, April 27, 1777, in Hastings, ed., *Public Papers of George Clinton*, v. 1, 745. There are many more references in the George Clinton papers to local committees who compalin about the leniency of the Com-

mittee to Detect Conspiracies. Some outlying localities complain as well that the committee never gets around to visiting their part of the state.

75. George Clinton to W. Malcolm, August 18, 1778, and George Clinton to the Commissioners for Detecting and Defeating Conspiracies, August 21, 1778, in Hastings, ed., *Public Papers of George Clinton*, v. 3, 656, 674; The Loyalists were not unaware of such leniency. In autumn 1779, two specially picked men from each provincial corps were to pretend to desert, blend back into their respective communities, and return if any important intelligence came up. See Patrick Ferguson to Henry Clinton, November 7, 1779, Henry Clinton Papers, v. 74, no. 11, Clements Library.

76. *The New York Packet*, May 28, 1778.

77. Rivington's *Royal Gazette*, May 16, 20, 1778.

78. Rivington's *Royal Gazette*, October 17, 1778.

79. Crèvecoeur to Roger Morris, February 17, 1779, British Headquarters Papers, #1756, DLAR; George Clinton to Alexander McDougall, December 25, 1778, in Hastings, ed., *Public Papers of George Clinton*, v. 4, 387; Bernhard A. Uhlendorf, trans. *Revolution in America: Confidential Letters and Journals 1776–1784 of Adjutant General Major Baurmeister of the Hessian Forces* (New Brunswick, N.J., 1957), 362.

80. Pocket Diary, 1776–81, Beekman Papers, folder 12, NYHS.

Chapter 2. The Web of Family

1. Catherine Alexander to Lord Stirling, September 6, 1778, William Alexander Papers, NYHS; Sarah Alexander to Lord Stirling, August 24, 1778, William Alexander Papers, NYHS.

2. For more on family and community during the revolution, see Joy Day Buel and Richard Buel, Jr., *The Way of Duty: A Woman and Her Family in Revolutionary America* (New York, 1984). See also Jonathan Clark, "The Problem of Allegiance in Revolutionary Poughkeepsie," in David D. Hall, John M. Murrin, and Thad W. Tate, eds., *Saints and Revolutionaries: Essays on Early American History* (New York, 1984), 285–317. For the depoliticizing effect of war on a community, see Sung Bok Kim, "The Limits of Politicization in the American Revolution: The Experience of Westchester County, New York," *The Journal of American History* 80 (December 1993), 868–89. For more on armies and their effect on civilians in the southern campaign, see John Shy, *A People Numerous and Armed: Reflections on the Military Struggle for American Independence* (Ann Arbor, Mich., 1990), 231–34; For more on Americans and personal opportunity, see Jack P. Greene, "Limits of the American Revolution" in Greene, ed. *The American Revolution: Its Character and Limits* (NY, 1987), 1–13.

3. Mary Ogden to a son, May 16, 1775, Bancker Family Papers, NYHS.

4. Howard J. Banker, *A Partial History and Genealogical Record of the Bancker or Banker Families of America* (Rutland, Vt., 1909). For the Address to the Howe Brothers with Evert, Jr.'s signature, see Mercantile Library Association, *From New*

York City During the American Revolution: A Collection of Original Papers from the Manuscripts in the Possession of the Mercantile Library Association of New York City (New York, 1861); Mary Bancker to Evert Bancker, Jr., November 26, 1777, and Adrian Bancker to Evert Bancker, Jr., April 20, 1779, The Bancker Papers, NYHS.

5. Ann Fenwick to Elizabeth Gates, December 3, 1778; November 13, 1779; December 3, 1779; May 2, 1780; Horatio Gates Papers, reels 8, 11, NYHS. The Phillips sisters' predicament also highlights the difficulty of ascertaining women's political allegiance. Some women were forced to join their husbands who fled to the other side. See Sally Medless petition, August 11, 1777, Governor William Livingston Miscellaneous Papers 1776–1790, Box 1, Item 71, New Jersey State Archives. At times, women refused to join their husbands, electing to stay with their birth families. See Freelove Birdsall to Congress, April 16, 1777, and Jean Seaman to Congress, April 21, 1777, *Journals of the Provincial Congress* (Albany, 1845), v. 1, 417. See also Catherine Turnbull to George Clinton, May 4, 1778, in Hugh Hastings, ed., *Public Papers of George Clinton* (Albany, 1902), v. 3, 271. In other instances, like that of Mary Watts, a wife dutifully remained with her husband and suffered the consequences of separation from mother and sister. When Mary Watts gave birth to two babies who did not survive infancy, she mourned without the support of the most important female connections of her life. Her sister wrote in 1778 that Mary's "political principles are perfectly rebellious." Her mother opined that Mary wished "to be with me, but duty to her husband must keep her where she is." See Catherine Alexander to Lord Stirling, September 6, 1778, and Sarah Alexander to Lord Stirling, August 24, 1778, William Alexander Papers, reel 2, NYHS.

6. Peter Elting to Richard Varick, January 12, 1777, Richard Varick Papers, 1777 folder, NYHS; John Varick, Jr., to Richard Varick, November 15, 1777, ibid.; Richard Varick to Philip Van Rensselaer, October 30, 1778, Richard Varick Papers, NYHS. John Varick, Jr., was a medical student in New York. He eventually returned to New Jersey before the war's end.

7. "Reminiscences of John Pintard," Box 3, Pintard Papers, NYHS. It was certainly convenient to have relatives and friends in the city just as city dwellers benefited from contacts in the country. Such mutual aid raises the question of whether families purposely set up bases in both camps as a way of hedging their bets. When people made decisions in 1775 and 1776 about their stand in the upcoming struggle, both sides felt confident of a short war. It may have made sense to install a person in the city to protect property, even in an abbreviated conflict, but the evidence does not support such forethought. To opt for the Whigs or Loyalists, or to remain neutral, seems to have been an individual decision, not part of a grand family strategy. While some individuals could make a choice about staying in or leaving the city, other families opted to remain in town because the only property they owned was there and the prospect of support in the hinterland proved unpromising. So an array of economic, emotional, and political reasons entered into a person's decision to stay or leave the city; few could guess the scope or length of the conflict, knowledge of which might have provoked more all-encompassing family planning. Later in the war, there is evidence that wives of Loyalist men stayed at home in an effort to protect property. See Mary Beth Nor-

ton, *Liberty's Daughters: The Revolutionary Experience of American Women, 1750–1800* (Boston, 1980), 218; Linda K. Kerber, *Women of the Republic: Intellect and Ideology in Revolutionary America* (Chapel Hill, N.C., 1980), 51, 75, 123–36.

8. Vincent Pearse Ashfield pension claim, A012/13/61, American Loyalist Claims, David Library of the American Revolution.

9. Lydia Robbins's deposition for the pension application of Henry Clapp, W22804, reel 548, Revolutionary War Pension Applications Files, DLAR.

10. Abraham Leggett, *The Narrative of Abraham Leggett* (New York, 1971), 20.

11. There were limits to British complaisance concerning women and prisoners of war. It was generally acceptable for individual women to aid a relative or friend; this was a private act. But when a woman raised her charity to public notice, she faced a riskier situation. Deborah Morris Franklin, an affluent Quaker woman in the city, developed a reputation for helping American prisoners confined in the sugar houses and prison ships. A newspaper article in 1893 quoted a 1780 document (uncited) in which the British commander, "no longer able to hear or to bear the daily account of her contributing with unbounded liberality to the relief of her fellow citizens, banished her, without regard to her station, her sex, or the inclemency of the season, from the city." See "Old-Time New-York Friends: Services of the 'Plain People' in Revolutionary Days," *The New York Times*, November 19, 1893.

12. Memorial of Mary Allen, May 16, 1777, Revolutionary Documents, Item #38, New Jersey State Archives.

13. Day Book, Commandant Office, New York, 18, in James Pattison Papers, DLAR.

14. John L. C. Roome to Captain Thomas Ward, July 20, 1780, in James Pattison, "Official Lettesr of Major General James Pattison," in *NYHS Collections* (New York, 1875).

15. Wallace Brown, *The Good Americans: The Loyalists in the American Revolution* (New York, 1969), 86. For female spy ring sending messages through the type and position of laundry they hang up on the line, see Carol Berkin, *First Generations: Women in Colonial America* (New York, 1996), 190–91; women made very effective spies for the British as well. Ann Bates was described by General Clinton's intelligence-disbursement officer as an ace informant whose "information as to Matter and Fact was by far superior to every other intelligence." See Treasury Office (TI-611), PRO. General Maxwell claimed that the wife of the Episcopal rector in Elizabethtown, New Jersey, was the most effective spy in town; see Harry M. Ward, *General William Maxwell and the New Jersey Continentals* (Westport, Conn., 1997), 119. For more on women spies, particularly Ann Bates, see John Bakeless, *Turncoats, Traitors, and Heroes* (Philadelphia, 1959).

16. Even if disposed to spy or to convey information, women were thought to be hampered by their essential make-up and their "natural" inclination towards nonpolitical matters. Charles Inglis, the Anglican minister of New York City, expressed this opinion in trying to effect the release of his wife and children from American-occupied territory. He felt that women could not provide the same level of quality information as men could. "I am of Opinion," he wrote, "that there is much better Intelligence conveyed to both armies in this unhappy Contest than could be given or communicated by women." Charles Inglis to General William

Heath, December 11, 1776, William Heath Papers, reel 2, Massachusetts Historical Society (hereafter MHS). This could be a strategy to extract his wife from rebel custody, but even if Inglis did not believe what he wrote, he obviously thought he would strike a chord in the Americans' mind. He successfully managed to get his family back to New York.

17. Sabine, ed., *Historical Memoirs*, v. 1, 71, 373, 68.

18. Cynthia A. Kierner, *Traders and Gentlefolk: The Livingstons of New York, 1675–1790* (Ithaca, N.Y., 1992), 218.

19. Sabine, ed., *Historical Memoirs*, v. 1, 81, 131, 423.

20. Ibid., 81. Philip Ranlet believes that the Patriots deliberately fed Smith information they wanted the British to hear. See Ranlet, *The New York Loyalists* (Knoxville, Tenn., 1986), 96–97.

21. Sabine, ed., *Historical Memoirs*, v. 1, 170, 358, 368.

22. Ibid., 121.

23. Ibid., 277.

24. Ibid., 402.

25. Ibid., 279.

26. Ibid., v. 3, 184. Later on, Smith attends Mrs. White's tea table. Women with information continue in his diary (they bring news of the fall of Charlestown, the state of Continental army rations, and a mutiny in the New Jersey line) but they do not appear as frequently as they did in Smith's stay at the manor.

27. John Kellogg to Ebenezer Sage, July 22, 1776, Misc. Mss., Ebenezer Sage folder, NYHS; Bakeless, *Turncoats, Traitors, and Heroes*, 125.

28. Sabine, ed., *Historical Memoirs*, v. 1, 397, 401.

29. Ibid., v. 3, 314, 386, 424.

30. Kemble, "Journal," July 27, 1777.

31. George Clinton to Col. Pawling, February 24, 1777, in Hastings, ed., *Public Papers of George Clinton*, v. 1, 623–25. Another of Cadwalader Colden's sons in New York City wrote to John André that his wife had obtained permission to come to town "and return to the country." See Cadwalader Colden, Jr., to John André, November 16, 1779, Henry Clinton Papers, Clements Library.

32. Johannes Jos. Blauveldt to George Clinton, April 26, 1777, in Hastings, ed., *Public Papers of George Clinton*, v. 1, 735; William Livingston to George Washington, December 21, 1778, in Carl E. Prince et al., eds., *The Papers of William Livingston* (Trenton, 1980), v. 2, 519; Pattison to Major Lumm, February 1, 1780, in Pattison, "Official Letters"; *Journals of the Continental Congress*, September 29, 1780, v. 18, 874–75. Officials around occupied Philadelphia also complained of illegal movement in and out of the city; see William Livingston to Isaac Collins, November 25, 1777, in Prince et al., eds., *The Papers of William Livingston*, v. 2, 125.

33. "An Act to Prevent the Subjects of this State from going into, or coming out of, the Enemy's Lines, without Permissions or Passports, and for other Purposes therein mentioned," October 8, 1778, from *Records of the States of the United States* (N.J. B.2 reel 4), New Jersey State Archives (hereafter cited as *Acts of the New Jersey General Assembly*).

34. "An Act to Explain and Amend an Act intitled, An Act to Prevent the Subjects of the State from going into or coming out of the Enemy's Lines, without

Permissions or Passports and for other Purposes therein mentioned," dated December 11, 1778 (N.J. B.2 reel 4), *Acts of the New Jersey General Assembly*; "An Act to Prevent Persons from Passing through this State without proper Passports," dated June 10, 1779 (N.J. B.2 reel 4), *Acts of the New Jersey General Assembly*; William Livingston to George Washington, December 21, 1778, in Prince et al., eds., *The Papers of William Livingston*, v. 2; George Washington to General William Irvine, January 1, 1780, and Washington to Governor Trumbull, January 14, 1780, in John C. Fitzpatrick, ed., *Writings of George Washington* (Washington, D.C., 1936), v. 17, 338, 394.

35. "A Supplement to the Act intitled, An Act to explain and amend an Act, intitled, An Act to prevent the Subjects of this State from going into, and coming out of, the Enemy's lines without Permissions or Passports, and for other Purposes therein mentioned," dated December 25, 1779 (N.J. B.2 reel 4), *Acts of the New Jersey General Assembly*; "An Act more effectively to prevent the Inhabitants of this State from trading with the Enemy, or going within their Lines, and for other Purposes therein mentioned," dated December 21, 1780 (N.J. B.2 reel 4), *Acts of the New Jersey General Assembly*; "An Act to Amend the Act on Trade, etc," dated June 28, 1781 (N.J. B.2 reel 4), *Acts of the New Jersey General Assembly*; "An Act for Preventing an illicit Trade and Intercourse between the Subjects of this State and the Enemy," dated June 24, 1782 (N.J. B.2 reel 4), *Acts of the New Jersey General Assembly*; "An Act to amend an Act intitled An Act for preventing an illicit trade and Intercourse between the Subjects of this State and the Enemy," dated December 21, 1782 (N.J. B.2 reel 4), *Acts of the New Jersey General Assembly*.

36. Resolution of the Committee of Safety, November 7, 1776, in *Journal of the Committee of Safety*. There was also an August law about the restrictions on the State Convention in issuing passes: act dated June 30, 1780, *Laws of the State of New York*, Third Session, 1780 (New York, 1792). "An Act to prevent abuses in flags of truce, and for other purposes therein mentioned," dated March 8, 1779, *Laws of the State of New York*, Second Session. On abuses of flags, see George Clinton to William Denning, November 29, 1779; George Clinton to General Heath, December 2, 1779; George Clinton, "Orders Regulating the Conduct of a Flag of Truce," April 28, 1780, in Hastings, ed., *Public Papers of George Clinton*.

37. General Pattison to Major Benson, October 27, 1779, in Pattison, "Official Letters," 284.

38. General Pattison to Col. Buskirk, July 22, 1779, in Pattison, "Official Letters."

39. The Council of Safety Act, April 4, 1778, as cited in Prince et al., eds., *The Papers of William Livingston*, v. 2, 406; George Washington to Udney Hay, November 28, 1778, in Fitzpatrick, ed., *Writings of Washington*, v. 13, 329.

40. George Washington to Joseph Reed, February 12, 1779, in Fitzpatrick, ed., *Writings of Washington*, v. 13, 101.

41. WO71-153, September 5, 1781, December 13, 1781, PRO.

42. See William Livingston to Lord Stirling, September 25, 1779, in Prince et al., eds., *The Papers of William Livingston*, v. 3, 169; Mary Watts to William Livingston, August 5, 1777, William Livingston Papers, State Library of New Jersey.

43. Susannah Livingston to Sarah Jay, October 1, 1781, John Jay Papers, Columbia University. Mrs. Frederick Jay's visit was also a subject in the correspondence between John Jay and Egbert Benson. Apparently Mrs. Jay had not secured Governor Clinton's permission to go into town. See Egbert Benson to John Jay, September 30, 1781, and John Jay to Egbert Benson, December 8, 1781, in Richard B. Morris, *John Jay: The Winning of Peace, Unpublished Papers, 1780–1784* (New York, 1980). In April of 1782, a New York State Committee wanted Frederick Jay to give security for his wife's future behavior. The feisty Mrs. Jay would not consent to it. See Susannah French Livingston to Sarah L. Jay, April 21, 1782, in Robert R. Livingston Papers, NYHS.

44. Sabine, ed., *Historical Memoirs*, v. 2, 56; Benjamin Lightfoot to Israel Pemberton, November 10, 1777, Pemberton Papers, HSP.

45. Prince et al., eds., *The Papers of William Livingston*, v. 1, 175.

46. Ibid., v. 2, 519. George Clinton also noted the propensity of women to take "little articles" from New York City. See George Clinton to James Clinton, May 10, 1778, in Hastings, ed., *Public Papers of George Clinton*, v. 3, 291.

47. *New Jersey Gazette*, December 31, 1777.

48. William Livingston to Mary Martin, February 16, 1778, in Prince et al., eds., *The Papers of William Livingston*, v. 2, 232.

49. William Livingston to Lord Stirling, September 25, 1779, in Prince et al., eds., *The Papers of William Livingston*, v. 3, 169; Mary Watts to William Livingston, August 5, 1777, Livingston Papers, State Library of New Jersey; Pass #145, dated October 17, 1779, in "Day Book," in Pattison, "Official Records," DLAR. Elizabethtown continued to be the compromise meeting place for General Lord Stirling's female kin. See Catherine Duer to Mary Watts, October 15, 1781, and August 16, 1782, in Livingston-Stirling-Watts Papers, Rosenbach Museum and Library.

50. For those trying to circumvent Governor Livingston, see Garrit Rapalje to George Clinton, January 6, 1781, and William S. Livingston to George Clinton, March 12, 1781, in Hastings, ed., *Public Papers of George Clinton*, v. 6, 641, 681. For Livingston's request to Clinton, see William Livingston to George Clinton, August 18, 1780, in Hastings, ed., *Public Papers of George Clinton*, v. 5, 124.

51. William Livingston to George Washington, December 21, 1778, in Prince et al., eds., *The Papers of William Livingston*, v. 2, 519; William Livingston to Mary Martin, February 16, 1778, ibid., v. 2, 232; William Livingston to Anne Hoit, November 5, 1781, Livingston II Papers, reel 5, Massachusetts Historical Society.

52. William Livingston to Alida Hoffman, October 29, 1782, Livingston II Papers, reel 8, MHS.

53. Pattison to General Patterson, October 6, 1779, in Pattison, "Official Letters," 275.

54. Ibid., 367. It was not just thick ice and the occasional sightings of the French fleet that caused jitters in His Majesty's headquarters, but also the stream of female refugees and their children who managed to cross the lines. While some summoned a great deal of ingenuity to get there, others were simply shipped in by the Revolutionary state governments. Fewer mouths to feed in New Jersey meant more mouths to feed in New York. When the New Jersey truce boats delivered a large group to New York City in 1779, a joyless British general could see only a

logistical nightmare. "I am really at a loss what to say," the exasperated Pattison wrote, "with regard to the legions of women from the Jerseys—by your descriptions of them, I can consider them in no other light than as a swarm of locusts who will help to devour the fair crops of Long Island." See General Pattison to Major General Leslie, August 1, 1779, in Pattison, "Official Letters," 237.

55. Flushing Men's Monthly Meeting records, Haviland Record Room, Society of Friends, New York. In 1780, five Quakers married out of meeting, three women and two men; in 1782, four women and three men were married by priests. The upheaval of war and the presence of young officers in crisp uniforms seems to have emboldened the Quaker maidens.

56. Minutes of the Monthly Meeting at New York, Flushing, and Newtown, September 6, 1780, and October 5, 1780. Haviland Record Room.

57. For more on the liberating aspect of literature with respect to women in the post-revolutionary period, see Cathy N. Davidson, "The Novel as Subversive Activity: Women, Reading, Women Writing" in Alfred F. Young, ed., *Beyond the American Revolution: Explorations in the History of Radicalism* (Dekalb, Ill., 1993), 284–316.

58. Hannah Lawrence, "A Journal of a Lady's Courtship," Schieffelin Family Papers, New York Public Library; see also the Aquila Giles correspondence at NYHS for another example of a couple who conquer political differences to fall in love. Anna Rawle writes to her mother in November 1780, "Major Giles being married on Long Island is amazing. I should not have imagined so great a whig could like anything within the British lines." Anna Rawle to Rebecca Shoemaker, November 4, 1780, Shoemaker Family Letters and Diaries, Am. 13745, HSP.

Chapter 3. Gentlemen at War

1. William H. W. Sabine, ed., *Historical Memoirs of William Smith*, (New York, 1956), v. 1, 290. For more on the allegiances of Charles Lee, see John Shy, "American Strategy: Charles Lee and the Radical Alternative," in John Shy, *A People Numerous and Armed: Reflections on the Military Struggle for American Independence* (Ann Arbor, 1990), 133–62.

2. Works on civility in the military include Charles Royster's *A Revolutionary People at War: The Continental Army and American Character, 1775–1783* (New York, 1979). Royster discusses the elements of a gentleman-officer's persona and how that played out within the Continental army; see 79–96 and 197–211. See also "Military Leadership in the American Revolution" in Don Higginbotham, *War and Society in Revolutionary America: The Wider Dimensions of Conflict* (Columbia, S.C., 1988), 87–101. For more on paroles, see Larry G. Bowman, *Captive Americans: Prisoners During the American Revolution* (Athens, Ohio, 1976), 97–103. See also Charles H. Metzger, *The Prisoner in the American Revolution* (Chicago, 1962), 191–98. For the operation of civility outside the military sphere, see Lawrence E. Klein, *Shaftesbury and the Culture of Politeness* (Cambridge, 1994) and Richard L. Bushman, *The Refinement of America: Persons, Houses, Cities* (New York, 1993).

3. M. H. Keen, *The Laws of War in the Late Middle Ages* (London, 1965); Theodor Meron, "Shakespeare's Henry the Fifth and the Law of War," *American Journal of International Law*, 86 (1992): 1–45; Francois Grosse, Esq., *Military Antiquities Respecting a History of the English Army from the Conquest to the Present Time* (London, 1786). By the eighteenth century, the French still chose their officers from aristocrats while the British had opened up their officer corps to wealthy men.

4. Rivington's *Royal Gazette*, October 4, 1777.

5. *Pennsylvania Evening Post*, May 29, 1777, mentions Vertot's *Life of Gustavus*. The quotations in the text were taken from the Reverend Walter Harte's *The History of the Life of Gustavus Adolphus* (London, 1759). For Gustavus's importance as an example to the military, see Barbara Donagan, "Halcyon Days and the Literature of War: England's Military Education before 1642," *Past and Present* 147 (May 1995): 85. For a list of 1776 military reprints, see *The Pennsylvania Evening Post*, August 17, 1776, May 29, 1777. For an example of a military primer written by an Englishman, see Thomas Simes, *The Military Guide for Young Officers* (Philadelphia, 1776); for an American example, see Lewis Nicola, *A Treatise of Military Exercise Calculated for the Use of the Americans* (Philadelphia, 1776). Barbara Donagan reminds us that as late as the English Civil War, the rules of war, which included paroles, were as yet unwritten. See Barbara Donagan, "Atrocity, War Crime, and Treason in the English Civil War," *American Historical Review* 99 (October 1994): 1142.

6. *The New York Packet and the American Advertiser*, March 12, 1778; *Simcoe's Military Journal: A History of the Operations of a Partisan Corps Called the Queen's Rangers* (New York, 1844), 264–85.

7. George Clinton to George Washington, September 12, 1777, in Hugh Hastings, ed., *The Public Papers of George Clinton* (New York, 1899), v. 2, 319–20.

8. For examples of British attitudes on American officers, see E. A. Benians, ed., *A Journal by Thomas Hughes, 1778–1789* (Cambridge, 1947), 57. Also see John S. Littell, ed., *Memoirs of His Own Time with Reminiscences of the Men and Events of the Revolution by Alexander Graydon* (Philadelphia, 1846), 209. One notable exception to this systematized complaisance was the treatment accorded to Loyalist officers captured by the Americans. Using the distinction of prisoners of state versus prisoners of war, the American side often incarcerated commissioned Loyalist officers, offering no possibility of parole. At times, Washington thought it proper to have these men released from jail and put on parole, but not often enough for the Loyalists. When the Associated Loyalists was founded in 1781, its leaders promised all recruits that henceforth, all American captives would be treated as well or as badly as Loyalists in American custody. Such a statement would not have been necessary if Loyalists had received the same treatment as their British allies. For examples of these cases, see William Livingston to George Washington, August 15, December 1, 1777, in Carl E. Prince et al., eds., *The Papers of William Livingston* (Trenton, 1980), v. 2, 32, 128.

9. Angus McDonnell parole dated June 5, 1778, Horatio Gates Papers, reel 4, NYHS; John Witherspoon to Elias Boudinot, Princeton, March 9, 1778, Emmet Collection, reel 3, #2758, NYPL.

10. Lillian Miller, ed., *The Selected Papers of Charles Willson Peale and His Family* (New Haven, Conn., 1983), 306–7. Peale's brother-in-law returned to New York City when the British issued an order that all American prisoners on parole had to report immediately to the city. Peale's sister was allowed to accompany her prisoner husband to British New York, where they set up a household on Long Island. His confinement there did not prevent the prisoner from purchasing a house in Baltimore. For a languishing prisoner, see John Lamb to the Continental Congress, November 25, 1776, in Dennis Ryan, ed., *A Salute to Courage: The American Revolution as seen through the Wartime Writings of Officers in the Continental Army and Navy* (New York, 1979), 53. For those who honored parole, see "Journal Kept by J. Peebles, a British Officer" (hereafter "Peebles's Diary"), June 26, 1779, microfilm #440, DLAR, and also Sabine, ed., *Historical Memoirs*, v. 1, 219.

11. Littell, ed., *Memoirs of His Own Time by Alexander Graydon*, 259. The British justified the imprisonment of officers when they committed crimes.

12. *The New York Packet and American Advertiser*, September 23, 1779.

13. Sabine, ed., *Historical Memoirs*, v. 2, 219; Philip Skene's Loyalist Pension, Loyalist Claims, 012/24/118, DLAR. A considerable number of Americans in Virginia purposely crossed British lines to obtain paroles which would forbid them from taking up arms for the American army. Thomas Jefferson, then Governor of Virginia, issued a Proclamation dated January 19, 1781, in which he deplores such action and reminds his neighbors that such action is against the law. See Thomas Jefferson Proclamation, January 19, 1781, in Von Steuben Papers, reel 1, 446, DLAR; Thomas Gummersall claim, Loyalist Claims, 013/12/192–250.

14. Baron Von Steuben Papers, June 28, 1779, microfilm, DLAR. On occasion, exchanges were negotiated for those officers who broke their paroles. See George Washington to John Beatty, January 29, 1779 in John C. Fitzpatrick, ed., *Writings of George Washington* (Washington, D.C., 1936), v. 14, 53.

15. George Washington, "Circular to the States," August 26, 1779, in Fitzpatrick, ed., *Writings of Washington*, v. 16, 175.

16. William E. Dornemann, "A Diary Kept by Captain Waldeck During the Last War, Part II," *Journal of Johannes Schwalm Historical Association*, v. 2, 4 (1984): 46; Jonathan Gillet to Elizabeth Gillet, New York, December 2, 1776, American Revolution Box 1, Letters, Connecticut Historical Society; Henry Hardman to unknown recipient, Graves End, Long Island, June 14, 1778, Gates Papers, reel 4; General Pattison to aide-de-camp, New York, August 20, 1779, in James Pattison, "Official Letters of Major General James Pattison," in *NYHS Collections* (New York, 1875); James Heron to James Milligan, New York, September 9, 1777, Edward Hand Papers, HSP; Sabine, ed., *Historical Memoirs*, v. 2, 255.

17. John McNamara Hayes to Horatio Gates, Fishkill, June 5, 1778, Gates Papers, reel 4; Don Gerlach, *Proud Patriot: Philip Schuyler and the War of Independence, 1775–1783* (Syracuse, 1987), 324; Gareth Williams to Horatio Gates, Albany, October 25, 1777, Gates Papers, reel 6. This episode ended in some misunderstanding which is why it appears in Gates's papers.

18. Howard Peckham, ed., *Memoirs of the Life of John Adlum in the Revolutionary War* (Chicago, 1968).

19. Ibid., 128. It is interesting to note that Adlum does not discuss the downside of officer life on parole until after his section on imprisoned Americans. After his description of the horrors of prison life, he may well have felt obliged to point out that officer life was no picnic either.

20. Abner Everett, Revolutionary War Pensions, W6087, DLAR; James Morris, ibid., W2035, DLAR; Littell, ed., *Memoirs of His Own Time by Alexander Graydon*, 245–53; "A Small Account Book while a Prisoner on Long Island in the Year 1777," Kingston Collection Miscellaneous, Box 14, folder 2, New York State Library.

21. Peebles's Diary, April 28, 1777, microfilm, DLAR.

22. Peckham, ed., *Memoirs of John Adlum*, 79–134; John Heller, Revolutionary War Pensions, S8702. I am indebted to Greg Knouff for sharing some stories of his Pennsylvania veterans who ended up in prison in New York City. "Reminiscences of John Pintard," Box 3, Pintard Papers, NYHS. Although there is corroborating evidence for the tough conditions in the city's prisons, some stories seem exaggerated for propaganda purposes. This could be the case, particularly with Pintard's story about doctors in the hospital.

23. Elias Boudinot, *Journal or Historical Reflections of American Events During the Revolutionary War* (Philadelphia, 1894), 13–14. In 1781, Boudinot does complain to the British about the treatment of prisoners onboard the prison ships.

24. The American witnesses never mention whether French officers shared the common sailors' fate. Concerning the uniform treatment accorded American officers and seamen, the British may have made no distinction because the overwhelming number of sailors captured were off privateers, which in the eyes of the British were little more than pirate ships. Imprisoned Americans received little help from Washington as his authority did not extend to the marine department. Soldiers could not be exchanged for sailors. Prison ship testimonies include "The Revolutionary Adventures of Ebenezer Fox of Roxbury Mass," in Hugh F. Rankin, ed., *Narratives of the American Revolution* (Chicago, 1976); Albert Greene, ed., *Recollections of the Jersey Prison Ship from the Manuscript of Captain Thomas Dring* (New York, 1961); *The Pennsylvania Evening Post*, May 3, 1777; James Fulton et al. to Elias Boudinot, Ship Judith, May 1, 1778, Misc. Mss. Boudinot, NYHS. For a creative exercise in reconstructing the mindset of imprisoned sailors, see Jesse Lemisch, "Listening to the 'Inarticulate': William Widger's Dream and the Loyalties of American Revolutionary Seamen in British Prisons," *Journal of Social History* 3, 1 (Fall 1969): 1–29. For more on prison ship experiences, see Bowman, *Captive Americans*, 40–61; Metzger, *The Prisoner in the American Revolution*, 281–88.

25. Peckham, ed., *Memoirs of John Adlum*, 113; Jesse Coles, S12523, and Abraham Ryckman, R9124, Revolutionary War Pensions, DLAR.

26. Peckham, ed., *Memoirs of John Adlum*, 172; Abraham Leggett, *The Narrative of Abraham Leggett* (New York, 1971), 22.

27. Because the city of New York was occupied, there was no central headquarters to push for the interests of the privates in the army. In Philadelphia, a unique organization called "The Committee of Privates" agitated for lower-sort interests. See Steven Rosswurm, *Arms, Country, and Class: The Philadelphia Militia*

and "Lower Sort" During the American Revolution, 1775–1783 (New Brunswick, N.J., 1987), 49; Dirck Hansen et al., Petition to Horatio Gates, Albany, October 25, 1777, Gates Papers, reel 6.

28. James Thomas Flexner, *The Traitor and the Spy: Benedict Arnold and John André* (New York, 1953), 81; Robert McConnell Hatch, *Major John André: A Gallant in Spy's Clothing* (Boston, 1986), 50. One of the captured quartermasters was Major John André. While the American soldiers under Montgomery continued north and fought a devastatingly hard campaign in Canada, John André made a leisurely progress towards his place of incarceration at Lancaster, Pa. In the first days of his journey, he had a delightful conversation with Henry Knox at an inn, then stopped at Albany for nearly a month where he dined at Philip Schuyler's table from time to time. Then he dallied for a couple of weeks in Philadelphia and finally arrived at Lancaster over two months after the surrender at St. John.

29. Samuel Tenny to Peter Turner, October 19, 1780, Peter Turner Letters, Clements Library. For more on tensions between the rank and file and their officers, see Royster, *A Revolutionary People at War*, 91–95. See also Woody Holton, *Forced Founders: Indians, Debtors, Slaves, and the Making of the American Revolution in Virginia* (Chapel Hill, N.C., 1999), 180–81.

30. Rankin, *Narratives of the American Revolution*, 361.

31. For representative examples, see Isaac Belknap's deposition in Revolutionary War Pensions, John Anderson, S46682; John Brasher, S16057; Robert Bruis, S22663; Samuel Myer, S23331; Jacob Van Orden, S28920; Benjamin Romine, S4135. For debate on André's execution, see Joshua Hett Smith, Esq., *An Authentic Narrative of the Causes which led to the Death of Major André* (London, 1808), and Egbert Benson, *Vindication of the Captors of Major André* (New York, 1817). For more on memory and history, see David Thelen, *Memory and American History* (Bloomington, Ind., 1990).

32. For more on the Arnold-André affair, see Clare Brandt, *The Man in the Mirror: A Life of Benedict Arnold* (New York, 1994). For a treatment that is more interpretive, see Charles Royster, " 'The Nature of Treason': Revolutionary Virtue and American Reactions to Benedict Arnold," *William and Mary Quarterly* 36 (April 1979): 163–93. Royster explains the powerful reaction to the Arnold treason case as a symptom of guilt on the part of the American public whose Revolutionary virtue had flagged. Americans transferred their failings to Arnold's shoulders. See also Jay Fliegelman, *Prodigals and Pilgrims* (New York, 1982), 215–19. Fliegelman uses the posthumous writings about André's execution to reinforce his point about the father figure in the reconstituted family of the Revolution.

33. By September 1780, William Smith had been expelled from Livingston Manor and lived in New York City. For Joshua Hett Smith's version of that night, see his *An Authentic Narrative*; for his tenants' version, see "The Record of the General Court Martial of Joshua Hett Smith," *The Historical Magazine* (July–November 1866). The Court Martial found insufficient evidence to convict Hett Smith of treason.

34. Joshua King Deposition, Ridgefield, Ct., June 9, 1817, Connecticut Historical Society, reel 2. In 1833, Benjamin Tallmadge related that André's way of walking across the floor betrayed his identity as a military man. See Benjamin Tall-

madge to Jared Sparks, November 16, 1833, as quoted in Hastings, ed., *Public Papers of George Clinton*, v. 6, 259.

35. John André to George Washington, September 24, 1780, in *Proceedings of a Board of General Officers* (Philadelphia, 1780), Evans Early American Imprints #17043, 6–7.

36. Tom Paine later described Arnold's boarding of the British warship *Vulture* as "one vulture receiving another." See Brandt, *The Man in the Mirror*, 221.

37. General Orders, September 26, 1780, in Fitzpatrick, ed., *The Writings of George Washington*, v. 20, 94–95.

38. *The New York Packet and Daily Advertiser*, Fishkill, N.Y., September 28, 1780; Nathanael Greene to Catherine Greene, September 29, 1780, in Richard K. Showman et al., eds., *The Papers of General Nathanael Greene* (Chapel Hill, N.C., 1991), v. 6, 321.

39. For Tallmadge on André, see Hatch, *Major John André*, 253. For Hamilton on André, see Alexander Hamilton to Isaac Sears, 1780, in Benson, *Vindication*, 68–74; Nathanael Greene to Catherine Greene, September 29, 1780, in Showman et al., eds., *The Papers of General Nathanael Greene*, v. 6, 321.

40. For Washington intervening in cases under the original jurisdiction of William Livingston, the Governor of New Jersey, see William Livingston to Silvanus Seely, December 26, 1777; William Livingston to George Washington, December 1, 1777; William Livingston to George Washington, August 15, 1777, in Prince et al., eds., *The Papers of William Livingston*, v. 2, 128, 148, v. 3, 32–36. For Washington's tempering his officers' tendency to carry out capital punishments, see George Washington to Henry Lee, July 9, 1779, in Fitzpatrick, ed., *Writings of Washington*, v. 15, 388. For Washington's liberality with respect to pardons, see Holly A. Mayer, *Belonging to the Army: Camp Followers and Community During the American Revolution* (Columbia, S.C., 1996), 260.

41. The officers composing the Board of Officers were General Greene, Lord Stirling, St. Clair, Lafayette, Howe, Steuben, Parsons, Knox, Glover, Patterson, Hand, Huntingdon, and Starke. Only Knox had met André on a previous occasion. In 1775, en route to his captivity in Lancaster from Canada, André found a very crowded inn whose proprietor indicated only one available sleeping place next to a very portly individual. As André was slim, he mounted the stairs to find Henry Knox, at 300 pounds, still awake from the driving snowstorm outside. Knox had owned a bookstore before the war, and so the two men spent most of the night chatting about literature and poetry. Knox was en route to Ticonderoga to fetch the cannon for Washington at Cambridge. See Flexner, *The Traitor and the Spy*, 137; for Washington's power to declare André to be a spy and hang him, see Grosse, *Military Antiquities Respecting a History of the English Army from the Conquest to the Present Time* (London, 1786), v. 2, 198. See also Captain George Smith, *An Universal Military Dictionary* (London, 1779).

42. Daniel Newton, "Journal of Daniel Newton," Misc. microfilm, reel 5, NYHS; Abraham Brasher to John Fell, Morristown, September 29, 1780, in Pintard Papers, Box 8, folder 15, NYHS.

43. Nathanael Greene to Catherine Greene, September 29, 1780, in Showman et al., eds., *The Papers of Nathanael Greene*, 321. For Hamilton, see Benson, *Vindica-*

tion, 68. For judgment of Board, see *Proceedings*, 13. Flags of truce were sanctioned movements of military personnel in the interest of facilitating communication between the two armies. The messengers under such flags were immune from any persecutions from enemy soldiers.

44. *The Case of Major John André* (New York: James Rivington, 1780), 11–13. Both André's confession and the British high command's arguments strained to fit André's actions into "proper behavior" as defined by the commonly accepted standard of military comportment. Unfortunately for the prisoner in Mabie's Tavern, the stories were not the same.

45. *Proceedings*, 10. In its publication of the *Proceedings*, the Congress added Washington's September 30, 1780, letter to Clinton in the appendix, 15.

46. John Russell to Count Marbois, February 14, 1815, Accession #1351, New York State Library.

47. *Proceedings*, 18–19. On Robertson's contention that Clinton had never put an American to death for a breach of the rules of war, one is reminded of the Nathan Hale case. In the autumn of 1776, the Connecticut Captain volunteered for a mission behind the British lines. Disguised as a Dutch school teacher, Hale was captured and hanged the next day. To Washington, it might have been a fine distinction that General Howe, not General Clinton, ordered the execution. There is no evidence in the contemporary accounts that André's execution would serve as revenge for Hale's. Not until Benjamin Tallmadge's memoirs in the nineteenth century does Hale's name appear in connection with the André case. According to Tallmadge, who was a personal friend of Hale's, André asked Tallmadge what he could expect from the American tribunal. Tallmadge invoked the name of Nathan Hale, which put a damper on André's mood. There is also no mention in contemporary sources of André's prominent participation in two British surprise attacks that the Americans labeled "massacres," at Paoli and Tappan. André was hanged in Tappan, the scene of one of the massacres, but the headquarters of the American army just happened to be there at the end of September 1780. There is no evidence that the act was symbolic revenge. It is also unlikely that the Americans knew the identity of the author of a satirical poem that appeared in the *Royal Gazette* just a few days before André's capture. In "Cow Chase," André, under a pen name, poked fun at the American high command. For the text, see *Royal Gazette*, August 16, 1780; August 30, 1780; September 20, 1780.

48. Elias Boudinot, *Journal or Historical Reflections of American Events During the Revolutionary War* (Philadelphia, 1894), 90; Henry Lee's October 2, 1780, letter to Simcoe is found in *Simcoe's Military Journal*, 292. The letter begins with an impatient rebuff on the part of Lee concerning a gushy expression of Simcoe's gratitude for the aid that Lee had extended when Simcoe was a prisoner of the Americans. At such a fever-pitch time, when mail must have been opened routinely, Lee might well have been nervous about such expressions of fraternal reciprocity. "For heaven's sake," Lee wrote to Simcoe, "omit in future your expression of obligations conferred by me, as my knowledge of your character confirms my assurance that a similar visit of fortune to me, will produce every possible attention from you." For the French volunteer's comment, see Robert B. Douglas, ed., *The Chevalier de Pontigibaud: A French Volunteer of the War of Independence* (Port Washington, N.Y.,

1968), 61–62. Pontigibaud's mention of mutiny was an apposite one since the army had experienced three mutinies thus far in 1780. American General William Heath claimed that the situation was so critical that had André gotten through, "The most serious consequences to the American cause would very soon have taken place." See R. R. Wilson, ed., *Heath's Memoirs of the American War* (New York, 1904), 270. During the crisis, Washington pleaded to Governor George Clinton of New York that he had only a couple of days supply left. See George Washington to George Clinton, October 1, 1780, in Hastings, ed., *Public Papers of George Clinton*, v. 6, 270.

49. Andrew Kettel, "Diary," May 26, June 17, 19, September 11, 1780, in Revolutionary War Pensions, W13568, DLAR; Joshua Hett Smith, *An Authentic Narrative*, 66; Andrew Elliot to William Eden, October 4, 1780, Auckland Papers, reel 5, DLAR.

50. Andrew Elliot to William Eden, October 4, 1780, Auckland Papers, reel 5, DLAR.

51. For Arnold's October 1 letter, see *Proceedings*, 19. For Hamilton's comment, see Benson, *Vindication*, 74. For Washington's observation, see George Washington to the Comte de Rochambeau, October 10, 1780, in Fitzgerald, ed., *Writings of Washington*, v. 20, 151. Thomas Anburey in his memoirs, originally published in 1789, claimed that Washington wanted to accede to André's request to be shot, but was overruled by the Board of Officers. See Thomas Anburey, *Travels Through the Interior Parts of America* (New York, 1969), 478. Joshua Hett Smith claimed that Washington and the Board were disposed to accede to André's request, but General Greene insisted that André hang "for, said he, if he is shot, mankind will think there are circumstances in his case which intitled him to notice or indulgence." See Smith, *An Authentic Narrative*, 166. Neither Anburey or Hett Smith mention their sources.

52. Hatch, *Major John André*, 272–74.

53. Andrew Kettel, "Diary," in Revolutionary War Pensions, W13568, DLAR; W. Stevens to Betsy Stevens, October 1, 1780, Clinton Papers, v. 125, #5, Clements Library; John Shreve, "Personal Narrative of the Services of Lieut. John Shreve," *Magazine of American History* 3, 9 (September 1879): 574.

54. George Washington to the President of Congress, September 26, 1780, in Fitzpatrick, ed., *Writings of George Washington*, v. 20, 91; for the congressional reward, see Benson, *Vindication*, 59; John Paulding received Peter Huggeford's farm on Cortland Manor. Paulding later aided Huggeford in writing a deposition in support of the Loyalist's pension application to the British government, claiming that he did indeed receive Huggeford's land from the State of New York. See Loyalist Claims, Peter Huggeford, AO13/64/369.

55. "Reflections on the Catastrophe of Major André," from *The Public Advertiser* as reprinted in Rivington's *Royal Gazette*, March 14, 1781. This argument was supported by military manuals written before the André affair. In George Smith's *Universal Military Dictionary*, published in 1779, spies are defined as lower sorts who had to be well paid and whose fidelity could only be insured by taking hostages. Major André, the quintessential military gentleman, would not fit this definition.

56. Hatch, *Major John André*, 277.

57. Henry J. Raymond, *An Oration Pronounced before the Young Men of West-chester County on the Completion of a Monument Erected by Them to the Captors of Major André at Tarrytown, October 7, 1853*, (New York, 1853), 22–23. For controversy around the erection of a monument at the André execution site, see Robert E. Cray, Jr., "Major John André and the Three Captors: Class Dynamics and Revolutionary Memory Wars in the Early Republic, 1780–1831," *Journal of the Early Republic* 17 (1997): 371–97.

Chapter 4. The Eagle Eye of Profit

1. John Robinson to General Sir William Howe, October 22, 1776, British Headquarters Papers, 1747–83, microfilm, DLAR; James Pattison to Lord Viscount Townsend, January 10, 1779, in Pattison, "Official Letters," 1. According to Alexander Huston, a ship captain fitting out a new vessel in New York harbor, there were five arrivals of victualing ships from Cork between January 1778 and May 1779. He also notes the arrival of two fleets from England in this period. See Alexander Huston Diary, Public Archives of Nova Scotia.

2. "Estimate of the Quantity of Candles Necessary for 40,000 Men for the 26 Winter Weeks," dated April 20, 1778, British Headquarters Papers, 1115 (2), DLAR.

3. George Washington to George Clinton, October 1, 1780, in Hastings, ed., *Public Papers of George Clinton*, v. 6, 270. On Washington's refined tastes, see Marvin Kitman, *George Washington's Expense Account* (New York, 1970). Kitman's treatment is meant to be humorous, but he does reprint the actual expense book, and has studied the accompanying vouchers. Washington's correspondence indicates that although he may have ordered the niceties of life, he may not have gotten them promptly. In February 1779, Washington complains that his tin dishes were rusty and so he ordered a set of china, candlesticks, and table linen. By August 1779, he graduated from tin to iron plates. See George Washington to John Mitchell, February 17, 1779, and George Washington to Doctor Cochran, August 16, 1779, in Fitzgerald, ed., *Writings of Washington*, v. 14, 127, v. 15, 116.

4. Elias Boudinot, *Journal*, 22; Robert Morris to General Gates, October 27, 1776, Horatio Gates Papers, reel 4. McDougall's quote is in Pauline Maier, *The Old Revolutionaries: Political Lives in the Age of Samuel Adams* (New York, 1980), 99. Maier used McDougall's radical colleague, Isaac Sears, to support her contention that for New Yorkers like him, patriotism and profit went hand in hand. "Confident in the material implications of liberty, New Yorkers talked less of virtue than of interest, and turned naturally outward the language of business in the business of revolution." *The Old Revolutionaries*, 94.

5. For more on reconciling private interests and public virtue, see Cathy Matson, "Public Vices, Private Benefit: William Duer and His Circle, 1776–1792," in William Pencak and Conrad Edick Wright, eds., *New York and the Rise of Capitalism: Economic Development and the Social and Political History of an American State: 1780–1870* (New York, 1989), 72–123. For more on trade in and out of the occupied city, see Robert A. East, *Business Enterprise in the American Revolutionary Era* (Gloucester, Mass., 1964), 180–94. For business in another occupied city,

see Willard O. Mishoff, "Business in Philadelphia during the British Occupation, 1777–1778," *PMHB*, 61 (April 1937): 165–81. See also John W. Jackson, *With the British Army in Philadelphia, 1777–1778* (San Rafael, Calif., 1979).

6. Petitions dated July 10, 1775, and July 25, 1775, in *Calendar of Historical Manuscripts*, v. 1, 110–12; William Beekman to Isaac Sears, April 16, 1782, Beekman Papers, NYHS.

7. Petition dated March 2, 1776, in *Calendar of Historical Manuscripts Relating to the War of the Revolution*, (Albany, 1868), v. 1, 255. Christopher Smith to John Alsop, June 24, 1775, Misc. Mss., John Alsop, NYHS; Becker, *The History of Political Parties in the Province of New York, 1760–1776*, 152; Donald McLeod to Congress, June 8, 1775, in *Calendar of Historical Manuscripts Relating to the War of the Revolution* (Albany, 1868), v. 1, 100. For more on the foreign composition of the Continental army, see Charles Patrick Neimeyer, *America Goes to War: A Social History of the Continental Army* (New York, 1996). Historians today do not agree on certain individuals' leanings. Edward Countryman calls John Alsop a Royalist. Philip Ranlet claims that this is an unfair charge, that Alsop was as much a Patriot as John Dickinson. See Countryman, *A People in Revolution: The American Revolution and Political Society in New York, 1760–1790* (New York, 1981), 240, and Ranlet, *The New York Loyalists*, 7.

8. Petitions dated June 11, 1776, and June 13, 1776, in *Calendar of New York Historical Manuscripts*, 321–22.

9. Loyalist Claims, Samuel Burling, AO13/11/405.

10. Robert Harper to Congress, May 27, 1776, in *Journals of the Provincial Congress, Provincial Convention, Committee of Safety and Council of Safety of the State of New York: 1775–1776–1777*, v. 2, 112; Committee of New Windsor to Provincial Congress, May 31, 1776, in *Calendar of Historical Manuscripts*, v. 1, 312.

11. For more on the importance of the non-importation movement in American politics, see T. H. Breen, "'The Baubles of Britain': The American and Consumer Revolutions of the Eighteenth Century," *Past and Present* 119 (1988): 73–104. See also T. H. Breen, "Narrative of Commercial Life: Consumption, Ideology, and Community on the Eve of the American Revolution," *William and Mary Quarterly* 50 (July 1993): 471–501. For titles dealing specifically with New York, see Edmund S. Morgan and Helen M. Morgan, *The Stamp Act Crisis: Prologue to Revolution* (New York, 1953), and Joseph Tiedemann, *Reluctant Revolutionaries*.

12. Petitions from *Calendar of New York Historical Manuscripts*, 128. For First Continental Congress law on non-exportation, see Becker, *The History of Political Parties*, 152; *Journals of the Provincial Congress*, v. 1, 289. See also November 1, 1775, in *Journals of the Continental Congress, 1774–1789* (Washington, D.C., 1904–37), v. 3, 314.

13. Curson Seton to John Alsop, May 10, 1775, Misc. Mss., John Alsop, NYHS.

14. John Adams to George Washington, January 6, 1776, in Taylor, ed., *Papers of John Adams* v. 3, 395–96.

15. Wertenbaker, *Father Knickerbocker Rebels*, 70, 73.

16. The American Prohibitory Act, December 22, 1775, in English Historical Documents IX: American Colonial Documents to 1776, #167, microfilm, DLAR.

Although there is no mention in the act concerning the suspension of civilian government, the army used this act to deny New Yorkers the restoration of their civil government. For the reaction of an enraged American civilian, see DeLancey, ed., *History of New York by Thomas Jones*, v. 2, 98–119.

17. Loyalist Claims, Robert Gault, AO13/26/130–137.

18. De Lancey, ed., *History of New York by Thomas Jones*, v. 2, 13.

19. William Howe to Andrew Elliot, December 10, 1777, British Headquarters Papers, Doc. #794, microfilm, DLAR. The quote expressing doubt that the British could hold New York comes from Lord William Eden, one of the Peace Commissioners sent from England. He is quoted thus in Sabine, ed., *Historical Memoirs*, v. 2, 49.

20. DeLancey, ed., *History of New York by Thomas Jones*, v. 2, 122. For more on British corruption, see Wertenbaker, *Father Knickerbocker Rebels*, 151–71, 207. For a sympathetic treatment of Andrew Elliot, see Robert Ernst, "Andrew Elliot, Forgotten Loyalist of Occupied New York," *New York History* 57 (July 1976): 285–320.

21. Rivington's *Royal Gazette*, November 22, December 27, 1777; November 11, 1778; January 16, February 16, June 30, September 18, 1779; November 4, December 2, 1780; November 17, 1781. Alexander Huston Diary, May 9, 1778, Public Archives of Nova Scotia. For merchant quote, see Stephen Rapalje to Tench Coxe, May 2, 1778, Coxe Papers, Tench Coxe Section, HSP.

22. Proclamation dated January 27, 1777, in Stephen Kemble, "Journals," 441; Rivington's *Royal Gazette*, June 3, 1778; Proclamation dated October 24, 1780, in Milton Klein and Ronald W. Howard, eds., *The Twilight of British Rule in Revolutionary America: The New York Letter Book of General James Robertson, 1780–1783* (Cooperstown, 1983), 160.

23. DeLancey, ed., *History of New York by Thomas Jones*, v. 1, 269–70. The isthmus described by Jones is at the current town of Canoe Place, just east of Hampton Bays.

24. Rhinelander to Messrs. Rawlinsons and Chatley, December 28, 1776, and June 7, 1777; Rhinelander to Hodgson and Donaldson, October 1778, in Rhinelander Letter Book, 1774–84, NYHS.

25. Rhinelander Letter Book: May 28, September 2, October 28, 1780; January 20, April 17, July 14, 1781; January 25, April 17, May 1782, NYHS.

26. James Robertson to Admiral Arbuthnot, May 9, 1780, in Klein and Howard, eds., *The Twilight of British Rule*, 108; Edward Gould to Tench Coxe, May 1, 1778, Coxe Papers, Tench Coxe Section, HSP; Christopher Smith to Evert Bancker, Jr., April 27, 1779, Bancker Papers, NYHS.

27. "John Greenwood Manuscript, 1775–1783," 67, Clements Library.

28. Minutes, Flushing Quarterly Meeting, November 4, 1779. For instances of prize goods violation, see Monthly Meeting, May 15, 1782, August 7, 1782, Haviland Record Room; scrap dated June 16, 1779, Bancker Family Papers, NYPL. For more on women and privateering, see Wertenbaker, *Father Knickerbocker Rebels*, 208.

29. Sabine, ed., *Historical Memoirs*, v. 2, 113, 162.

30. "Deposition of James Smith," August 16, 1777, in Prince, ed., *The Papers*

of William Livingston, v. 2, 39; Joseph Stoddard to Horatio Gates, June 24, 1777, Horatio Gates Papers, microfilm, DLAR. Washington notes more illegal trade in 1779 by civilians in New Jersey who sell liquor to American soldiers in exchange for the soldiers' clothing provision. See George Washington to William Livingston, March 3, 1779, in Fitzgerald, ed., *Writings of Washington*, v. 14, 185.

31. Rivington's *Royal Gazette*, November 29, 1777; William Livingston to George Washington, November 22, 1777, in Prince, ed., *The Papers of William Livingston*, v. 2, 120; George Washington to Lord Stirling, October 21, 1778, in Fitzpatrick, ed., *Writings of George Washington*, 120.

32. George Washington to Lord Stirling, November 19, 1778; George Washington to General Charles Scott, October 3, 1778; George Washington to William Livingston, December 16, 1778, in Fitzpatrick, ed., *Writings of George Washington*, v. 13, 18, 284, 404. The trade-off between illegal trade and spying was again raised by Washington in late 1779. Those who were supposed to be spying, said Washington, "attend more to their own emolument than to the business with which they are charged." See Washington to General Parsons, December 18, 1779, in Fitzpatrick, ed., *Writings of George Washington*, v. 17, 285. For an example of use of spies acting as black market traders, see William Johnson's pension in John C. Dann, ed., *The Revolution Remembered: Eyewitness Accounts of the War for Independence* (Chicago, 1980), 354–57. For a pessimistic assessment of the situation in Monmouth County, see Major Richard Howell to Lord Stirling, November 1778, Papers of William Alexander, Lord Stirling, NYHS. For more on trade in Monmouth County during the war, see David Fowler, "Egregious Villains, Wood Rangers, and London Traders: The Pine Robber Phenomenon in New Jersey During the Revolutionary War," Ph.D. dissertation, Rutgers University, 1987.

33. Fitzpatrick, ed., *The Writings of George Washington*, v. 13, 496, 500; William Livingston to Gouverneur Morris and William Whipple, January 30, 1779, in Prince, ed., *The Papers of William Livingston*, v. 3, 26.

34. *The New York Packet and American Advertiser*, August 12, 1779.

35. "Court-Martial of Sylvanus Seely," May 27, 1780, in Prince, ed., *The Papers of William Livingston*, v. 3, 398–99. This is one of several examples of soldiers who seem to be accomplices of civilian smugglers. One is reminded of Washington's order to Lord Stirling to look into any soldier complicity in the smuggling at Shrewsbury.

36. "In Council, Philadelphia," dated December 23, 1779, William Livingston Papers, reel 1, Massachusetts Historical Society; Prince, ed., *The Papers of William Livingston*, v. 3, 281–84.

37. Charles Bushnell, ed., *The Adventures of Christopher Hawkins* (New York, 1968), 71; John Haring to George Clinton, December 11, 1780, in Hastings, ed., *Public Papers of George Clinton*, v. 6, 487.

38. William Heath to George Clinton, December 7, 1780, in Hastings, ed., *Public Papers of George Clinton*, v. 6, 480; Isaac Nicoll to George Clinton, February 19, 1781, ibid., v. 6, 647; George Clinton to unknown, February 2, 1780, ibid., v. 5, 473.

39. William Livingston to Abraham Lott, January 11, 1780, in Prince, ed., *The Papers of William Livingston*, v. 3, 290.

40. David Brearley to Lord Stirling, January 11, 1783, William Alexander papers, reel 2, NYHS; *The New York Mercury and General Advertiser*, January 3, 1783.

41. "An Act to Revive the Act entitled An Act to Prohibit the Exportation of Provisions from the State of New Jersey, June 20, 1777, *Acts of the New Jersey General Assembly*, Third session; "Proclamation," dated August 22, 1778, in Prince, ed., *The Papers of William Livingston*, v. 2, 421; *The New York Packet*, November 20, 1777; William Livingston to George Washington, September 21, 1778, in Prince, ed., *The Papers of William Livingston*, v. 2, 444. In this letter Livingston asks Washington's advice on how to treat this flag boat from the enemy. As a flag, it is immune from prosecution, but it did violate its charter and the laws of the state of New Jersey. Livingston is concerned that he follow the honorable course but he is not quite sure what that course is, so he asks Washington, who is knowledgeable on the Laws of Nations, about how to proceed, being "desirous of forbearing any step not supported by precedent or derogatory to the honour of America."

42. "Proclamation," dated August 22, 1778, in Prince, ed., *The Papers of William Livingston*, v. 2, 421; William Livingston to John Mead, February 5, 1779, in ibid., v. 3, 29; Samuel Huntington to George Clinton, November 17, 1780, in Hastings, ed., *Public Papers of George Clinton*, v. 6, 418. For Connecticut laws, see acts dated February 20, 1777, and April 1779, in Charles J. Hoadly, ed., *The Public Records of the State of Connecticut* (Hartford, 1894), 179, 222.

43. Peter Wilson to Richard Varick, April 16, 1781, Richard Varick Papers, NYHS.

44. D. Romeyn to Richard Varick, April 22, 1782, Richard Varick Papers, NYHS.

45. "An Act to amend an Act intitled An Act for Preventing an illicit Trade and Intercourse between the subjects of this state and the Enemy," *Acts of the New Jersey General Assembly*, December 21, 1782.

46. Jesse Waln case, September 5, 1781, WO 71-153, PRO; British commanders of posts in New Jersey (within the guns of New York) also regularly bartered with the "country people." Captain Ward received permission to carry silk hankies, tea, taffeta, lace, pins, and ribbons to Bergen Point. See Clinton Papers, 130–26, Clements Library.

47. "Letter from Rebecca Franks to Ann Harrison Paca, February 26, 1778," *PMHB* 16 (1892), 216–17. This exchange took place in occupied Philadelphia, but Rebecca continued to send and receive various items from beyond the lines while she was a resident of New York. In an August 1781 letter, she mentions receiving crackers, a ham, and checkers; she is about to send out a ragdoll dressed in the latest fashion, along with spangles and some thread. See "Letter from Rebecca Franks to Abigail Franks Hamilton, August 10, 1781," *PMHB* 23 (1899), 303–9.

48. For an example of this exchange, see Anna Rawle to Rebecca Shoemaker, November 4, 1780, Shoemaker Papers, HSP.

49. William Livingston to Thomas Handerson, John Covenhoven, and Thomas Seabrook, January 18, 1782, Livingston II Papers, reel 8, MHS.

50. Henry Brockholst Livingston to Susan Livingston, December 31, 1777, and January 12, 1778, Livingston II Papers, reel 8, MHS. Lady Harriet's family name is Acland, but in American sources her name is spelled "Ackland."

51. R. R. Livingston's 1782 letter quoted in DeLancey, ed., *History of New York*, lxx.

52. Bill dated New York, January 6, 1778, William Livingston Papers, reel 1, MHS.

53. DeLancey, ed., *History of New York*, lxx.

Chapter 5. Crossing Freedom's Line

1. Evert Byvanck, Memorandum, Misc. Mss., Evert Byvanck folder, NYHS.

2. Evert Byvanck to John Byvanck and Garret Abeel, January 20, 1778, Henry Bogart Papers, New York State Library, Albany, New York; "Description of New York, Long, and Staten Islands in 1776," in William L. Stone, ed., *Letters of Brunswick and Hessian Officers During the American Revolution* (Albany, 1891), 188–202; William E. Dornemann, trans., "A Diary Kept by Chaplain Waldeck During the Last War," *Journal of Johannes Schwalm Historical Association* 2, 3 (1983): 37; 1771 Census, Strachey Papers, Clements Library.

3. A. Leon Higginbotham, Jr., *In the Matter of Color: Race and the American Legal Process: The Colonial Period* (New York, 1978), 131–35. Historians disagree as to how to characterize the 1741 event. For a new interpretation of the uprising of 1741, see Serena R. Zabin, "Places of Exchange: New York City, 1700–1763," Ph.D. dissertation, Rutgers University, 2000.

4. Dorothy Rita Dillon, *The New York Triumvirate: A Study of the Legal and Political Careers of William Livingston, John Morin Scott, and William Smith, Jr.* (New York, 1949), 88; *New York Gazette and Weekly Mercury*, October 21, 1765.

5. Gary B. Nash and Jean R. Soderlund, *Freedom by Degrees: Emancipation in Pennsylvania and Its Aftermath* (New York, 1991), 54, 72.

6. Minutes of Monthly Meeting at New York, Flushing, and Newtown, February 2, 1775, Haviland Record Room, New York. The first two disowned were John Way and Samuel Doughty on September 2, 1778.

7. It is possible that blacks in New York had heard of the Sommersett decision whereby a British judge in 1772 ruled in favor of a slave whose master wanted to forcibly transport the man to Jamaica to be sold. The judge, Lord Mansfield, ruled that it was illegal for a foreign slavemaster to forcibly remove his slave from England. See Higginbotham, *In the Matter of Color*, 313–68.

8. Benjamin Quarles, *The Negro in the American Revolution* (Chapel Hill, N.C., 1961), 19. For effect of Dunmore's Proclamation on Boston King, a Virginia slave who eventually comes to New York, see excerpt from King's memoir in Graham Hodges, *Root and Branch: African Americans in New York and East Jersey, 1613–1863* (Chapel Hill, N.C., 1999), 139.

9. Quarles, *The Negro in the American Revolution*, 115.

10. Ibid., vii. For another instance of African Americans using upheaval in the white elite community for their own purposes, see Douglas R. Egerton, *Gabriel's Rebellion: The Virginia Slave Conspiracies of 1800 and 1802* (Chapel HIll, N.C., 1993), 34–49.

11. Quarles, *The Negro in the American Revolution*, 120.

12. Ibid., 115; Billy G. Smith, "Runaway Slaves in the Mid-Atlantic Region During the Revolutionary Era," in Ronald Hoffman and Peter J. Albert, eds., *The Transforming Hand of Revolution: Reconsidering the American Revolution as a Social Movement* (Charlottesville, Va., 1995), 225.

13. Pocket diary, December 23, 1776, folder 12; William Beekman to Hugh Gaine, December 23, 1776, folder 8; Abraham Delanoy to William Beekman, March 10, 1783, Folder 14, all in William Beekman Correspondence, Box 17, NYHS.

14. For mention of Howe's Proclamation, see Graham Hodges, *Root and Branch*, 140; "Orders relative to Refugee Negroes," Daniel Jones, June 7, 1779, in James Pattison Papers, microfilm, DLAR; Proclamation, June 30, 1779, Sir Henry Clinton, in Rivington's *Royal Gazette*, July 3, 1779; James Pattison to Abraham Cuyler, May 25, 1780, in James Pattison, "Official Letters of Major General James Pattison," *NYHS Collections* (New York, 1875), 397.

15. *The New York Packet* (Fishkill), June 25, 1778; *New York Packet*, June 25, 1778; Rivington's *Royal Gazette*, September 21, 1782, March 15, 1783; *New York Packet*, September 2, 1779.

16. William Beekman to James Beekman, November 27, 1778; unknown Beekman to brothers, August 11, 1777; Gerard Beekman to William Beekman, August 3, 11, 31, 1778, in Box 17, folder 9 of William Beekman Correspondence, NYHS.

17. William Livingston to Richard Bache, May 22, 1777, in Carl E. Prince et al., eds., *The Papers of William Livingston*, (Trenton, 1980), v. 2, 338; George Clinton to George Washington, September 7, 1778, in Hugh Hastings, ed., *Public Papers of George Clinton* (Albany, 1902), v. 4, 7.

18. "An Act more effectually to prevent the Inhabitants of this State from Trading with the Enemy, or going within their Lines, and for other Purposes therein Mentioned," in *Acts of the New Jersey General Assembly*, State Library of New Jersey; "An Act for Preventing an Illicit Trade and Intercourse between the Subjects of this State and the Enemy," sixth session.

19. "A Supplement to the Act intitled an Act to explain and amend an Act intitled An Act to Prevent the Subjects of this State from going into, or coming out of, the Enemy's Lines without Permissions or Passports, and for other Purposes therein mentioned," December 25, 1779 (N.J. B.2 reel 4), *Acts of the New Jersey General Assembly*. Clinton's Proclamation might have been a reaction to proposed American offers in the Southern colonies. See Ellen Gibson Wilson, *The Loyal Blacks* (New York, 1976), 29.

20. William H. W. Sabine, ed., *Historical Memoirs of William Smith* (New York, 1971), 270; William Beekman to Mr. Hardenburgh, April 6, 1777, William Beekman Correspondence, NYHS; William Walton to Cornelia Walton, September 1, 1783, NYHS. See Chapter 6 for fate of Mrs. Walton's slaves.

21. David King, Loyalist Claims, 013/114/685. There is some question as to why King would flee to Rhode Island. Newport was not occupied by the British until December 1776.

22. John Jackson, Loyalist Claims, 013/114/532; John Ashfield, Loyalist Claims, 012/99/135.

23. Abraham Bancker to his father, September 17, 1776, Bancker Papers, NYHS.

24. Rivington's *Royal Gazette*, November 22, 1777; September 2, 1780. For more on black women's experiences during the war, see Jacqueline Jones, "Race, Sex, and Self-Evident Truths: The Status of Slave Women During the Era of the American Revolution," in Ronald Hoffman and Peter J. Albert, eds., *Women in the Age of the American Revolution* (Charlottesville, Va., 1989), 293–337.

25. Rivington's *Royal Gazette*, August 26, 1780. There were over twice as many ads in Rivington's paper for females as for males. Almost all the males sold in occupied New York were young boys, aged fourteen or less. With respect to runaways, ads for males outnumbered those for women by three to one.

26. Rivington's *Royal Gazette*, August 15, 1778; August 19, 1780; August 23, 1780.

27. Rivington's *Royal Gazette*, October 11, 1777; November 1, 1777; March 6, 1779; July 17, 1779; August 16, 1780.

28. Loyalist Claims, Thomas Wood, 013/25/539–41; Petition, Dinah Archey, August 8, 1783, Henry Clinton Papers, Clements Library.

29. Loyalist Claims, John Jackson, 013/114/532.

30. Loyalist Claims, Thomas Farmer, 012/99/167; Petition, Inchu Moore, February 10, 1779, Henry Clinton Papers, v. 52, #25, Clements Library.

31. Graham Russell Hodges, *New York City Cartmen, 1667–1850* (New York, 1986), 64; Quarles, *The Negro in the American Revolution*, 134; "Orders for Commissioners of Captures," Clinton Papers, v. 65, #13, Clements Library.

32. Loyalist Claims, Samuel Burke, 012/19/339.

33. Orderly Book, 27–28, Captain De Peyster's Papers, 1741–1836, NYHS; Quarles, *The Negro in the American Revolution*, 131.

34. Testimony, October 29, Mermaid Loo to Henry Clinton, Clinton Papers, v. 127, #14; David Ogden Petition, July 20, 1777, Revolutionary Documents, Item #38, New Jersey State Archives. With respect to the Ogden story, one must keep in mind that he is trying to get back into the good graces of the American Revolutionaries so that he can return home. Still, the flight of three slaves would hardly help Mr. Ogden's case. For Hessian soldier testimony, see Von Krafft, "The Journal of John Charles Philip Von Krafft, 1776–1784," in *NYHS Collections* (New York, 1882), 82. For Whitecuff's spying, see Quarles, *The Negro in the American Revolution*, 142.

35. One of the more effective bands of volunteers was a multiracial group led by a black named Tye. For more on this extraordinary character, see Graham Russell Hodges, "Black Revolt in New York City and the Neutral Zone: 1775–83," in Paul A. Gilje and William Pencak, eds., *New York in the Age of the Constitution, 1775–1800* (New York, 1989), 20–47; see also Quarles, *The Negro in the American Revolution*, 147. Here, Tye's band is characterized as a group operating "in a somewhat free-lance fashion," suggesting that it was not formally recognized by the British.

36. William Bayard to Captain Murray, November 14, 1780, Clinton Papers, v. 130, #14, Clements Library; Petition, December 5, 1780, Clinton Papers, Clements Library.

37. "Abstract of the Evidence of James Stringham, with regard to the Quantity of Wood Cut," Clinton Papers, v. 189, #22; Loyalist Claims, 013/87/104.

38. *New York Mercury and General Advertiser*, February 8, 1782; June 21, 1782.

39. D. Romeyn to R. Varick, July 20, 1782, Richard Varick Papers, NYHS; Court Martial of Samuel Doremus et al., August 12, 1782, WO71-154, PRO.

40. Evert Bancker to Abraham Bancker, September 23, 1780, and Abraham Bancker to Evert Bancker, October 7, 1780, Bancker Papers, NYHS. It has been claimed that slaves in New York City had some freedom to select their own masters in the colonial period, particularly before the beginning of mass importations of slaves directly from Africa. See Ira Berlin, *Many Thousands Gone: The First Two Centuries of Slavery in North America* (Cambridge, Mass., 1998), 53.

41. Mary Beekman to William Beekman, March 7, 1782, William Beekman correspondence, NYHS.

42. Petition to Governor George Clinton, March 28, 1780, and Jesse Woodhull to George Clinton, undated, in Hastings, ed., *Public Papers of George Clinton*, v. 5, 568, 555; Memorial of Freeholders of the Township of Flatlands, undated, Schenck Family Papers, NYHS.

43. Rivington's *Royal Gazette*, February 10, 1779; March 10, 1779. Owner complaisance and nervousness could have been fostered by possible slave rebellions like the one foiled in Elizabethtown in June 1779. See *New Jersey Archives*, Second Series, v. 3, 460.

44. Rivington's *Royal Gazette*, January 26, 1782; October 30, 1782; November 19, 1783.

45. Rivington's *Royal Gazette*, July 6, 1782. *New York Mercury*, July 5, 1782. The text of the advertisement is as follows: "Massa, me see in a newspaper, Mr. B—d—e advertise poor Venu for runaway. True, Massa, me live with Mr. B—e. Mr. H— brought me from Philadelphia and sold me to Mr. B—d—e. I had ten pounds that was given by my old Massa to Mr. B—d—e to keep me. Masa tell me, 'Venus, you work, get more money to buy yourself free.' My husband and me get forty pounds, by working very hard; me give all to Mr. B—d—e; me ask Mr. B—d—e, 'Me be free.' 'No, you black [devil?], you get no money.' Me tink no right for a French gentleman to cheat poor Negro. Now Mr. B—d—e, as you a French gentleman, please give back the money to my poor husband, then me comes home again."

46. Charles I. Bushnell, *The Adventures of Christopher Hawkins* (New York, 1968), 99–100.

47. Andrew Breasted letter, September 1, 1780, Lamb Misc. Family Letters, reel 3, NYHS. Breasted's letter is to Jack's owner. On the defensive because he had not notified the owner of Jack's presence at the Breasted farm until nine months later, Mr. Breasted described Jack as a burden rather than a valuable extra hand at a time when labor was scarce.

48. Rivington's *Royal Gazette*, November 4, 1780, July 12, 1782. The double standard applies not only to enforced wage work but also to supplies. When the British ran low on flour, they reserved the dwindling supply for the white population while doiling out substitutes to the African Americans. See Brook Watson to George Rose, March 15, 1783, in TI/581, PRO.

49. Jacobus Van Zandt to Robert Morris, November 18, 1777, Miscellaneous Van Zandt, NYHS; Court Martial of Captain John Howard, September 24, 1777, in WO71-148, PRO; *New Jersey Gazette*, February 11, 1778. The British court martial records also feature African Americans who testify in trials and are acquitted of crimes in which their accusers are white. See the case of Isaac Richardson, undated, and Mary Bassford et al., November 25, 1778, both in WO71-149; see also the case of Plato, WO71-148.

50. Milford Smith to Robert S. Jones, August 5, 1778, and Margaret Childe to the Members of Congress for the State of New York, August 18, 1778, in Hastings, ed., *Public Papers of George Clinton*, v. 3, 610, 662. It is also possible that someone else wrote the letter for Smith.

51. Rivington's *Royal Gazette*, February 27, 1779; August 29, 1781; August 17, 1782; September 17, 1783. For more on slave naming, see Ira Berlin, *Slaves Without Masters: The Free Negro of the Antebellum South* (New York, 1974), 51–52. For development of slave naming after the revolution, see Gary Nash, "Forging Freedom: The Emancipation Experience in the Northern Seaport Cities, 1775–1820," in Ira Berlin and Ronald Hoffman, *Slavery and Freedom in the Age of the American Revolution* (Charlottesville, Va., 1983), 20–27.

52. Rivington's *Royal Gazette*, January 19, 1782. The letter writer then made fun of the African American attempts at clever speech.

53. Dornemann, trans., "A Diary Kept by Chaplain Waldeck," 35.

54. Testimony, Murphy Steel, August 16, 1781, Clinton Papers, v. 170, #27, Clements Library.

55. Bernhard A. Uhlendorf, ed., *Revolution in America: Confidential Letters and Journals 1776–1784 of Adjutant General Major Baurmeister of the Hessian Forces* (New Brunswick, N.J., 1957), 569.

56. John André, "Expenditures on the Public Account," February 21–September 1780, Clinton Papers, v. 86, 5a, Clements Library. It should be noted that other African Americans were inspired by the Whig rhetoric of independence and freedom and made significant advances, particularly in Massachusetts. See Higginbotham, *In the Matter of Color*, 85–99. One of the more notable cases in New York concerned a black man who worked for Benedict Arnold while the General commanded at West Point. After treason was uncovered, this African American was one of the men who unwittingly rowed Arnold down the Hudson to the British ship. Once in New York, the black man was told that he was to serve as a coachman to Mrs. Arnold when she arrived. He refused, insisting that he return to West Point. Arnold threw his servant into a prison ship in the New York harbor until the black man relented. No sooner released and fitted out with a complete suit of livery, Arnold's man fled the British lines. Such behavior, noted the white woman who wrote about it, evinced "few stronger instances of attachment and honor" to the cause. See Kitty Livingston, May 12, 1781, John Jay Papers, Columbia University.

57. Shane White, *Somewhat More Independent: The End of Slavery in New York City, 1770–1819* (Athens, Ga., 1991); Hodges, *Root and Branch*, 162–86.

Chapter 6. The Late Unhappy Commotions

1. Diary of Rebecca Shoemaker, September 28, 1781, Am. 13745, HSP; *Royal Gazette*, September 26, 29, 1781, and October 6, 1781. Forty nine years after his visit to New York City, Prince William would become William IV, the King of England.

2. William H. W. Sabine, ed., *Historical Memoirs of William Smith* (New York, 1971), v. 3, October 24, 1781, and November 3, 1781.

3. Ibid., v. 3, August 2, 3, 1782.

4. Beverly Robinson to Henry Clinton, August 8, 1782, Clinton Papers, v. 195, 33, Clements Library.

5. Rivington's *Royal Gazette*, November 10, 1781, January 2, 1782.

6. Abraham Bancker to Abraham Bancker, May 22, August 22, 1782, Bancker Family Papers, NYHS. Family lore maintains that Abraham Bancker of Staten Island was a spy for the Americans. See Howard James Banker, *A Partial History and Genealogical Record of the Bancker Families of America* (Rutland, Vt., 1909), 285. See also John Bakeless, *Turncoats, Traitors, and Heroes* (Philadelphia, 1959), 180.

7. Cornelia Walton to William and Jacob Walton, April 8, 1782; Cornelia Walton to James Robertson, April 8, 1782, and William Walton to Cornelia Walton, April 23, 1782, Beekman Papers, Box 22, folder 5, NYHS; Abraham Delanoy to Cornelia Walton, March 28, 1783, Beekman Papers, NYHS.

8. William Walton to Cornelia Walton, New York, April 24, 1783, Beekman Papers, NYHS.

9. Cornelia Walton to William Walton, November 12, 1783, Beekman Papers, NYHS.

10. American Loyalist Claims, AO13/25/505–9. As William had hoped, the Walton family name survived unsullied after the revolution. Although sued in his aunt's will for annuities still due her, he inherited his aunt's mansion when she died in 1786 thanks to his uncle's will. By the time William's son was an old man in 1832, the Walton family name had been completely restored to its former glory, along with notable deletions in its history. In 1832, the *New York Mirror* ran a series on the "Antiquities of New York" which featured the "still noble" Walton mansion. According to the article, the Walton family was "one of the most respectable of this city," no mention being made of its Loyalist tendencies during the war. Cornelia Walton did not figure at all in this family history. She was purposely excluded. The article described her husband as a man "who lived and died a bachelor" and bequeathed his estate to his nephew. Cornelia's family had written her out of existence. See *The New York Mirror*, March 17, 1832, NYHS.

11. Shoemaker's concealed messages to his family begin in the March 14, 1781, edition of Rivington's *Royal Gazette*. (The September 1779 to April 1, 1780, editions look mysteriously cut off, so he may have begun his secret communications before the above-mentioned edition). His secret scribbles on prisoners of war are contained in the following editions: March 31, December 22, 1781; February 2, February 16, February 23, June 22, July 20, and November 27, 1782; January 1, February 5, February 22, February 26, March 1, and March 22, 1783. Library Company of Philadelphia. I am indebted to Christine Hucho for providing the lead that eventually opened to me this remarkable source. Like Shoemaker, William Smith devel-

oped a sudden concern for American prisoners as well in the last year of the war. He worked to better conditions in the city's prisons, hoping that "these measures will recommend me beyond the lines." See Sabine, ed., *Historical Memoirs*, v. 3, 568.

12. Rivington's *Royal Gazette*, February 12, 1783.

13. "To All Adherents to the British Government and Followers of the British Army Commonly called TORIES who are at present within the City and County of New-York." August 15, 1783. Broadside Collection, NYHS.

14. W. S. Smith to George Clinton, October 20, 1783, in Hugh Hastings, ed., *Public Papers of George Clinton* (Albany, 1902), v. 8, 265–66. For Hamilton quote, see Harold C. Syrett and Jacob E. Cooke, eds., *The Papers of Alexander Hamilton* (New York, 1962), v. 3, 431.

15. "To William Smith, Charles Inglis, Frederick Philipse, Isaac Low, Hugh and Alexander Wallace, Theophilact Bache, James Rivington, etc. etc etc.," July 10, 1783, Early American Imprints 17871. In the galaxy of communities that vowed never to take Loyalists back, there was one possible exception in 1783: Connecticut. See Sabine, ed. *Historical Memoirs*, v. 3, 600.

16. Rivington's *Royal Gazette*, January 4, January 15, 1783. The Loyalists also predicted that Ireland, the Isle of Man, Scotland, and Wales would want to follow suit. See *Royal Gazette*, March 15, 1783.

17. "A Dialogue between a Country Justice and a Committeeman Concerning the Loyalists." *Royal Gazette*, October 15, 1783. Note that the slander used to discredit the lower-class radicals is not unlike that used to vilify the three militiamen who captured André.

18. Rivington's *Royal Gazette*, November 20, 1782, May 10, 1783.

19. Quote of Rivington's *Royal Gazette* in *Pennsylvania Packet*, December 23, 1783; Abraham Beekman to William Beekman, August 23, 1783, Beekman Papers, NYHS.

20. Cadwallader Colden to George Clinton, July 26, 1783, in Hastings, ed., *Public Papers of George Clinton*, v. 8, 221.

21. *New York Journal and State Gazette*, April 1, 22, 1784; Byline from New York in *Pennsylvania Packet*, January 8, 1783; *New York Independent Gazette*, December 23, 1783.

22. Henry Addison to Jonathan Boucher, April 14, 1783, Addison Papers, Clements Library; Sabine, ed., *Historical Memoirs*, April 19, April 20, 1783.

23. Elias Boudinot to Lewis Pintard, April 8, 1783, Misc. Mss., Elias Boudinot, NYHS; William Floyd to George Clinton, March 25, 1783, in Hastings, ed., *Public Papers of George Clinton*, v. 8, 93; John Morin Scott to George Clinton, April 19, 1783, ibid., v. 8, 148. It is interesting to note that a radical like John Morin Scott would think that "friendly intercourse" and "assimilation" with the then-current inhabitants of New York was a positive development. For more on the tensions produced by the impression that gentry had garnered unfair advantage over the poorer sort in entering the city and resolving their affairs, see Staughton C. Lynd, "The Revolution and the Common Man: Farm Tenants and Artisans in New York Politics, 1777–1788," Ph.D. dissertation, Columbia University, 1962.

24. Rivington's *Royal Gazette*, February 19, April 9, 1783; Sabine, ed., *Historical Memoirs*, April 19, 1783; Rebecca Shoemaker to Anna, May 1, 1783, Am.

13745, HSP; John Von Krafft, "Journal of Lt. John Charles Philip Von Krafft, 1776–1784," in *NYHS Collections* (New York, 1882); Henry Addison to Jonathan Boucher, April 28, 1783, Addison Papers, Clements Library; Margaret Beekman Livingston to Robert R. Livingston, April 30, 1783, Robert R. Livingston Papers, microfilm, NYHS.

25. Abraham Bancker to Abraham Bancker, April 21, 1783, Bancker Papers, NYHS; William Beekman to one of his brothers, July 1, 1783, Beekman Papers, NYHS.

26. Philip Van Rensselaer to George Clinton, June 7, 1783, Historic Cherry Hill Papers: Philip Van Rensselaer Papers, New York State Library; William Livingston to John Livingston, June 30, 1783, in Prince et al., eds., *The Papers of William Livingston*, v. 5, 30.

27. From *London Chronicle*, May 17–20, 1783, as quoted in Phelps Stokes, ed. *Iconography of Manhattan Island* (New York, 1915), v. 5, 1159.

28. Ibid.

29. Henry Addison to Jonathan Boucher, October 29, 1783, Henry Addison Papers, Clements Library. Addison was from Maryland.

30. In Rivington's *Royal Gazette*, May 17, 1783, there is a note that real estate was bought at one-twentieth of its value. See Loyalist Claims, Misper Lee (AO12/24/6). For quote on sellers' market, see Peter Elting to Richard Varick, July 31, 1783, Richard Varick Papers, NYHS. For examples of complications with respect to last-minute deals, see Loyalist Claims, Henry Watkeys, AO12/16/253–258, and scrap dated December 16, 1783, Beekman Papers, NYHS. For Shoemaker letter, see Rebecca Shoemaker to Anna, April 18, 1783, Shoemaker Papers, HSP. Mrs. Shoemaker feared that her son "may not approve this plan" possibly because they would be profiting from the misfortune of an old acquaintance.

31. Information taken from Rivington's *Royal Gazette*. In the last year of occupation, eighteen males were sold, compared to only twelve in the period from December 1777 to November 1782. On the female side, twenty-two were sold in the last year of occupation while fifty-two were sold in the war years before that. The number of runaways too, particularly women, shot up in the last year of war.

32. Baroness Von Riedesal's narrative in Hugh F. Rankin, *Narratives of the American Revolution* (Chicago, 1976), 419–20.

33. Abraham Delanoy to Abraham and William Beekman, March 10, 1783, Beekman Family Papers, Box 17, folder 14, NYHS; Abraham Delanoy to Cornelia Walton, March 20, 1783, Abraham Delanoy to William Beekman, July 31, 1783, Beekman Family Papers, NYHS. John decided to go back to the Beekmans.

34. "Payments due to the children of Amanda Ashton," undated, Beekman Papers, Box 22, NYHS; Cornelia Walton to William Walton, August 28, September 17, 1783; William Walton to Cornelia Walton, September 1, 1783; Abraham Delanoy to William Beekman, September 9, 1783; William Walton to Cornelia Walton, September 1, 1783, all in Beekman Papers, NYHS. Cornelia Walton, dated March 1786, proved June 1786, Probate Section, Surrogate Court, New York City. The pull of personal connections and the comfort of the familiar probably induced slaves like Hanover, John, and Mando to stay. It is possible too that masters offered

special inducements to slaves to stay. William Beekman freed John and bequeathed to him 100 Spanish dollars. See William Beekman, dated 1794, proved November 1795, Probate Section, Surrogate Court, New York City.

35. Evert Byvanck to Sir Guy Carlton, April 13, 1783, British Headquarters Papers, DLAR.

36. Jacob Duyree Trial, July 11, 1783, WO71-155, PRO. When referring to the victim, Duyree and his witnesses called him "Frank." The British typically added the surname. Frank Griffin lost no time insuring his freedom. He left New York City on a British ship just two weeks after his trial. See Graham Russell Hodges, *The Black Loyalist Directory: African Americans in Exile after the American Revolution*, (New York, 1996), 98.

37 For estimate on the black exodus, see Hodges, ed., *The Black Loyalist Directory* xv.

38. Sabine, ed., *Historical Memoirs*, May 9, 1783. For a few instances where the British gave back blacks who did not qualify for freedom under the British proclamations before 1782, see Ellen Gibson Wilson, *The Loyal Blacks* (New York, 1976), 68, and Graham Russell Hodges, *Root and Branch: African Americans in New York and East Jersey, 1613–1863* (Chapel Hill, N.C., 1999), 157.

39. The Americans refused to compensate Loyalists because they claimed the British never compensated the slaveowners for the slaves who departed with the British.

40. Rhinelander to Vigor and Stevens and also to Hodgson and Donaldson, February 17, 1783, Rhinelander Letter Book, NYHS.

41. George Stonehouse to Rhinelander, June 1783; Cooke and [Relpty?] to Rhinelander, July 1, 1783; Thomas Pomeroy to Rhinelander, July 2, 1783; Pierce and Browne, December 1783, in James Beekman Business Correspondence, NYHS. *Royal Gazette*, September 24, 1783.

42. Alexander Hamilton to R. R. Livingston, August 13, 1783, in Syrett and Cooke, eds., *The Papers of Alexander Hamilton*, v. 3, 431. In this letter, Hamilton felt obliged to explain why he went to the British-occupied city. Ever the gallant, young Hamilton was "induced" to go by a lady. Only "in complaisance to her" did he "pass through New York."

43. Sabine, ed., *Historical Memoirs*, v. 3, 586.

44. William Smith to Jonathan Trumbull, August 23, 1783, in Sabine, ed., *Historical Memoirs*, v. 3, 600; *Royal Gazette*, May 12, 1783. On the subject of the number of people who fled the city, the British commissary, Brook Watson, recorded on November 24, 1783, that 29,244 men, women, and children departed for Canada. See Robert Ernst, "A Tory-Eye View of the Evacuation of New York," *New York History*, 44 (October 1983): 377–93.

45. Loyalist Claims: Martin Lawler, AO13/26/228; Francis Staple, AO13/15/459; Mary Airy, AO12/24/78.

46. *London Chronicle*, October 2–4, 1783, in Stokes, ed., *Iconography*, v. 5, 1167.

47. *Pennsylvania Packet*, September 4, 1783, in Stokes, ed., *Iconography*, v. 5, 1167.

48. Stephen Skinner to Effingham Lawrence, June 11, 1783, Stephen Skinner

Letter book, NYHS; David Colden, "Letter from David Colden to Henrietta Maria Colden, September 15, 1783," *American Historical Review* 25, 1 (October 1919): 79–86.

49. Rivington's *Royal Gazette*, January 25, 1783, and July 19, 1783. By July 1783, several families had returned to New York, claiming they "would sooner return here and stand a chance to be hung here" than return to Canada. See Abraham Beekman to William Beekman, July 23, 1783, Beekman Papers, NYHS. The British may have encouraged emigration to Canada by freely publishing all the unwelcoming news from the American mainland concerning the prospects of the Loyalists returning to their homes.

50. For Carleton on violence, see *Royal Gazette*, September 13, 1783. For Gouverneur Morris quote, see Sabine, ed., *Historical Memoirs*, v. 3, 591.

51. Rivington's *Royal Gazette*, September 10, 1783; *Pennsylvania Packet*, September 18, 1783; "Reminiscences of John Pintard," Pintard Papers, Box 3, 83, NYHS; *Royal Gazette*, October 1, 1783, for list of prisoners in the Provost. The British started to publish lists of prisoners in the Provost in February 1783 as a gesture of goodwill to the Americans. As of early March, there were no more military prisoners. The last naval prisoners were gone by early May. See Sabine, ed., *Historical Memoirs*, v. 3, January 29, 1783.

52. Rivington's *Royal Gazette*, November 20, 1782, November 15, 1783; Abraham Bancker to Abraham Bancker, October 2, 1783, Bancker Papers, NYHS. For a particularly vivid articulation of this bitterness, see the introduction Edward Floyd DeLancey, ed., *History of New York During the Revolutionary War and of the Leading Events in the other Colonies during that Period* (New York, 1879).

53. Abraham Beekman to William Beekman, August 23, 1783, Beekman Papers, NYHS; Sabine, ed., *Historical Memoirs*, v. 3, September 13, 1783.

54. Christopher Moore, *The Loyalists: Revolution, Exile, Settlement* (Toronto, 1984), 153; Sabine, ed., *Historical Memoirs*, v. 3, November 29, 1783.

55. Sabine, ed., *Historical Memoirs*, v. 3, December 2, 1783; Abraham Beekman to William Beekman, November 7, 1783, Beekman Papers, NYHS; New York byline, dated November 22, 1783, in *Pennsylvania Packet*.

56. New York byline, dated November 26, in *Pennsylvania Packet*, December 2, 1783. It should be noted that Washington had dismissed most of the army before Evacuation Day.

57. Rivington's *Royal Gazette*, December 3, 1783.

58. "Reminiscences of John Pintard," Pintard Papers, Box 3, 82; "Benjamin Tallmadge Memoir," in Dennis Ryan, ed., *A Salute to Courage* (New York, 1979), 290; Abraham Delanoy to William Beekman, November 25, 1783, in Beekman Papers, NYHS.

59. Brockholst Livingston to Susan Livingston, December 3, 1783, Livingston II Papers, reel 5, Massachusetts Historical Society; *Royal Gazette*, December 3, 1783.

60. Ryan, ed., *A Salute to Courage*, 291; George Washington to Andrew Elliot, December 1, 1783, in John C. Fitzpatrick, ed., *Writings of George Washington* (Washington, D.C., 1936), v. 27, 251–52. Tories too noted the calm of the American take-

over. Jonathan Odell wrote off Staten Island that the evacuation was orderly and that "the town we hear continues in quiet under the American military." Ward Chipman, a Loyalist functionary about to leave New York with the British, visited town after the evacuation. Although he never saw "a more shabby ungentlemanlike crew," he went "unmolested" in his peregrinations through the town. See Jonathan Odell to Edward Winslow, December 3, 1783, and Ward Chipman to Edward Winslow, November 29, 1783, in Winslow Papers, Harriet Irving Library, University of New Brunswick; for two instances of disturbances during Evacuation Day, see Paul A. Gilje, *The Road to Mobocracy: Popular Disorder in New York City, 1763–1834* (Chapel HIll, N.C., 1987), 75–76.

61. *Independent New York Gazette*, December 13, 1783; *The Pennsylvania Packet*, January 8, 1784.

62. *Independent Gazette*, May 27, 1784.

63. Testament, dated February 4, 1784, Misc. Mss., Box 14, #54, NYHS: Loyalist Claims, Thomas White, AO13/16/298–352. For Gaine ad, see *Independent Gazette*, February 26, 1784. For Rivington material, see *Independent Gazette*, December 27, 1783. For Rivington as possible spy for the Americans, see Catherine Snell Crary, "The Tory and the Spy: The Double Life of James Rivington," *William and Mary Quarterly*, 3d ser., 16 (1959): 61–71. For Gaine as possible American spy, see Howard Peckham, ed. *Memoirs of the Life of John Adlum in the Revolutionary War* (Chicago, 1968), 105. For Bayley material, see *Independent Gazette*, December 20, 1783.

64. *Independent Gazette*, December 13, 1783, December 27, 1783; New York byline, in *Pennsylvania Packet*, December 23, 1783.

65. Robert R. Livingston to Robert Morris, December 12, 1783, Robert R. Livingston Papers, NYHS; Robert Livingston to John Jay, January 25, 1784, in Richard B. Morris, ed., *John Jay: The Winning of Peace, Unpublished Papers, 1780–1784* (New York, 1980), 679; Alexander Hamilton to Gouverneur Morris, April 7, 1784, in Syrett and Cooke, eds., *The Papers of Alexander Hamilton* (New York, 1962), v. 3, 529. Hamilton's was one of the few to raise objections in public to the radical agenda. See his Letters from Phocion, dated January 1–27, 1784, and April 1784, in Syrett and Cooke, eds., *The Papers of Alexander Hamilton*, v. 3, 483–97 and 530–58. "A Mechanic" responded to Hamilton's first essay, calling him a "ridiculous earwig of our late worthy general," a "stripling delegate," and "the Jack-Daw of Public affairs." See *New York Journal and State Gazette*, March 25, 1784.

66. *Independent Gazette*, December 20, December 27, 1783.

67. *New York Journal and State Gazette*, April 1, 1784; *Independent Gazette*, December 13, 1783.

68. *New York Journal and State Gazette*, March 18, 1784.

69. *New York Packet and the American Advertiser*, March 18, 1784.

70. *Independent Gazette*, December 13, 1783. Particularly illuminating in this regard was a handbill written by a moderate who advocated the election of Isaac Sears and John Morin Scott, men whom the author identified as moderates. There was, of course, an angry response to this handbill by one who scoffed at the thought that Sears and Morin might find common cause with Tory sympathizers. The idea

that the new men in the power structure were not as committed to substantive change as were the radicals of post-evacuation New York did not occur to the Whig author.

71. For the new men in the legislature, see Edward Countryman, *A People in Revolution: The American Revolution and Political Society in New York, 1760–1790* (New York, 1981).

72. Lewis Morris to Judge Wyncoop, February 14, 1784. The legislature passed an Alien Bill in the 1783 session, but the Council of Revision vetoed this bill. When it later came up for another vote in February 1784, the legislature did not vote for its passage." An Act for the Regulation of Sales by Public Auction," *Laws of New York*, February 20, 1784; "Sale of Attainted Houses," signed by Gerard Bancker, Treasurer, undated, De Peyster Papers, v. 9, NYHS.

73. Article Six of the peace treaty guarantees that no future confiscations or prosecutions would commence against any person for the role he or she played in the war. See The Definitive Treaty of Peace, signed at Paris on September 3, 1783; Robert Watts to John Watts, Sr., July 6, 1784, Robert Watts Papers, Box 3, NYHS. The terms of the definitive peace treaty stipulated that Congress would recommend to the states that property be restored to Loyalists who had not taken up arms. Those Loyalists would have a year to try to recover their property, paying to the current owners the price that the current owners paid for the property. No state adoped this policy. For more on Treaty of Paris, see Ronald Hoffman and Peter J. Albert, eds., *Peace and the Peacemakers: The Treaty of 1783* (Charlottesville, Va., 1986).

74. "An Act for the relief of Elizabeth Bend and Grove Bend, and their creditors," *Laws of New York*, May 10, 1784. Grove Bend did have relatives in New Jersey during the war.

75. "An Act to Preserve the Freedom and Independence of this State," dated May 12, 1784, and "An Act respecting certain prosecutions existing in the supreme court of judicature of this State," dated November 23, 1784, in *Laws of New York*. The government of the City of New York was equally wanting in any radical vision with respect to the slavery issue. In March 1784, "A Law for Regulating Negro and Mulatto slaves" stipulated that no slave could walk the streets after 9 P.M. without a lantern or a lighted candle. See *The New York Packet and the American Advertiser*, March 11, 1784. In September, the Common Council of New York ordered a special census of blacks, paying particular attention to those who claimed to be free. See *Minutes of the Common Council of the City of New York, 1784–1831* (New York, 1917), 68.

76. Another sign of the times occurred in New York City, where an exiled American woman sued for damages against a Tory man who had occupied her house during the Revolution. Egbert Benson argued for the plaintiff, Elizabeth Rutgers. Alexander Hamilton argued for the defendant, Joshua Waddington. James Duane, the Mayor of New York and judge in this case, ruled in favor of Waddington, saying that the law under which Mrs. Rutgers sued was in violation of the Treaty of Paris. Although some angry assemblymen voiced their outrage over this nullification of state law, the Rutgers-Waddington decision stood. See Countryman, *A People in Revolution*, 249–50.

77. Richard Varick to Philip Van Rensselaer, March 27, 1783, Richard Varick Papers, NYHS.

78. Rebecca Shoemaker to Samuel Shoemaker, January 14, 1784, December 13, 1783, Shoemaker Papers, HSP.

79. Loyalist Claims: Cadwallader Colden, Jr., AO13/12/64–92; John Franklin, AO13/4/86–103; Thomas White, AO13/16/298–352; Peter Huggeford, AO13/64/369.

80. David Colden, "Letter from David Colden to Henrietta Maria Colden, September 15, 1783," *American Historical Review* 25, 1 (October 1919): 85. The Banishment Act refers to a part of the 1779 Forfeiture Act which banished certain named individuals.

81. Christopher to Thomas Miller, October 10, 1783, Loyalist Claims, Ao13/115/330.

82. Elizabeth Galloway to Abel James, Owen Jones, and Henry Drinker, September 25, 1785, Elizabeth Galloway correspondence, HSP.

83. Will of William Crucher, dated 1784, Probate Section, Surrogate Court, New York City.

84. Nomination for Office, dated July 21, 1784, Cadwalader Collection, Judge John Cadwalader Legal, Bancker, HSP. For survey book, see BV Bancker, Evert Jr., NYHS.

85. *Royal Gazette*, November 12, 1783; *Minutes of the Common Council of the City of New York, 1784–1831*, v. 1, 52.

86. "Address and Instructions to the Representatives in Assembly for the City of New York," *Independent Gazette*, April 8, 1784.

87. Gerard Walton to Peter Van Schaack, May 7, 1784, Nicholas Law Papers, NYHS. Countryman notes that although the New York delegation saw the ouster of its radical members, upstate counties continued to support its more liberal representatives; see Countryman, *A People in Revolution*, 251. Joseph Tiedemann, in his study of Revolutionary Queens County, makes the point that the state did not seriously attempt to punish those charged with the crime of loyalism. See Joseph S. Tiedemann, "Response to Revolution: Queens County, New York, during the Era of the American Revolution," Ph.D. dissertation, City University of New York, 1976, 213.

88. While Americans celebrated the final release of America from British trade controls, the British countered with trade restrictions on the Americans and began the long policy of harassment of American shipping on the high seas. Trade opportunity captured the imaginations of two of New York's most famous radicals. Alexander McDougall became the President of the First Bank of New York. Isaac Sears traveled on the first American ship to China and died in Canton. See Pauline Maier, *Old Revolutionaries: Political Lives in the Age of Samuel Adams* (New York, 1980), 92.

89. John Shy, "Armed Loyalism: The Case of the Lower Hudson Valley," *A People Numerous and Armed: Reflections on the Military Struggle for American Independence* (Ann Arbor, 1990), 183–92.

90. Joseph S. Tiedemann, "Patriots by Default: Queens County, New York, and the British Army, 1776–1783," *William and Mary Quarterly* 43 (1986): 35–63;

Milton M. Klein, "Why Did the British Fail to Win the Hearts and Minds of New Yorkers?" *New York History* 44 (October 1983): 357–75; Henry Addison to Jonathan Boucher, March 25, 1782, Addison Papers, Clements Library.

91. In assessing the war's character as revolution, Robert Palmer has pointed out that the number of exiles per capita was greater in the American Revolution than it was in the French, suggesting that the Americans were more violently disposed toward the Tories. But if New Yorkers can be taken as fairly representative of those Tories who left America in 1783, one sees a substantive difference in the motivation for their departure. Many Americans left not because they were convinced that they would lose their lives, but rather because they had no faith in the incoming American government. French aristocrats faced the real threat of the guillotine. See R. R. Palmer, *The Age of the Democratic Revolution: A Political History of Europe and America, 1760–1800* (Princeton, N.J., 1959), 188.

92. Countryman, *A People in Revolution*, 254–63.

93. New York byline, in *Pennsylvania Packet*, December 25, 1783.

94. For use of Tory name calling in politics, see Howard B. Rock, "The American Revolution and the Mechanics of New York City: One Generation Later," *New York History* 57 (July 1976): 380–86. For an example of a 1794 incident featuring revolutionary symbols, see Gerard G. Beekman to P. Van Cortlandt, February 11, 1794, Van Cortlandt–Van Wyck Papers, NYPL. For pining Thomas Jones, see Thomas Jones to Mrs. Floyd, May 5, 1782, Jones Papers, Museum of the City of New York. For request of American products, see Thomas Jones to David R. Floyd, May 11, 1786, Jones Papers, Museum of the City of New York.

Bibliography

MANUSCRIPT COLLECTIONS

William L. Clements Library, Ann Arbor, Michigan

Henry Addison Papers
Loftus Cliffe Papers
Henry Clinton Papers
Fenno-Hoffman Family Papers
Nicholas Fish Papers
John Greenwood Manuscript
William Howe—Orderly Book
King's American Regiment—Orderly Book
Miscellaneous Collection
Rogers-Carver Correspondence
Henry Strachey Papers
Peter Turner Letters

Columbia University, Rare Book and Manuscript Library

John Jay Papers
Gouverneur Morris Papers

Connecticut Historical Society

American Revolution: Letters
Diary of Prudence Punderson

David Library of the American Revolution, Washington's Crossing, Pennsylvania

American Loyalist Claims Commission
Auckland Papers
British Headquarters Papers (Sir Guy Carleton)
English Historical Documents IX: American Historical Documents to 1776
    (microfilm)

"Official Records Compiled by General Pattison's Staff" (microfilm 47)
James Pattison Papers
John Peebles, Diary
Revolutionary War Pension Application Files
Society for the Propagation of the Gospel in Foreign Parts (SPG)
Von Steuben Papers (microfilm)
War Office Papers, Public Records Office, London (PRO)

Haviland Record Room, Society of Friends, New York

Elias Hicks Papers
Minutes of the Flushing Monthly Meeting
Minutes of the Ladies' Meeting
Minutes of the Quarterly Meeting

Historical Society of Pennsylvania

Boudinot Papers
Clifford-Pemberton Papers
Coxe Papers
Dreer Collection
Elizabeth Galloway Correspondence
Edward Hand Papers
Lardner Family Papers
Pemberton Papers
William Rawle Papers
Shoemaker Letters and Diaries

Harriet Irving Library, University of New Brunswick

Benjamin Marston Diary
Moore Family Papers
Winslow Papers

Library Company of Philadelphia

Samuel Shoemaker Notes in *Royal Gazette*

Maryland Historical Society

Revolutionary War Collection

Massachusetts Historical Society

William Heath Papers
William Livingston Papers
Livingston II Papers
Sedgwick II Papers

Museum of the City of New York

De Lancey Family Papers
Jones Papers
Munro Papers
National Maritime Museum, Greenwich, Conn.
Revolutionary Documents

New Jersey Historical Society

James Abeel Papers
Hugh Hughes Letterbook

New Jersey State Archives, Trenton

Council of Safety Records
Governor William Livingston Miscellaneous Papers, 1776–1790
Miscellaneous Correspondence
Records of the States of the United States
Revolutionary Documents

New-York Historical Society

William Alexander Papers
William Allison, Miscellaneous Manuscripts
John Alsop, Misc. Mss.
Bancker Family Papers
Beekman Family Papers
James Beekman Business Correspondence
William Beekman Correspondence
Christopher Benson, Misc. Mss.
Anthony Bleecker, Misc. Mss.
Elias Boudinot, Misc. Mss.
Broadside Collection

Church-Schuyler Collection
Donald Clark Collection
J. Cogswell, Jr., Misc. Mss.
Enoch Crosby, Misc. Mss.
John Cruger, Misc. Mss.
Henry Cuyler, Misc. Mss.
Samuel De La Plaine Papers
Oliver De Lancey
De Peyster Papers
Demarest, Misc. Mss.
Duane Papers
Gates Papers
Aquila Giles Correspondence
Garish Harsin, Misc. Mss.
William Hull, Misc. Mss.
Samuel Jones, Misc. Mss.
Lamb Misc. Family Letters
Robert R. Livingstone Papers
Nicholas Low, Misc. Mss.
McDougall Papers
John Moore, Misc. Mss.
New York City—Misc. Mss.
Daniel Newton, Misc. microfilm
John Pintard Papers
Poetry Collection
Cornelius Ray, Misc. Mss.
Rhinelander Letter Book
Ebenezer Sage, Misc. Mss.
Schenk Family Papers
Stephen Skinner Letterbook
Christopher Smith, Misc. Mss.
Van Zandt, Miscellaneous
Richard Varick Papers
Robert Watts Papers

New York Public Library

Emmet Collection
Myers Collection
Schieffelin Family Papers
William Smith Papers
Van Cortlandt–Van Wyck Papers

New York State Library, Albany

Henry Bogart Papers
Leonard Bronk Lampman Papers
George Clinton Papers
Historic Cherry Hill Papers
Israel Keith Papers
Kingston Collection
Rebecca Shoemaker, Diary

Public Archives of Nova Scotia

Diary of Alexander Huston

Queensborough Public Library

Parsons Collection

Rosenbach Museum and Library, Philadelphia

Livingston-Stirling-Watts Papers

Rutgers University, New Brunswick, N.J.

General Grey's Orderly Book

Surrogate Court, New York City

Probate Section

PUBLISHED PRIMARY SOURCES

Adams, Charles Francis, ed. *The Works of John Adams*. Boston: Little, Brown, 1850.
Albion, Robert G. and Leionidas Dodson, eds. *Philip Vickers Fithian: Journal 1775–1776 Written on the Virginia-Pennsylvania Frontier and in the Army Around New York*. Princeton, N.J.: Princeton University Press, 1934.
Allen, Ethan. *A Narrative of Colonel Ethan Allen's Captivity Containing His Voyages and Travels*. New York: The Georgian Press, 1930.
Anburey, Thomas. *Travels Through the Interior Parts of America by Thomas Anburey*. New York: Arno Press, 1969.

Andrews, Frank D., ed. *Philip Vickers Fithian of Greenwich NJ, Chaplain in the Revolution, 1776: Letters to His Wife, Elizabeth Beatty Fithian.* Vineland, N.J.: Smith Printing House, 1932.

Bangs, Edward, ed. *Journal of Lieutenant Isaac Bangs.* Cambridge: John Wilson and Sons, 1890.

Benians, E. A., ed. *A Journal by Thomas Hughes, 1778-1789.* Cambridge: Cambridge University Press, 1947.

Biddle, James S., ed. *Autobiography of Charles Biddle.* Philadelphia: E. Claxton, 1883.

Boudinot, Elias. *Journal or Historical Reflections of American Events During the Revolutionary War.* Philadelphia: F. Bourquin, 1894.

Bourdin, Henri L., Ralph H. Gabriel, and Stanley T. Williams, eds. *Sketches of Eighteenth Century America by St. John De Crèvecoeur.* New York: Benjamin Blom, Inc., 1972.

Bushnell, Charles I., ed. *The Adventures of Christopher Hawkins.* New York: New York Times, 1968.

Calendar of Historical Manuscripts Relating to the War of the Revolution. Albany: Weed & Parsons Co., 1868.

The Case of Major John André. New York: James Rivington, 1780.

Colden, David. "Letter from David Colden to Henrietta Maria Colden, September 15, 1783." *American Historical Review* 25 (October 1919): 79-86.

Collections of the New York Historical Society. New York: Printed for the New York Historical Society, 1872, 1875, 1876, 1882, 1883.

Cresswell, Nicholas. *The Journal of Nicholas Cresswell, 1774-1777.* New York: The Dial Press, 1924.

Dann, John C., ed. *The Revolution Remembered: Eyewitness Accounts of the War for Independence.* Chicago: University of Chicago Press, 1980.

De Lancey, Edward Floyd, ed. *History of New York During the Revolutionary War and of the Leading Events in the other Colonies during that Period by Thomas Jones.* New York: Printed for the New York Historical Society, 1879.

Dornemann, William E., trans. "A Diary Kept by Captain Waldeck During the Last War." *Journal of the Johannes Schwalm Association* 2, 3 (1983): 23-49 and 2, 4 (1984): 28-64.

Douglas, Robert B., ed. *The Chevalier de Pontgibaud: A French Volunteer of the War of Independence.* Port Washington, N.Y.: Kennikat Press, 1968.

Fitzpatrick, John C., ed. *Writings of George Washington.* Washington, D.C.: United States Government Printing Office, 1936.

Force, Peter, ed. *American Archives,* 4th and 5th Series. Washington, D.C.: Published under authority of an Act of Congress, 1837-53.

Franks, Rebecca. "Letter from Rebecca Franks to Abigail Franks Hamilton, August 10, 1781," *Pennsylvania Magazine of History and Biography* 23 (1899): 303-9.

———. "Letter from Rebecca Franks to Ann Harrison Paca, February 26, 1778," *Pennsylvania Magazine of History and Biography* 16 (1892): 216-17.

"General Court Martial of Joshua Hett Smith." *The Historical Magazine* July–November 1866.

Greene, Albert, ed. *Recollections of the Jersey Prison Ship from the Manuscript of Captain Thomas Dring*. New York: Corinth Books, 1961.

Grosse, Francois, Esq. *Military Antiquities Respecting a History of the English Army from the Conquest to the Present Time*. London: I. Stockdale, 1786.

Hastings, Hugh, ed. *Public Papers of George Clinton*. Albany: State of New York, 1899–1904.

Hicks, Elias. *Journal of the Life and Religious Labors of Elias Hicks*. New York: Isaac T. Hopper, 1832.

Hoadly, Charles J., ed. *The Public Records of the State of Connecticut*. Hartford: Case, Lockwood & Brainard, 1894.

Hodges, Graham Russell, ed. *The Black Loyalist Directory: African Americans in Exile After the American Revolution*. New York: Garland Publishing, Inc., 1996.

Hubbs, V. C., ed. "Journal of the Brunswick Corps in America Under General Von Riedesel." In Howard H. Peckham, ed., *Sources of American Independence: Selected Manuscripts from the Collections of the William L. Clements Library*. Chicago: University of Chicago Press, 1978.

Hubbs, Valentine C., ed. *Hessian Journals: Unpublished Documents of the American Revolution*. Columbia, S.C.: Camden House, 1981.

Jones, Daniel P., ed. "From War to Peace: Letters of William Peartree Smith." *New Jersey History* 104 (Fall 1986): 49–77.

Journals of the Continental Congress. Washington, D.C.: United States Government Printing Office, 1904–37.

Journals of the Provincial Congress, Provincial Convention, Committee of Safety and Council of Safety of the State of New York, 1775–1777. Albany: Thurlow Weed, 1845.

Kemble, Stephen. "Journals of Lieut.-Col. Stephen Kemble." In *NYHS Collections*. New York: Printed for the Society, 1883.

Klein, Milton, ed. *The Independent Reflector or Weekly Essays on Sundry Important Subjects More Particularly Adapted to the Province of New-York*. Cambridge, Mass.: The Belknap Press, 1963.

Klein, Milton M. and Ronald W. Howard, eds. *The Twilight of British Rule in Revolutionary America: The New York Letter Book of General James Robertson, 1780–1783*. Cooperstown: The New York State Historical Association, 1983.

Laws of the State of New York. New York: Thomas Greenleaf, 1792.

Lee, Charles. "The Lee Papers." In *Collections of the New York Historical Society*. New York: Printed for the Society, 1872.

Leggett, Abraham. *The Narrative of Abraham Leggett*. New York: New York Times, 1971.

Littell, John S., ed. *Memoirs of His Own Time with Reminiscences of the Men and Events of the Revolution by Alexander Graydon*. Philadelphia: Lindsay and Blakiston, 1846.

Mercantile Library Association. *From New York City During the American Revolution: A Collection of Original Papers from the Manuscripts in the Possession of the Mercantile Library Association of New York City*. New York: Printed for the Association, 1861.

Miller, Lillian, ed. *The Selected Papers of Charles Willson Peale and His Family*. New Haven, Conn.: Yale University Press, 1983.

Minutes of the Commissioners for Detecting and Defeating Conspiracies in the State of New York: Albany County Sessions, 1778–1781. 2 vols. New York: De Capo Press, 1972.

Minutes of the Common Council of the City of New York, 1784–1831. New York: City of New York, 1917.

Morris, Richard B., ed. *John Jay: The Winning of Peace, Unpublished Papers, 1780–1784*. New York: Harper and Row, 1980.

New Jersey Archives. Trenton: John L. Murphy, 1901.

Nicola, Lewis. *A Treatise of Military Exercise Calculated for the Use of Americans*. Philadelphia: Styner and Cist, 1776.

O'Callaghan, E. B., ed. *The Documentary History of the State of New York*. Albany: Weed Parsons and Company, 1857.

Pattison, James. "Official Letters of Major General James Pattison." In *NYHS Collections*. New York: Printed for the Society, 1875.

Peckham, Howard, ed. *Memoirs of the Life of John Adlum in the Revolutionary War*. Chicago: The Caxton Club, 1968.

Prince, Carl E. et al., eds. *The Papers of William Livingston*. 5 vols. Trenton and New Brunswick, N.J.: Rutgers University Press, 1979–88.

Proceedings of a Board of General Officers. Philadelphia: Francis Bailey, 1780.

Rankin, Hugh F., ed. *Narratives of the American Revolution*. Chicago: R. R. Donnelly and Sons Company, 1976.

Raymond, Henry J. *An Oration Pronounced before the Young Men of Westchester County on the Completion of a Monument Erected by Them to the Captors of Major André at Tarrytown, October 7, 1853*. New York: Samuel T. Callahan, 1853.

Richards, Samuel. *Diary of Samuel Richards: Captain of Connecticut Line, War of the Revolution*. Philadelphia: Leeds and Biddle, 1909.

Richardson, John. "Letters of Lt. John Richardson, 1776." *Pennsylvania Magazine of History and Biography* 16 (1892): 202–6.

Richardson, Samuel. *The History of Sir Charles Grandison*. New York: Croscup and Sterling, 1901.

Roberts, Lemuel. *Memoirs of Captain Lemuel Roberts*. New York: Arno Press, 1969.

Robson, Eric, ed. *Letters from America, 1773 to 1780 Being the Letters of a Scots Officer, Sir James Murray to His Home during the War of American Independence*. New York: Barnes and Noble, 1950.

Ryan, Dennis, ed. *A Salute to Courage: The American Revolution as Seen Through the Wartime Writings of Officers in the Continental Army and Navy*. New York: Columbia University Press, 1979.

Sabine, William H. W., ed. *Historical Memoirs of William Smith*. New York: Arno Press, 1971.

Schaukirk, Ewald Gustav. *Occupation of New York City by the British*. New York: New York Times and Arno Press, 1969.

Scott, Winfield. *Memoirs of Lieut. Gen. Scott, LL.D*. New York: Sheldon and Company, 1864.

Showman, Richard K. et al., eds. *The Papers of General Nathanael Greene*. Chapel Hill: University of North Carolina Press, 1991.

Shreve, John. "Personal Narrative of the Services of Lieut. John Shreve." *Magazine of American History* 3, 9 (September 1879): 564–76.

Simcoe's Military Journal: A History of the Occupations of a Partisan Corps Called the Queen's Rangers. New York: Bartlett and Welford, 1844.

Simes, Thomas, Esq. *The Military Guide for Young Officers*. Philadelphia: Humphreys, Bell and Aitken, 1776.

Smith, George. *An Universal Military Dictionary*. London: J. Millan, 1779.

Smith, Joshua Hett. *An Authentic Narrative of the Causes Which Led to the Death of Major André*. London: Matthews and Leigh, 1808.

Smyth, J. F. D. *A Tour in the United States of America*. Dublin: G. Perrin, 1784.

Stokes, I. N. Phelps, ed. *The Iconography of Manhattan Island*. New York: Robert H. Dodd, 1915.

Stone, William L., ed. *Letters of Brunswick and Hessian Officers During the American Revolution*. New York: De Capo Press, 1970.

Stone, William L., trans. *Memoirs of Major General Riedesal*. Albany: Arno Press, 1969.

Syrett, Harold C. and Jacob E. Cooke, eds. *The Papers of Alexander Hamilton*. New York: Columbia University Press, 1962.

Tallmadge, Benjamin. *Memoir of Col. Benjamin Tallmadge*. New York: Thomas Holman, 1858.

Tatum, Edward H., Jr., ed. *The American Journal of Ambrose Serle, secretary to Lord Howe 1776–1778*. San Marino, Calif.: The Huntington Library, 1940.

Taylor, Robert J., ed. *Papers of John Adams*. Cambridge, Mass.: The Belknap Press of Harvard University Press, 1979.

Uhlendorf, Bernhard A., ed. *Revolution in America: Confidential Letters and Journals 1776–1784 of Adjutant General Major Baurmeister of the Hessian Forces*. New Brunswick, N.J.: Rutgers University Press, 1957.

Von Krafft, John. "Journal of Lt. John Charles Philip Von Krafft, 1776–1784." In *NYHS Collections*. New York: Printed for the Society, 1882.

Willard, Margaret Wheeler, ed. *Letters on the American Revolution, 1774–1776*. Port Washington, N.Y.: Kennikat Press, 1925.

Wilson, Rufus Rockwell. *Heath's Memoirs of the American War*. New York: A. Wessels Company, 1904.

NEWSPAPERS

The Independent New York Gazette
New Jersey Gazette
New York Gazette and Weekly Mercury
New York Journal and State Gazette
New York Mercury and General Advertiser
New York Mirror

New York Packet and the American Advertiser, Fishkill
Pennsylvania Evening Post
Pennsylvania Packet
Rivington's Royal Gazette

SECONDARY SOURCES

Anderson, Fred. *Crucible of War: The Seven Years' War and the Fate of Empire in British North America, 1754–1766*. New York: Alfred A. Knopf, 2000.
———. *A People's Army: Massachusetts Soldiers and Society in the Seven Years' War*. New York: W. W. Norton, 1984.
Bailyn, Bernard. *Ideological Origins of the American Revolution*. Cambridge: The Belknap Press, 1967.
———. *The Ordeal of Thomas Hutchinson*. Cambridge: The Belknap Press of Harvard University Press, 1874.
Bakeless, John. *Turncoats, Traitors, and Heroes*. Philadelphia: J. B. Lippincott, 1959.
Banker, Howard J. *A Partial History and Geneaological Record of the Bancker or Banker Families of America*. Rutland, Vt.: The Tuttle Company, 1909.
Barck, Oscar T. *New York City During the War for Independence*. New York: Columbia University Press, 1931.
Beck, Gordon Eugene. "British Military Theatricals in New York City During the Revolutionary War." Ph.D. dissertation, University of Illinois, 1964.
Becker, Carl Lotus. *The History of Political Parties in the Province of New York*. Madison: University of Wisconsin Press, 1968.
Benson, Egbert. *Vindication of the Captors of Major André*. New York: Kirk and Mercein, 1817.
Benton, William A. *Whig-Loyalism: An Aspect of Political Ideology in the American Revolutionary Era*. Rutherford, N.J.: Fairleigh Dickinson University Press, 1969.
———. "Peter Van Schaak: The Conscience of a Loyalist." In Robert East and Jacob Judd, eds., *The Loyalist Americans: A Focus on Greater New York*. Tarrytown, N.Y.: Sleepy Hollow Restorations, 1975.
Berkin, Carol. *First Generations: Women in Colonial America*. New York: Hill and Wang, 1996.
Berlin, Ira. *Many Thousands Gone: The First Two Centuries of Slavery in North America*. Cambridge, Mass.: The Belknap Press of Harvard University Press, 1998.
———. *Slaves Without Masters: The Free Negro of the Antebellum South*. New York: Pantheon Books, 1974.
Berlin, Ira and Ronald Hoffman. *Slavery and Freedom in the Age of the American Revolution*. Charlottesville: University Press of Virginia, 1983.
Billias, G. A., ed. *George Washington's Generals*. New York: William Morrow and Company, 1964.
———. *George Washington's Opponents: British Generals and Admirals in the American Revolution*. New York: William Morrow and Company, 1969.
Bliven, Bruce, Jr. *Battle for Manhattan*. New York: Henry Holt and Company, 1955.

Bodle, Wayne. "This Tory Labyrinth: Community, Conflict, and Military Strategy During the Valley Forge Winter." In Michael Zuckerman, ed., *Friends and Neighbors: Group Life in America's First Plural Society*. Philadelphia: Temple University Press, 1982, 222–50.

Bonomi, Patricia U. *A Factious People: Politics and Society in Colonial New York*. New York: Columbia University Press, 1971.

Bowman, Larry. *Captive Americans: Prisoners During the American Revolution*. Athens: Ohio University Press, 1976.

Brandt, Clare. *The Man in the Mirror: A Life of Benedict Arnold*. New York: Random House, 1994.

Breen, T. H. "'Baubles of Britain': The American and Consumer Revolutions of the Eighteenth Century." *Past and Present* 119 (1988): 73–104.

———. "Narrative of Commercial Life: Consumption, Ideology, and Community on the Eve of the American Revolution." *William and Mary Quarterly* 50 (July 1993): 471–501.

Brown, Jared. *The Theatre in America During the Revolution*. Cambridge: Cambridge University Press, 1995.

Buel, Joy Day and Richard Buel, Jr. *The Way of Duty: A Woman and Her Family in Revolutionary America*. New York: W. W. Norton, 1984.

Buel, Richard, Jr. *Dear Liberty: Connecticut's Mobilization for the Revolutionary War*. Middletown, Conn.: Wesleyan University Press, 1980.

Burrows, Edwin G. and Mike Wallace. *Gotham: A History of New York City to 1898*. New York: Oxford University Press, 1999.

Bushman, Richard L. *The Refinement of America: Persons, Houses, Cities*. New York: Vintage Books, 1993.

Calhoon, Robert McCluer. *The Loyalists in Revolutionary America: 1760–1781*. New York: Harcourt Brace Jovanovich, 1973.

———. "The Reintegration of the Loyalists and the Disaffected." In Jack P. Greene, ed. *The American Revolution: Its Character and Limits*. New York: New York University Press, 1987.

Carp, Wayne. *To Starve the Army at Pleasure: The Continental Army Administration and American Political Culture, 1775–1783*. Chapel Hill: University of North Carolina Press, 1984.

Clark, Jonathan. "The Problem of Allegiance in Revolutionary Poughkeepsie." In David D. Hall, John M. Murrin, and Thad W. Tate, eds., *Saints and Revolutionaries: Essays on Early American History* New York: W. W. Norton, 1984.

Collins, James F. "Whaleboat Warfare on Long Island Sound." *New York History* 25 (1944): 195–201.

Conway, Stephen. "To Subdue America: British Army Officers and the Conduct of the Revolutionary War." *William and Mary Quarterly* 43 (July 1986): 381–407.

Countryman, Edward. *A People in Revolution: The American Revolution and Political Society in New York, 1760–1790*. New York: W. W. Norton, 1981.

Crane, Elaine Forman. *A Dependent People: Newport, Rhode Island in the Revolutionary Era*. New York: Fordham University Press, 1985.

Crary, Catherine Snell. "The Tory and the Spy: The Double Life of James Rivington." *William and Mary Quarterly* 16 (January 1959): 61–71.

Cray, Robert E. "Major John André and the Three Captors: Class Dynamics and the Revolutionary Memory Wars in the Early Republic, 1780–1831." *Journal of the Early Republic* 17 (Fall 1997): 371–97.

Davidson, Cathy N. "The Novel as Subversive Activity: Women Reading, Women Writing." In Alfred F. Young, ed., *Beyond the American Revolution* (De Kalb: Northern Illinois University Press, 1993), 284–316.

Dillon, Dorothy Rita. *The New York Triumvirate: A Study of the Legal and Political Careers of William Livingston, John Morin Scott, and William Smith, Jr.* New York: Columbia University Press, 1949.

Donagan, Barbara. "Atrocity, War Crime, and Treason in the English Civil War." *American Historical Review* 99 (October 1994): 1137–66.

———. "Halycon Days and the Literature of War: England's Military Education before 1642." *Past and Present* 147 (May 1995): 65–100.

Dowd, Gregory Evans. *A Spirited Resistance: The North American Indian Struggle for Unity, 1745–1815.* Baltimore, Md.: Johns Hopkins University Press, 1992.

Duer, William Alexander. *New York as It Was During the Latter Part of the Last Century.* New York: Stanford and Swords, 1849.

East, Robert and Jacob Judd, eds. *The Loyalist Americans: A Focus on Greater New York.* Tarrytown, N.Y.: Sleepy Hollow Restorations, 1975.

East, Robert A. *Business Enterprise in the American Revolutionary Era.* Gloucester, Mass.: Peter Smith, 1964.

Egerton, Douglas. *Gabriel's Rebellion: The Virginia Slave Conspiracies of 1800 and 1802.* Chapel Hill: University of North Carolina Press, 1993.

Ernst, Robert. "Andrew Elliot, Forgotton Loyalist of Occupied New York." *New York History* 57 (July 1976): 285–320.

———. "A Tory-Eye View of the Evacuation of New York." *New York History* 64 (October 1983): 377–93.

Evans, Elizabeth. *Weathering the Storm: Women of the American Revolution.* New York: Charles Scribner's Sons, 1975.

Ferling, John E. *A Wilderness of Miseries: War and Warriors in Early America.* Westport, Conn.: Greenwood Press, 1980.

Flexner, James Thomas. *The Traitor and the Spy: Benedict Arnold and John André.* New York: Harcourt Brace, 1953.

Fliegelman, Jay. *Prodigals and Pilgrims: The American Revolution Against Patriarchal Authority, 1750–1800.* New York: Cambridge University Press, 1982.

Fowler, David. "Egregious Villains, Wood Rangers, and London Traders: The Pine Robber Phenomenon in New Jersey During the Revolutionary War." Ph.D. dissertation, Rutgers University, 1987.

Frey, Sylvia R. *The British Soldier in America: A Social History of Military Life in the Revolutionary Period.* Austin: University of Texas Press, 1981.

———. *Water from the Rock: Black Resistance in a Revolutionary Age.* Princeton, N.J.: Princeton University Press, 1991.

Friedman, Jerome. *Miracles and the Pulp Press During the English Revolution: The Battle of the Frogs and Fairford's Flies.* London: UCL Press, 1993.

Gerlach, Don. *Proud Patriot: Philip Schuyler and the War for Independence, 1775–1783.* Syracuse, N.Y.: Syracuse University Press, 1987.

Gilbert, Arthur N. "Law and Honour Among Eighteenth-Century British Army Officers." *The Historical Journal* 19, 1 (1976): 75–87.

Gilje, Paul A. "Loyalty and Liberty: The Ambiguous Patriotism of Jack Tar in the American Revolution." *Pennsylvania History* 67, 2 (Spring 2000): 165–93.

———. *The Road to Mobocracy: Popular Disorder in New York City, 1763–1834.* Chapel Hill: University of North Carolina Press, 1987.

Gilje, Paul A. and William Pencak, eds. *New York in the Age of the Constitution, 1775–1800.* Rutherford, N.J.: Fairleigh Dickinson Press, 1992.

Greene, Jack P. "Limits of the American Revolution." In *The American Revolution: Its Character and Limits.* New York: New York University Press, 1987.

Gross, Robert A. *The Minutemen and Their World.* New York: Hill and Wang, 1976.

Hall, David D., John M. Murrin, and Thad W. Tate, eds. *Saints and Revolutionaries: Essays on Early American History.* New York: W. W. Norton, 1984.

Harrington, Virginia D. *The New York Merchants on the Eve of the Revolution.* New York: Columbia University Press, 1935.

Harte, Walter. *The History of the Life of Gustavus Adolphus.* London, 1759.

Hatch, Robert McConnell. *Major John André: A Gallant in Spy's Clothing.* Boston: Houghton Mifflin, 1986.

Henretta, James A., Michael Kammen, and Stanley N. Katz, eds. *The Transformation of Early American History: Society, Authority, and Ideology.* New York: Knopf, 1991.

Higginbotham, A. Leon, Jr. *In the Matter of Color: Race and the American Legal Process: The Colonial Period.* New York: Oxford University Press, 1978.

Higginbotham, Don. "The Early American Way of War: Reconnaissance and Appraisal." *William and Mary Quarterly* 44 (April 1987): 230–73.

———. *War and Society in Revolutionary America: The Wider Dimensions of Conflict.* Columbia: University of South Carolina Press, 1988.

———, ed. *Reconsiderations on the Revolutionary War: Selected Essays.* Westport, Conn.: Greenwood Press, 1978.

———. *The War of American Independence: Military Attitudes, Politics, and Practice, 1763–1789.* New York: Macmillan, 1971.

Hodges, Graham Russell. "Black Revolt in New York City and the Neutral Zone: 1775–83." In Paul A. Gilje and William Pencak, eds., *New York in the Age of the Constitution, 1775–1800.* Rutherford, N.J.: Fairleigh Dickinson Press, 1992, 20–47.

———. *New York City Cartmen, 1667–1850.* New York: New York University Press, 1986.

———. *Root and Branch: African Americans in New York and East Jersey, 1613–1863.* Chapel Hill: University of North Carolina Press, 1999.

Hoffman, Ronald. *A Spirit of Dissension: Economics, Politics, and the Revolution in Maryland.* Baltimore: Johns Hopkins University Press, 1973.

Hoffman, Ronald and Peter J. Albert, eds. *Peace and the Peacemakers: The Treaty of 1783.* Charlottesville: University Press of Virginia, 1986.

———. *The Transforming Hand of Revolution: Reconsidering the American Revolution as a Social Movement.* Charlottesville: University Press of Virginia, 1995.

————. *Women in the Age of the American Revolution*. Charlottesville: University Press of Virginia, 1989.

Holton, Woody. *Forced Founders: Indians, Debtors, Slaves, and the Making of the American Revolution in Virginia*. Chapel Hill: University of North Carolina Press, 1999.

Isaac, Rhys. *The Transformation of Virginia, 1740–1790*. Chapel Hill: University of North Carolina Press, 1982.

Jackson, John W. *With the British Army in Philadelphia*. San Rafael, Calif.: Presidio Press, 1979.

Jameson, J. Franklin. *The American Revolution Considered as a Social Movement*. Boston: Beacon Press, 1956.

Jones, Jacqueline. "Race, Sex, and Self-Evident Truths: The Status of Slave Women During the Era of the American Revolution." In Hoffman and Albert, eds. *Women in the Age of the American Revolution*. Charlottesville: University Press of Virginia, 1989, 293–337.

Judd, Jacob. "The Unknown Philip Van Cortlandt: Loyalist." *New York History* 64 (October 1983): 395–407.

Keen, M. H. *The Laws of War in the Late Middle Ages*. Toronto: University of Toronto Press, 1965.

Kerbert, Linda K. *Women of the Republic: Intellect and Ideology*. Chapel Hill: University of North Carolina Press, 1980.

Kierner, Cynthia A. *Traders and Gentlefolk: The Livingstons of New York, 1675–1790*. Ithaca, N.Y.: Cornell University Press, 1992.

Kim, Sung Bok. "The Limits of Politicization in the American Revolution: The Experience of Westchester County, New York." *Journal of American History* 80 (December 1993): 868–89.

Kitman, Marvin. *George Washington's Expense Account*. New York: Ballantine Books, 1970.

Klein, Lawrence E. *Shaftesbury and the Culture of Politeness*. Cambridge: Cambridge University Press, 1994.

Klein, Milton. *The American Whig: William Livingston of New York*. New York: Garland Publishing, Inc., 1993.

————. "An Experiment That Failed: General James Robertson and Civil Government in British New York, 1779–1783." *New York History* 51 (1980): 229–54.

————. "Why Did the British Fail to Win the Hearts and Minds of New Yorkers?" *New York History* 64 (October 1983): 357–75.

Knight, Betsy. "Prisoner Exchange and Parole in the American Revolution." *William and Mary Quarterly*, 48, 2 (April 1991): 201–22.

Knouff, Gregory. *The Common People's Revolution: Class, Race, Masculinity, and Locale in Pennsylvania, 1775–1783*. Ph.D. dissertation, Rutgers University, 1996.

Kwasny, Marl V. *Washington's Partisan War, 1775–1783*. Kent, Ohio: Kent State University Press, 1996.

Lee, Jean B. *The Price of Nationhood: The American Revolution in Charles County*. New York: W. W. Norton, 1994.

Leiby, Adrian C. *The Revolutionary War in the Hackensack Valley: The Jersey Dutch and the Neutral Ground*. New Brunswick, N.J.: Rutgers University Press, 1962.

Lemisch, Jesse. "Listening to the 'Inarticulate': William Widgers' Dream and the Loyalties of American Revolutionary Seamen in British Prisons." *Journal of Social History* 3,1 (Fall 1969): 1–29.

Lustig, Mary Lou. *Privilege and Prerogative: New York's Provincial Elite, 1710–1776*. Madison, N.J.: Fairleigh Dickinson University Press, 1995.

Lynd, Staughton Craig. "The Revolution and the Common Man: Farm Tenants and Artisans in New York Politics, 1777–1788." Ph.D. dissertation, Columbia University, 1962.

MacKinnon, Janice Potter. *While the Women Only Wept: Loyalist Refugee Women*. Montreal: McGill-Queen's University Press, 1993.

Maier, Pauline. *From Resistance to Revolution: Colonial Radicals and the Development of American Opposition to Britain, 1765–1776*. New York: Alfred A. Knopf, 1972.

———. *The Old Revolutionaries: Political Lives in the Age of Samuel Adams*. New York: Alfred A. Knopf, 1980.

Martin, James Kirby. "A 'Most Undisciplined Profligate Crew': Protest and Defiance in the Continental Ranks, 1776–1783." In Ronald Hoffman and Peter J. Albert, eds., *Arms and Independence: The Military Character of the American Revolution*. Charlottesville: University Press of Virginia, 1984.

Matson, Cathy. "Public Vices, Private Benefit: William Duer and His Circle, 1776–1792." In William Pencak and Conrad Edick Wright, eds., *New York and the Rise of American Capitalism: Economic Development and the Social and Political History of an American State, 1780–1870*. New York: New-York Historical Society, 1989.

Mayer, Holly A. *Belonging to the Army: Camp Followers and Community During the American Revolution*. Columbia: University of South Carolina Press, 1996.

McCowen, George Smith, Jr. *The British Occupation of Charleston, 1780–1782*. Columbia: University of South Carolina Press, 1972.

Meadows, R. Darrell. "Engineering Exiles: Social Networks and the French Atlantic Community, 1789–1809." *French Historical Studies* 23 (Winter 2000): 67–102.

Meron, Theodor. "Shakespeare's Henry the Fifth and the Law of War." *American Journal of International Law* 86 (1992): 1–45.

Metzger, Charles H. *The Prisoner in the American Revolution*. Chicago: Loyola University Press, 1962.

Mishoff, Willard O. "Business in Philadelphia During the British Occupation, 1777–1778," *Pennsylvania Magazine of History and Bibliography* 61 (April 1937): 165–81.

Moore, Christopher. *The Loyalists: Revolution, Exile, Settlement*. Toronto: McClelland and Stewart, 1984.

Morgan, Edmund S. *American Slavery, American Freedom: The Ordeal of Colonial Virginia*. New York: W. W. Norton, 1975.

———. *The Birth of the Republic, 1763–1789*. Chicago: University of Chicago Press, 1956.

Morgan, Edmund S. and Helen M. Morgan. *The Stamp Act Crisis: Prologue to Revolution*. New York: Collier Books, 1953.

Nash, Gary B. "Forging Freedom: The Emancipation Experience in Northern Sea-port Cities, 1775–1820." In Ira Berlin and Ronald Hoffman, eds., *Slavery and Freedom in the Age of the American Revolution*. Charlottesville: University Press of Virginia, 1983.

————. *The Urban Crucible: Social Change, Political Consciousness, and the Origins of the American Revolution*. Cambridge, Mass.: Harvard University Press, 1979.

Nash, Gary B. and Jean R. Soderlund. *Freedom by Degrees: Emancipation in Penn-sylvania and Its Aftermath*. New York: Oxford University Press, 1991.

Neimeyer, Charles Patrick. *America Goes to War: A Social History of the Continental Army*. New York: New York University Press, 1996.

Norton, Mary Beth. *The British Americans: The Loyalist Exiles in England, 1774–1789*. Boston: Little, Brown, and Company, 1972.

————. *Liberty's Daughters: The Revolutionary Experience of American Women, 1750–1800*. Boston: Little, Brown, and Company, 1980.

Palmer, R. R. *The Age of the Democratic Revolution: A Political History of Europe and America, 1760–1800*. Princeton, N.J.: Princeton University Press, 1959.

Pancake, John S. *The Destructive War: The British Campaign in the Carolinas*. University, Ala.: University of Alabama Press, 1985.

Pencak, William. *War, Politics, and Revolution in Provincial Massachusetts*. Boston: Northeastern University Press, 1981.

Pencak, William and Conrad Edick Wright, eds. *New York and the Rise of American Capitalism: Economic Development and the Social and Political History of an American State, 1780–1870*. New York: New York Historical Society, 1989.

Pointer, Richard W. "Religious Life in New York During the Revolutionary War." *New York History* 66 (October 1985): 357–73.

Quarles, Benjamin. *The Negro in the American Revolution*. Chapel Hill: University of North Carolina Press, 1961.

Ranlet, Philip. *The New York Loyalists*. Knoxville: University of Tennessee Press, 1986.

Robson, Eric. "Purchase and Promotion in the British Army in the Eighteenth Century." *History* 36 (1951): 57–72.

Rock, Howard B. "The American Revolution and the Mechanics of New York City: One Generation Later." *New York History* 57 (July 1776): 367–94.

Rosswurm, Steven. *Arms, Country, and Class: The Philadelphia Militia and "Lower Sort" During the American Revolution, 1775–1783*. New Brunswick: Rutgers University Press, 1987.

Rothschild, Nan A. *New York City Neighborhoods: The Eighteenth Century*. San Diego: Academic Press, 1990.

Royster, Charles. " 'The Nature of Treason': Revolutionary Virtue and American Reactions to Benedict Arnold." *William and Mary Quarterly* 36 (April 1979): 163–93.

————. *A Revolutionary People at War: The Continental Army and American Char-acter, 1775–1783*. New York: W. W. Norton, 1979.

Shy, John. *A People Numerous and Armed: Reflections on the Military Struggle for American Independence*. Ann Arbor: University of Michigan Press, 1990.

———. *Toward Lexington: The Role of the British Army in the Coming of the American Revolution*. Princeton, N.J.: Princeton University Press, 1965.

Silverman, Kenneth. *A Cultural History of the American Revolution*. New York: T. Y. Crowell, 1976.

Smith, Barbara Clark. "Food Rioters and the American Revolution." *William and Mary Quarterly* 51 (January 1994): 3–38.

Smith, Billy. "Runaway Slaves in the Mid-Atlantic Region During the Revolutionary Era." In Ronald Hoffman and Peter J. Albert, eds., *The Transforming Hand of Revolution: Reconsidering the American Revolution as a Social Movement*. Charlottesville: University Press of Virginia, 1995, 199–230.

Smith, Paul H. "New Jersey Loyalists and the British 'Provincial' Corps in the War for Independence." *New Jersey History* 87 (Summer 1969): 69–78.

Smith, Thomas E. V. *The City of New York in the Year of Washington's Inauguration*. Riverside, Conn.: The Chatham Press, 1972.

Sweets, John F. *Choices in Vichy France: The French Under Nazi Occupation*. New York: Oxford University Press, 1986.

Thelen, David. *Memory and American History*. Bloomington: Indiana University Press, 1990.

Thompson, Peter. *Rum Punch and Revolution: Taverngoing and Public Life in Eighteenth-Century Philadelphia*. Philadelphia: University of Pennsylvania Press, 1999.

Tiedemann, Joseph S. "Loyalists and Conflict Resolution in Post-Revolutionary New York: Queens County as a Test Case." *New York History* 68 (January 1987): 27–43.

———. "Patriots by Default: Queens County, New York, and the British Army, 1776–1783." *William and Mary Quarterly* 43 (1986): 35–63.

———. *Reluctant Revolutionaries: New York City and the Road to Independence, 1763–1776*. Ithaca, N.Y.: Cornell University Press, 1997.

———. "Response to Revolution: Queens County, New York, During the Era of the American Revolution." Ph.D. dissertation, City University of New York, 1976.

Ward, Harry M. *General William Maxwell and the New Jersey Continentals*. Westport, Conn.: Greenwood Press, 1997.

Weigley, Russell F. *The American Way of War: A History of U. S. Military Strategy and Policy*. New York: Macmillan, 1973.

Wertenbaker, Thomas Jefferson. *Father Knickerbocker Rebels: New York City During the Revolution*. New York: Charles Scribner's Sons, 1948.

White, Donald Wallace. *A Village at War: Chatham, New Jersey, and the American Revolution*. Rutherford, N.J.: Fairleigh Dickinson University Press, 1979.

White, Shane. *Somewhat More Independent: The End of Slavery in New York City*. Athens, Ga.: University of Georgia Press, 1991.

Wickwire, Franklin and Mary Wickwire. *Cornwallis: The American Adventure*. Boston: Houghton Mifflin, 1970.

Willcox, William B. *Portrait of a General: Sir Henry Clinton in the War of Independence*. New York: Alfred A. Knopf, 1964.

Wilson, Ellen Gibson. *The Loyal Blacks*. New York: G. P. Putnam's Sons, 1976.

Wood, Gordon S. *The Creation of the American Republic, 1776–1787*. New York: W. W. Norton, 1969.

———. "A Note on Mobs During the American Revolution." *William and Mary Quarterly* 23 (October 1966): 635–42.

———. *The Radicalism of the American Revolution*. New York: Vintage Books, 1991.

Wrong, Dennis. *Power: Its Forms, Bases, and Uses*. New York: Harper Colophon Books, 1979.

Young, Alfred F., ed. "American Historians Confront 'The Transforming Hand of Revolution.'" In Ronald Hoffman and Peter J. Albert, eds., *The Transforming Hand of Revolution: Reconsidering the American Revolution as a Social Movement*. Charlottesville: University Press of Virginia, 1995, 346–492.

———. *The American Revolution: Explorations in the History of American Radicalism*. De Kalb: Northern Illinois University Press, 1976.

———. *Beyond the American Revolution: Explorations in the History of American Radicalism*. De Kalb: Northern Illinois University Press, 1993.

Zabin, Serena R. "Places of Exchange: New York City, 1700–1763." Ph.D. dissertation, Rutgers University, 2000.

Zeichner, Oscar. "The Loyalist Problem in New York after the Revolution." *New York History* 21 (July 1940): 284–302.

———. "The Rehabilitation of Loyalists in Connecticut." *The New England Quarterly* 11 (1938): 308–30.

Zuckerman, Michael. "A Different Thermidor: The Revolution Beyond the American Revolution." In James A. Henretta, Michael Kammen, and Stanley N. Katz, eds., *The Transformation of Early American History: Society, Authority, and Ideology*, 170–93.

———, ed. *Friends and Neighbors: Group Life in America's First Plural Society*. Philadelphia: Temple University Press, 1982.

Index

Acknowledgments

It was "wonderful terrible" to write this book. The manuscript took shape through financial crisis, teaching responsibilities, and family tragedy. Without the support of many friends along the way, this work would never have seen the light of day. I owe an enormous debt to the people who plucked me out of my books and papers to enjoy restorative, convivial moments that recharged the batteries.

On the academic side of life, I am beholden first and foremost to Patricia Bonomi, my teacher, role model, and dissertation advisor. From Pat, more than anyone else, I learned the craft of my profession. She allowed me a great deal of latitude in my work while extending the great gifts of her critical eye, graceful prose, and patient reasoning.

Other friends and colleagues have provided illuminating commentary on various drafts of this project. In the early stages, my colleagues at the McNeil Center for Early American Studies helped to shape the manuscript. Many thanks to Jacquelyn Miller, Camilla Townsend, Jeff Mullins, Dallett Hemphill, Nancy Mykoff, Greg Knouff, Tom Humphrey, and George Boudreau. The members of my dissertation committee at New York University, Karen Kupperman, William Pencak, Carl Prince, and Dave Reimers, provided enormously helpful advice that launched me forth into the postdoctoral shaping of the manuscript. I received valuable suggestions on later versions of the book from Robert Calhoon, Richard Dunn, Paul Gilje, Don Higginbotham, Karen Pastorello, Dan Richter, Joseph Tiedemann, and Donald Wright. Friends from outside the professional history field read parts of my manuscript for clarity and comprehensibility. Many thanks to Nancy Frick, Stephanie Muntone, Diane Zaremba, Susan Dixon, and Bill Van Buskirk.

I would like to acknowledge my debt to the McNeil Center for Early American Studies, the Gilder Lehrman Institute of American History, the Nuala Drescher Affirmative Action Leave Program funded by the State of New York and the United University Professions' Affirmative Action Committee, the Clements Library, the David Library of the American Revolution, the Sons of the Revolution, the Society of the Cincinnati, the Cortland College Foundation, and the English Speaking Union for their financial support during the research and writing of this project.

I would also like to thank all the archivists who made my research labors much lighter, particularly Megan and Richard Fraser at the New York Historical Society, Elizabeth Moger at the Haviland Records Room, and John Dann and Arlene Shy at the Clements Library.

I am especially lucky to have worked with Bob Lockhart, Erica Ginsburg, and Audra Wolfe at the University of Pennsylvania Press, who encouraged me in my desire to write a book that would appeal to a wide audience and would privilege the voices of the Revolution's participants. I am grateful as well to Berchie Rafferty and David Cousineau, who helped to prepare the manuscript for submission to the press.

I often wonder how such an unlikely candidate as I should write a book. But when I take stock of my closest friends, the mystery begins to unravel. Since the second grade, Diane Zaremba has encouraged me to kick the odds and strike out in new directions. My brother, Bill, has inspired me with his humor, his wise counsel, and his love of words. We gave the rockers on my mother's porch a good workout over many seasons of great talk. But my deepest debt of gratitude goes to my mother, Jean Van Buskirk. Little did my mother know that when she stopped the household chores to listen intently to her children expressing themselves, she would produce dancers, poets, actors, and one historian. She also secured for me all the advantages she never had, insisting that her daughter have the same educational opportunities as her sons. I have looked into her eyes for wisdom, perspective, and the silver lining. She has never failed me. This book is a testimony to her spirit.